Vault Reports Guide to the Top Consulting Firms

TEAM

DIRECTORS
H.S. Hamadeh Samer Hamadeh Mark Oldman

EXECUTIVE EDITOR
Marcy Lerner

MANAGING EDITOR
Edward Shen

SENIOR WRITERS
Doug Cantor
Andrew Gillies
Chandra Prasad
Nikki Scott

ART DIRECTION
Robert Schipano
Jake Wallace
Amy Wegenaar

INFORMATION SYSTEMS
Todd Kuhlman

MARKETING
Roberta Griff
Thomas Nutt
Katrina Williams
Noah Zucker

CUSTOMER RELATIONS
Slavica Naumovska
Agatha Ponickly

RESEARCH ASSISTANTS
Kofo Anifalaje
Alex Apelbaum
Al Gatling
Kevin Salgado

Candice Mortimer
Thomas Lee
Joan Lucas
Kelly Guerrier

Sylvia Kovac
Austin Shau
Angela Tong

VAULT REPORTS, INC.
80 Fifth Avenue ♦ 11th Floor ♦ New York, NY 10011 ♦ (212) 366-4212 ♦ www.VaultReports.com

Vault Reports Guide to the Top Consulting Firms

MARCY LERNER, CHANDRA PRASAD, NIKKI SCOTT
AND SAMER HAMADEH

Copyright © 1999 by Vault Reports, Inc. All rights reserved.

All information in this book is subject to change without notice. Vault Reports makes no claims as to the accuracy and reliability of the information contained within and disclaims all warranties. No part of this book may be reproduced or transmitted in any form or by any means, electronic or mechanical, for any purpose, without the express written permission of Vault Reports, Inc.

Vault Reports, and the Open Vault logo are trademarks of Vault Reports, Inc.

For information about permission to reproduce selections from this book, contact Vault Reports Inc., P.O. Box 1772, New York, New York 10011-1772, (212) 366-4212.

Library of Congress CIP Data is available.

ISBN 1-58131-039-0

Printed in the United States of America

ACKNOWLEDGEMENTS

Warm thanks to:

Hernie, Glenn Fischer, Carol and Bart Fischer, Lee Black, Jay Oyakawa, Ed Somekh, Todd Kelleher, Bruce Bland, Celeste and Noelle, Rob Copeland, Muriel and Stephanie, Michael Kalt, Ravi Mhatre, Tom Phillips, Bryan Finkel, Geoff Baum, Gary Mueller, Ted Liang, Brian Fischer, Glen and Dorothy Wilkins, Sarah Griffith, Russ Dubner, Kirsten Fragodt, Aldith and Robert Scott-Asselbergs, C., J. Nilsson, Geoff Vitale, Dana Evans, Olympia, the king of burgers, White Castle (33rd St. and 5th Ave.) and Salon Bob (Elderidge St. between Houston and Stanton).

And to:

Amy Wegenaar, Angela Tong, Kofo Anifalaje, Alex Apelbaum, Al Gatling, Kevin Salgado, Candice Mortimer, Samir Shah, Thomas Lee, Joan Lucas, Kelly Guerrier, Sylvia Kovac, and Austin Shau

And Artists:

Robert Schipano and Jake Wallace

CONSULTING JOB SEEKERS:

Have job openings that match your criteria e-mailed to you!

VAULTMATCH™
FROM VAULT REPORTS

A free service for Consulting job seekers!

Vault Reports will e-mail job postings to you which match your interests and qualifications. This is a free service from Vault Reports. Here's how it works:

1 You visit www.VaultReports.com and fill out an online questionnaire, indicating your qualifications and the types of positions you want.

2 Companies contact Vault Reports with job openings.

3 Vault Reports sends you an e-mail about each position which matches your qualifications and interests.

4 For each position that interests you, simply reply to the e-mail and attach your resume.

5 Vault Reports laser prints your resume on top-quality resume paper and sends it to the company's hiring manager within 5 days.

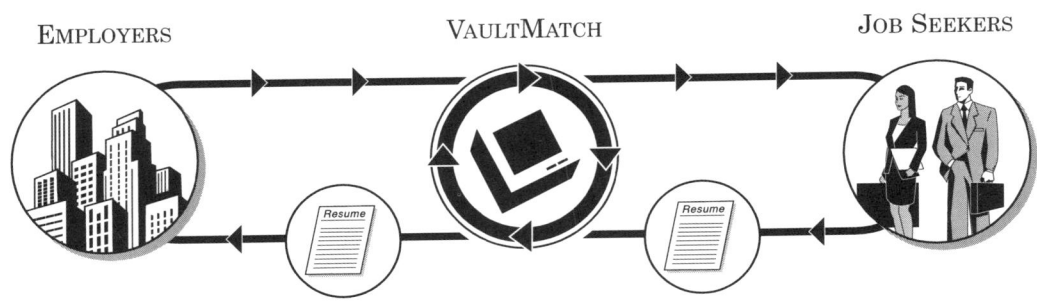

EMPLOYERS: PUT VAULTMATCH TO WORK FOR YOU. CONTACT VAULT REPORTS AT 888-562-8285.

www.VaultReports.com

Contents

INTRODUCTION   1

Our 1999 Top Ten Consulting Firms 5
Types of Consulting 7
Industry Rankings 13
Key Industry Terms 17

THE VAULT REPORTS TOP 10

McKinsey & Company 22
Boston Consulting Group 30
Bain & Company 38
Monitor Company 46
Booz•Allen & Hamilton 54
Mercer Management Consulting 62
Andersen Consulting 70
A.T. Kearney 78
Mitchell Madison Group 86
Marakon Associates 94

LEADING CONSULTING FIRMS

The Advisory Board 105
American Management Systems (AMS) 111
American Practice Management (APM) 117
Arthur Andersen 123
Arthur D. Little 129
Buck Consultants 135
Cambridge Technology Partners 139
Charles River Associates 145
Computer Sciences Corporation (CSC) 151
Dean & Company 155

Vault Reports Guide to the Top Consulting Firms

Contents

Deloitte Consulting	161
DFI/Aeronomics	167
Diamond Technology Partners	171
Edgar, Dunn & Company	177
Ernst & Young Consulting	181
First Manhattan Consulting Group (FMCG)	187
Gartner Group	193
Gemini Consulting	199
Greenwich Associates	205
Hewitt Associates	209
ICF Kaiser	214
Integral	219
KPMG Consulting	223
Kurt Salmon Associates	229
LEK/Alcar Consulting	235
Mars & Company	241
Oliver, Wyman & Company	247
Parthenon Group	251
Pittiglio Rabin Todd & McGrath (PRTM)	255
PricewaterhouseCoopers	259
Renaissance Worldwide	265
San Francisco Consulting Group	271
Stern Stewart & Company	275
Strategic Decisions Group	281
Towers Perrin	287
Vertex Partners	295
Watson Wyatt Worldwide	299
William Kent International	303
ZS Associates	309

A Guide to this Guide

If you're wondering what all those snazzy icons in our company entries are for, or how we developed our information, read on. Here's a guide to the information you'll find in each entry of our book.

THE METERS

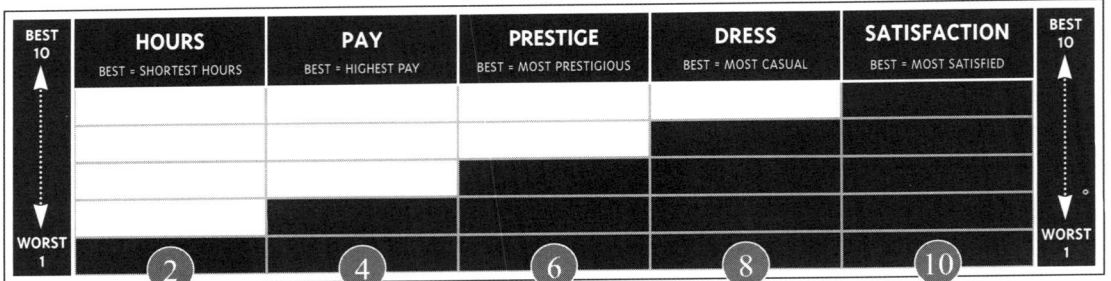

The Vault Reports Meters are scored on a 1-10 scale, with 10 being the highest. The scores are based upon how a particular firm compares to the average employer (including industries other than consulting). A firm with a score of "5" in pay signifies that the firm has an average salary. In determining our ratings, we looked at both company data and our own surveys and benchmarking of companies (derived from years of research).

The meters attempt to give an at-glance look at a company. However, keep in mind that the issues they measure are complex, and a closer look at the entry is necessary for a fuller view.

Work Hours: The shorter the workweek, the higher the score. We did not adjust these scores to account for company locations or the long hours in the consulting industry in general. Working 60 hours a week may be a vacation at some New York consulting firms, but it's still a mighty long workweek.

Pay: A company's pay score is based on home office pay, with bonuses (and likelihood of achieving them) factored in. We did not factor in cost of living or stock options.

Prestige: The higher the score, the more prestigious the firm. This score is based on our written and online surveys of consultants (see our description of our rankings on p. 5), as well as our interviews with consultants.

Dress: The higher the score, the more casual the dress code. A score of 10 means shorts and ripped T-shirts; a score of 1 means strict business formal.

Satisfaction: Employee satisfaction is based on our extensive interviews and surveys of consultants at each firm.

THE BUZZ

In surveys that we used to compile our prestige rankings, we asked our respondents not only to rank firms, but also to give us their impressions of each company listed. We've collected a sampling of their comments in "The Buzz." We did this in order to gauge the nuances of the reputations of the top consulting firms. In choosing three or four quotes for each firm to include, we tried to include quotes representative of the common perception of the firms, even if the quotes, in our opinion (based on interviews with insiders at that company), did not accurately describe the firm. Some of the comments are fair, some rather nasty, a few hilarious.

THE GRAPHS

The information given in the graphs for each firm are drawn from a variety of sources. Some of the basic financial and employment data (net revenues, number of employees, etc.) comes from business information provider Hoover's Online. We also relied on information compiled by other organizations, (such as Kennedy Information, which follows management consulting firms). Finally, in many cases, the companies and firms themselves supplied data.

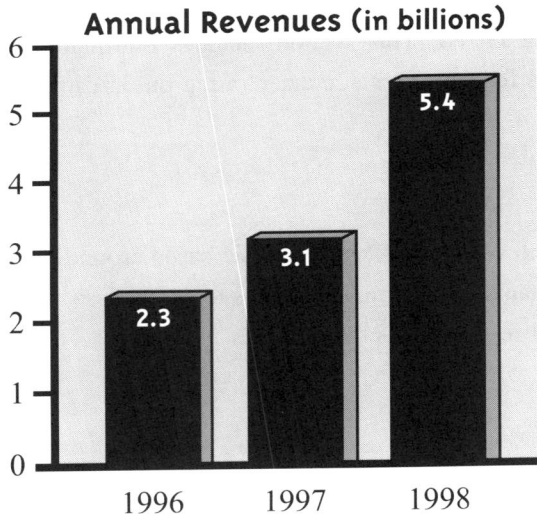

Vault Reports Guide to the Top Consulting Firms

A Guide to this Guide

THE ENTRIES

Each of our entries is broken into three sections: The Scoop, Getting Hired, and Our Survey Says.

The Scoop: This section includes information about the firm's history, strategy and organization, recent business performance, and other points of interest.

Getting Hired: This section includes information about the firm's hiring process for consultants, concentrating on on-campus recruiting and summer programs.

Our Survey Says: This section is based around quotes and comments from consultants at the firm, and covers topics such as company culture, pay, perks, social life, as well as many others.

Introduction

What is consulting – besides one of the boom industries of the 1990s? Basically, consultants are hired by a company (or sometimes, a government entity or a nonprofit) to help assess its problems, plan its future or improve operations. These companies believe that consultants are neutral outsiders, sometimes with more overall industry experience than the client itself. Teams of consultants then work on projects – usually called "engagements" – for the client that can last anywhere from a couple of weeks to several years.

Because consultants are always moving to new engagements and learning new information about their clients and their industries, management consulting – whether focused on strategy, operations or information technology – is a unique career that offers the chance to work within many industries and companies, rub shoulders with CEOs, and travel throughout the country and the world. Consultants sell knowledge, and their skill and expertise. Expect to work long hours, don't make any firm weekend plans, and get an insider's view of sick and hypochondriac companies and organizations around the world.

LIFESTYLE IN THE INDUSTRY: AN OVERVIEW

Consulting salaries are high – for college graduates, they start at $40,000 to $50,000, not including signing bonuses. For MBAs, salaries start at $75,000 and go up – up to $140,000, including bonuses. In 1998, the average MBA consulting employee earned $88,000 in base salary, not including bonuses. Many firms pay year-end bonuses, tied to the performance of the consultant as well as the firm's overall performance. Some consulting firms offer performance bonuses of up to 100 percent of annual salary, though figures of 20 to 30 percent of base salary are more common.

Consultants aren't paid this money for nothing – they work hard and long hours. The typical consultant works 50 to 70 hours per week. Due to the cyclical nature of consulting, however hours can shoot up to 100 hours towards the end of assignments. However, during lulls between assignments, consultants are said to be "on the beach" – and normally spend this time writing assignment proposals, leaving work early, and squeezing in doctor's appointments and haircuts.

RAPID HIRING & RISING SALARIES: CAN'T GET ENOUGH!

The field of consulting has boomed in the past few decades. Revenues have risen 44 percent since 1996, and industry projections show that business will probably be up 15 percent a year at least until the millenium. What this means is that consulting firms are eager, even desperate, to hire new consultants. "Mental horsepower" (a phrase beloved by consultants) is, after all, the main product of a consulting firm. Kennedy Information has calculated that the industry will need to hire a quarter of a million new consultants to meet demand by the year 2000. McKinsey alone now hires roughly a seventh of the graduating class of Harvard Business School each year (that's 100 consultants!).

It just so happens that this increased demand for consultants comes at the same time that many prospective consultants are becoming disenchanted with the field. It's not because consulting pays out paltry wages – the average starting salary for an MBA, complete with signing bonuses, tops $120,000. It's because the monetary rewards in fields ranging from investment banking to high tech are even greater. Consulting, unlike high tech, doesn't routinely pay enormously lucrative stock options, and unlike I-banking, doesn't pay out massive year-end bonuses to reward the completion of multibillion dollar deals. Consulting firms are under no illusions that their employees intend to stay with them for life; the average tenure of a consultant is now less than three years.

GOING PUBLIC

While investment banks have long gone public (the last high-profile holdout, Goldman Sachs, announced plans for an IPO in 1998), consulting firms have traditionally shunned the idea of going public. Now, it looks like that stance is changing. The massive consultancy KPMG (currently working on a $186 million, 15-year project for NASA) is considering putting a 30 percent share of its U.S.-based consulting business up for either an IPO or sale to a private investor. The sale would bring in hundreds of millions of dollars in capital. Andersen Consulting is also rumored to be considering going public. A smaller firm, Diamond Technology Partners, already has gone public (and Diamond consultants have profited – stock has risen from $5.50 a share at the time of IPO to around $20 a share today). Consultants at IT consulting firm Cambridge Technology Partners also profited when that firm went public. What's next, publicly traded law firms?

DIVIDING AND COMBINING

Like outsized amoebae, consulting firms continue to expand and divide. Perhaps the most celebrated divorce has been that of Andersen Consulting and Arthur Andersen, a painful saga worse than *Gone With the Wind* which has been raging since January 1998. But while Andersen Consulting and Arthur Andersen have been not-so-fondly waving goodbye, other firms have been saying hello. Price Waterhouse and Coopers & Lybrand merged their operations, including their consulting units, under the Frankenstein-like moniker of "PricewaterhouseCoopers." (The combined firm comes complete with a bizarre corporate logo; industry insiders joke that Price Waterhouse and Coopers & Lybrand paid $10 million to create their new name and logo, upon which Andersen Consulting paid the designers $20 million to screw it up.)

THE IT CONSULTING BOOM: THANKS TO THE MILLENNIUM...

Consulting firms with information technology competencies are seeing business boom, especially as companies and governments around the world scurry to catch up with the looming millennium bug (Year 2000, or "Y2K" within the industry). One researcher estimates it may cost as much as $500 billion to update the world's computers for the new millennium. The trouble derives from a programming fix in the 1960s when, to save then-scarce programming space, dates were entered in two digits, not four (e.g., 69 instead of 1969). This works fine in the 20th century, but in the year 2000, all dates will revert to 00 – and computers will assume it's the year 1900. If uncorrected, this may mean that major computer systems will shut down – ATMs, air traffic control systems, and so on. Consulting firms are cashing in, hiring hordes of information technology consultants to wade through millions of lines of code to alter date instructions. In 1997, IT gurus Andersen Consulting and Deloitte Consulting showed 21 and 30 percent growth in revenues, respectively. (Strategy ships like McKinsey and BCG didn't do too badly either, with growth of 10 and 9 percent respectively.) It remains to be seen how robust the Y2K market will remain in 1999.

OUR 1999 TOP TEN CONSULTING FIRMS

As part of the *Vault Reports Guide to the Top Consulting Firms*, we've selected what we believe to be the most prestigious ten consulting firms in the country. Our picks are based on the results of a battery of hundreds of prestige surveys we've administered at consulting firms and our interviews and conversations with hundreds of management consultants. Our choices range from the largest consulting firm in the world, to some of the best-known, to a consultancy with a mere 220 consultants. We believe our 1999 Top Ten offers an accurate view of the most desirable and prestigious consulting firms in America in 1999.

Rank	Firm	Headquarters
1	McKinsey & Company	New York
2	Boston Consulting Group	Boston
3	Bain & Company	Boston
4	Monitor Company	Cambridge, MA
5	Booz·Allen & Hamilton	New York
6	Mercer Management Consulting	New York
7	Andersen Consulting	New York
8	A.T. Kearney	Chicago
9	Mitchell Madison Group	New York
10	Marakon Associates	Stamford, CT

VAULTMATCH™

A free service from Vault Reports!

Job Seekers: VaultMatch from Vault Reports is free, convenient way to help you in your job search. We will e-mail you job openings which match your criteria and qualifications. Here's how it works:

1. You, the job seeker, visit www.vaultreports.com and fill out a simple online questionnaire, indicating your qualifications and the types of positions you want.
2. Top companies contact Vault Reports with job openings.
3. Vault Reports sends you an e-mail about each position which matches your qualifications and interests.
4. For each position you are interested in, simply reply to the e-mail and attach your resume.
5. Vault Reports laser prints your resume on top-quality resume paper and sends it to the company's hiring manager.

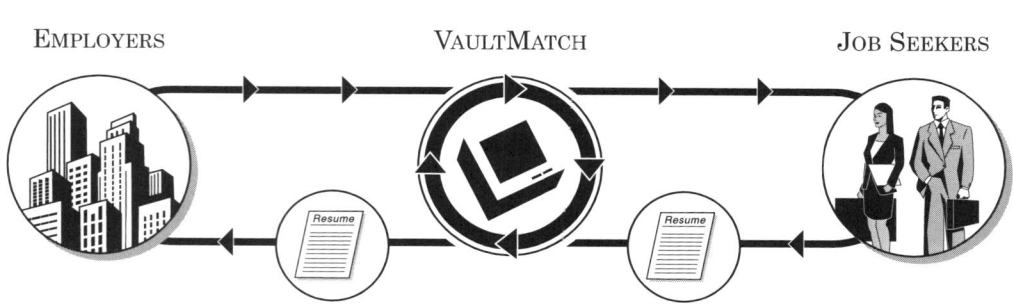

To find out more about using VaultMatch from Vault Reports, visit www.VaultReports.com

Types of Consulting

The types of consulting that firms offer can be divided roughly into three categories: strategy, operations and information technology. There are also specialty areas, such as human resources consulting. These categories often overlap, and many times one consultancy offers two or three different areas of consulting. For example, a single consulting firm may formulate an overall strategy for a client, look closely at the efficiency of its operations, and implement the appropriate information technology solutions to improve operations.

To order the 150-page Vault Reports Guide to Management Consulting call 1-888-JOB-VAULT or visit www.VaultReports.com

The Vault Reports Guide to Management Consulting includes detailed discussion of job responsibilties, career path, industry segments, and industry trends.

Vault Reports Guide to the Top Consulting Firms

Types of Consulting

Strategy Consulting

Strategy consulting is aimed at helping senior client executives (for instance, the CEO and board of directors) understand and face the strategic challenges of running their companies or organizations. Strategy consultants typically work with the client's most senior management, since those at the top normally set a company's strategy and long-term plans.

Strategy consultants employ different models of analysis which allow them to understand a client's business concerns, and determine the direction a client should take. What factors drive cost? How high are the client's costs compared to those of its competitors? Who are the client's major competitors? What are their capabilities, strategies and strategies? Who are the client's biggest customers, and why are these customers drawn to the client?

While strategy consulting firms have historically made their recommendations, presented a "deck" (a report detailing the issues and recommendations) and walked away, their clients are increasingly expecting the strategists to stick around and make sure their suggestions actually bear fruit. That means more and more consulting firms are touting their "implementation" capabilities.

EXAMPLES OF TYPICAL STRATEGY CONSULTING ENGAGEMENTS

- Figuring out why Broadway theaters have been losing money, and how the theaters can reposition themselves to capitalize on new markets.

- Positioning a snack manufacturer to enter China. Assessing what kind of snacks the Chinese will want and predicting how much they will pay for these snacks.

- Assessing the current state of the satellite communications market and possible expansion opportunities around the world.

- Evaluating a possible acquisition for an investment management firm and deciding on a price.

LEADING STRATEGY CONSULTING FIRMS

- Bain & Company
- The Boston Consulting Group
- McKinsey & Company
- Monitor Company

Operations Consulting

Operations consulting examines a client's internal workings, such as production processes, distribution, order fulfillment, and customer service. While strategy sets the firm's goals, operations ensures that a client can reach these goals. Operations consultants may investigate its client's customer service response times, cut operating or inventory backlog costs, investigate resource allocation, improve distribution, heighten product quality, or restructure entire departments and organizations (a specialty of the "re-engineering" craze in consulting in the early 1990s). Unlike strategy consultants, who are still more likely to hand off their findings to the client and leave, operations consultants are more likely to assist in making sure their suggestions are properly executed (a process called "implementation" by consulting insiders).

EXAMPLES OF TYPICAL OPERATIONS CONSULTING ENGAGEMENTS

- Streamlining the equipment purchasing process of a major manufacturer.
- Determining where a restaurant chain can save on its ingredient cost without changing its menu.
- Working with a newly-merged commercial bank to increase its customer response efficiency.
- Creating a new logistical database for a tire manufacturer.

LEADING OPERATIONS CONSULTING FIRMS

- Andersen Consulting
- Arthur D. Little
- Gemini Consulting
- Mitchell Madison Group

Vault Reports Guide to the Top Consulting Firms

Types of Consulting

Information Technology

Information Technology (or "IT") consultants tap into the world of technology to help clients achieve their business goals. IT consultants (also called "systems consultants") work with corporations and other clients to understand how technology can work for the organizations, design custom software or networking solutions, ensure that all systems and programs are compatible, and see to it that the new systems are properly implemented. The changeover from mainframes to networked PCs, and the rush to upgrade computers systems before the millenium bug hits (many computers are still unable to process years that do not begin with 19) have boosted the fortunes of IT consultants in recent years.

EXAMPLES OF TYPICAL IT CONSULTING ENGAGEMENTS

- Advising a mutual fund company on how to provide its clients with access to account information online.
- Working with a telecommunications company to avoid the "Year 2000" bug.
- Switching a major law firm from WordPerfect to Windows.
- Troubleshooting on a major SAP software installation.

CONSULTING FIRMS WITH MAJOR IT PRACTICES

- American Management Systems
- Arthur Andersen
- Cambridge Technology Partners
- Deloitte Consulting
- Diamond Technology Partners

Human Resources Consulting

It helps to have a good plan, but the best business strategies, the most up-to-date tech and the most streamlined operations won't mean anything if the right people aren't there to put them into place. That's why the field of human resources consulting is on the upswing. Increasingly, companies have determined that investing in their human capital pays off just like in other aspects of their operations. Human resources consultants are called upon to maximize the value of human workers while placing the right people in the right roles. This may involve "change navigation" designed to develop or alter work cultures, "managing relationships" to ensure focus on customers and open communication, building "competencies" through better and more efficient training programs, or fostering employee creativity through "process innovation." Another growing area of human resources consulting, now that large-scale downsizing is a way of life, is counseling and processing laid-off employees.

LEADING HUMAN RESOURCES CONSULTING FIRMS

- Buck Consultants
- Hewitt Associates
- Towers Perrin
- Watson Wyatt Worldwide

Industry Rankings

POSITION QUADRANTS

KEY TO CONSULTING FIRMS

ADL = Arthur D. Little
AMS = American Management Systems
Andersen = Andersen Consulting
Bain = Bain & Company
BCG = Boston Consulting Group
EY = Ernst & Young
MMG = Mitchell Madison Group
Monitor = Monitor Company
PwC = Price Waterhouse Coopers
Towers = Towers Perrin

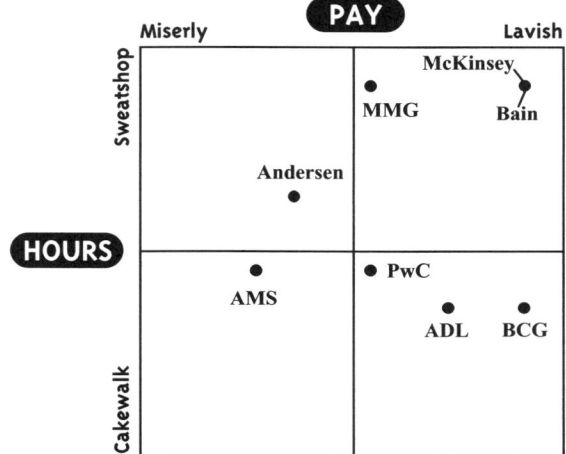

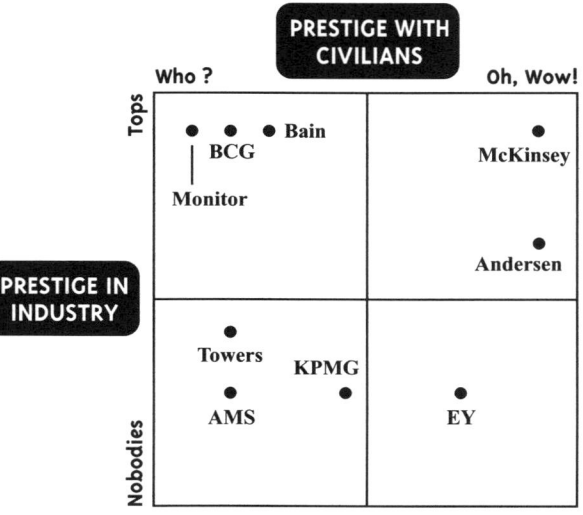

Source: Vault Reports research

Vault Reports Guide to the Top Consulting Firms

Industry Rankings

TOP 50 GLOBAL CONSULTING FIRMS BY REVENUES

Rank	Firm	1997 Revenues
1	Andersen Consulting	$ 5,726,000,000
2	CSC	$ 3,000,000,000
3	Ernst & Young	$ 2,680,000,000
4	Coopers & Lybrand*	$ 2,400,000,000
5	Deloitte Consulting	$ 2,300,000,000
6	McKinsey & Company	$ 2,200,000,000
7	KPMG	$ 2,011,000,000
8	Cap Gemini	$ 1,648,000,000
9	Price Waterhouse*	$ 1,400,000,000
10	Mercer Consulting Group	$ 1,338,000,000
11	Towers Perrin	$ 1,120,000,000
12	A.T. Kearney	$ 1,100,000,000
13	Booz·Allen & Hamilton	$ 1,075,000,000
14	Arthur Andersen	$ 953,000,000
15	Sema Group	$ 888,000,000
16	IBM Consulting	$ 880,000,000
17	American Management Systems	$ 791,000,000
18	Hewitt Associates	$ 709,000,000
19	Watson Wyatt Worldwide	$ 673,000,000
20	The Boston Consulting Group	$ 655,000,000
21	MCI Systemhouse	$ 620,000,000
22	Arthur D. Little	$ 589,000,000
23	Logica	$ 570,000,000
24	Keane	$ 560,000,000
25	Aon Consulting	$ 553,000,000

* Since merged to form PricewaterhouseCoopers

Source: Consultants News and Kennedy Information

Top 50 Global Consulting Firms (cont'd)

Rank	Firm	1997 Revenues
26	Bain & Company	$ 480,000,000
27	Delphi Group	$ 466,000,000
28	Debis Systemhaus	$ 448,000,000
29	Renaissance Worldwide	$ 428,000,000
30	CMG	$ 413,000,000
31	Cambridge Technology Partners	$ 407,000,000
32	Woodrow Milliman	$ 405,000,000
33	PA Consulting Group	$ 381,000,000
34	Origin	$ 380,000,000
35	Grant Thornton	$ 351,000,000
36	Bellcore	$ 340,000,000
37	Roland Berger & Partner	$ 338,000,000
38	Sedgwick Noble Lowndes	$ 334,000,000
39	AT&T Solutions	$ 325,000,000
40	Buck Consultants	$ 304,000,000
41	CTG	$ 265,000,000
42	Hay Group	$ 265,000,000
43	CIBER	$ 262,000,000
44	Cotelligent Group	$ 218,000,000
45	Tata Consultancy	$ 201,000,000
46	Mitchell Madison Group	$ 200,000,000
47	Mastech Corporation	$ 196,000,000
48	Perot Systems	$ 195,000,000
49	Monitor Company	$ 186,000,000
50	Whittman-Hart	$ 174,000,000

Source: Consultants News and Kennedy Information

Consulting Job Seekers: Receive free e-mailed job postings matching your interests & qualifications! Register at www.VaultReports.com

Key Industry Terms

Even consultants can't always tell what they're talking about. That's why we compiled this glossary.

Bananagram: A graph showing profitability (the typical measure of profitability for this graph is return on capital employed, or "ROCE" [pronounced roachy]) vs. relative market share. The graph shows that the higher market share, the higher the profits.

BCG matrix: A portfolio assessment tool developed by BCG. Also called a growth/share matrix.

Benchmarking: Measuring a value or practice or other business measure (such as costs) against other companies in the industry.

Blank slide: Initial sketch on paper for a slide to be used in a consulting case presentation called blank because it does not include data until analysts put it in.

Brainteaser: A type of consulting interview question in which the job seeker is asked to solve a logic problem.

Case interview: The most common type of management consulting interview, in which the job seeker is asked to suggest solutions to a business scenario. For sample case interview questions with model answers, read the *Vault Reports Guide to Case Interviews*.

Case team: Team that works on a consulting project for a client. Usually composed of one partner, one consultant and two or more analysts.

Change management: One of the services provided by consulting firms, in which the firm helps a company cope with a period of significant change (such as a merger, downsizing or restructuring).

Key Industry Terms

Convergence: The trend toward media, information, and telecommunications technologies uniting. (For example, cable TV customers may someday be able to place telephone calls using cable technology, while telephone customers may be able to receive television through phone lines.)

Core competencies: The areas in which a company excels. Consultants believe a company should enter only those businesses that are part of its core competencies.

DCF: Discounted Cash Flow. The present value of a future cash flow.

Engagement: A consulting assignment received by a consulting firm. Also called a "case" or "project."

Experience curve: The principle that a company's costs decline as its production increases. One assumption used by consultants is that a company's costs decline by roughly 25 percent for every doubling in production (i.e., a company's 200th unit of a product costs 75 percent of the 100th unit's cost).

Guesstimate: A type of consulting interview question. Guesstimates require candidates to make educated estimates (often of the size of the market for a particular product or service) using basic calculations.

Hoteling: Consultants move around so much that in some firms they are not assigned permanent offices, just a voice mail extension. Each week, they must call up the office nearest them to request a desk. This is called "hoteling."

Implementation: The process by which a consulting firm ensures that the advice it gives to a client company is enacted.

Learning curve: The rate at which a consultant acquires background information or industry knowledge needed for a case. A "steep" curve is a good thing.

Key Industry Terms

NPV: Net present value. The sum of a series of discounted cash flows. Used to assess the profitability of making an investment or undertaking a project.

O'Hare Test: A test consultants use to assess personality "fit" in interviews. If I was stuck overnight with this person at O'Hare airport, would I have fun?

On the beach: For consultants, the spare time between assignments when their work hours decline drastically. Consultants between assignments are said to be "on the beach" (not literally). This expression originated at McKinsey.

Out-of-the-box thinking: Creativity.

Outsourcing: Taking a process normally performed within a company and hiring an outside vendor to perform the task, often at a lower cost and with better results. Examples of processes that are commonly outsourced include: payroll, data processing, recruitment, and document processing. Outsourcing is a growing trend among corporations.

Re-engineering: A largely discredited fad of the early 1990s, which advocates a complete overhaul (and usually downsizing) of a company's strategies, operations, and practices.

Rightsizing: A clever new term for "downsizing."

Robust: A commonly used word among consultants. It means "good."

Shareholder value: The total net wealth of a company's stockholders. The primary goal of consultants in undertaking any engagement is to maximize shareholder value.

Total Quality Management: Also known as TQM. Management with the purpose or intent of producing a product or offering a service of the highest quality, with zero tolerance for defects. (Until recently, Motorola was considered the king of TQM).

Value migration: The flow of economic and shareholder value away from obsolete business models to new, more effective designs.

Value-added: Used to define a service or product in a marketplace that adds value to a preexisting product or way of doing things.

Work plan: A schedule for completing a consulting engagement.

White space opportunity: An opportunity for a company to make money in an area in which it is currently generating zero revenue (for example, launching a new product line, licensing an existing brand or technology, or entering a new geographic market).

The Vault Reports
TOP 10

McKinsey & Company

VAULT REPORTS RANKING 1

55 East 52nd Street
New York, NY 10022
(800) 221-1026
Fax: (212) 446-7200
www.mckinsey.com

McKinsey & Company

LOCATIONS

New York, NY (HQ)
Atlanta, GA • Boston, MA • Chicago, IL • Cleveland, OH • Dallas, TX • Los Angeles, CA • Minneapolis, MN • Pittsburgh, PA • San Francisco, CA • Washington, DC • Barcelona, Spain • Berlin, Germany • Buenos Aires, Argentina • Dublin, Ireland • Hong Kong • Mexico City, Mexico • Paris, France • Tokyo, Japan • Toronto, Canada • Vienna, Austria • Other offices worldwide

DEPARTMENTS

Consulting
Information Technology

THE STATS

Annual Revenues: $2.2 billion (1997)
No. of Employees: 4,500 (worldwide)
No. of Offices: 75 (worldwide)
A privately-held company
CEO: Rajat Gupta

KEY COMPETITORS

- Andersen Consulting
- Bain & Company
- Booz•Allen & Hamilton
- Boston Consulting Group
- Mercer Management Consulting
- Monitor & Company

THE BUZZ
What consultants at other firms are saying about McKinsey

- "Hires the brightest but most insecure"
- "Competitive, slick"
- "The gold standard"
- "CEO-level"

Vault Reports Guide to the Top Consulting Firms

McKinsey & Company

UPPERS
- High pay
- Extensive job training
- Worldwide prestige

DOWNERS
- Frequent travel
- Somewhat square and snobbish consultants
- "Up-or-out" stress

EMPLOYMENT CONTACT

Recruiting Administrator
McKinsey & Company
55 East 52nd Street
New York, NY 10022

(212) 446-7993
baus_recruit@mckinsey.com

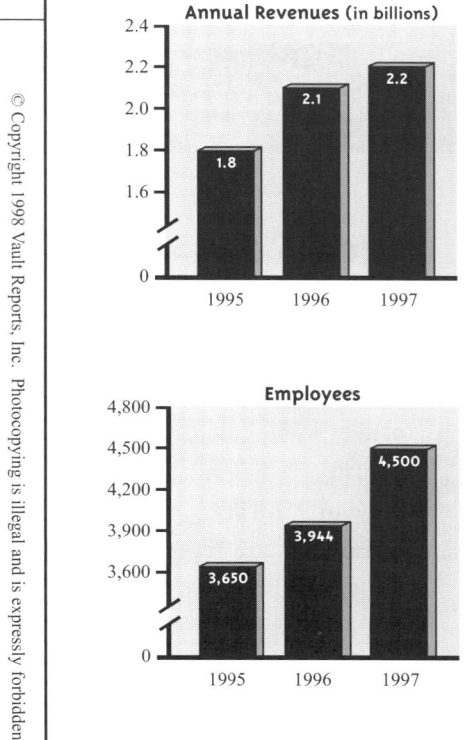

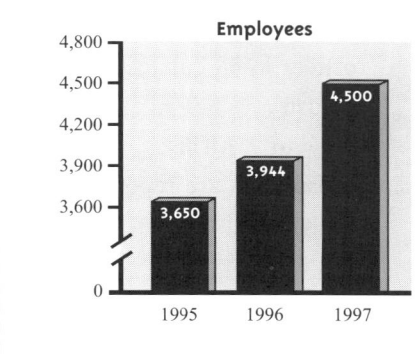

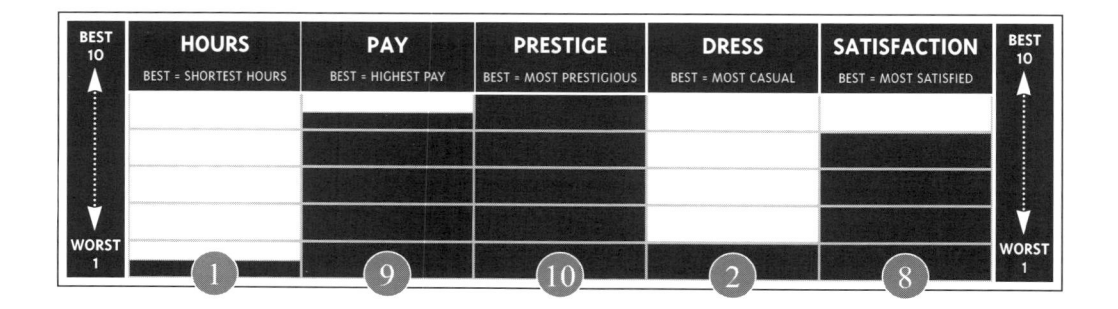

Annual Revenues (in billions)
- 1995: 1.8
- 1996: 2.1
- 1997: 2.2

Employees
- 1995: 3,650
- 1996: 3,944
- 1997: 4,500

© Copyright 1998 Vault Reports, Inc. Photocopying is illegal and is expressly forbidden.

	HOURS BEST = SHORTEST HOURS	PAY BEST = HIGHEST PAY	PRESTIGE BEST = MOST PRESTIGIOUS	DRESS BEST = MOST CASUAL	SATISFACTION BEST = MOST SATISFIED	
BEST 10 / WORST 1	1	9	10	2	8	BEST 10 / WORST 1

Consulting Job Seekers: Receive free e-mailed job postings matching your interests & qualifications! Register at www.VaultReports.com

www.vaultreports.com

THE SCOOP

NOTHING COMPARES TO YOU, MCKINSEY

In an industry with a handful of leaders, McKinsey & Company has come to be regarded as the most influential consulting firm in the world. Founded by James O. McKinsey in 1926, McKinsey earns more money per consultant than any other consulting firm. Now with 75 offices in 38 countries and more than 4000 professional employees, McKinsey dominates its industry. When rival consulting firms want to give themselves a boost, they say they're second only to McKinsey. McKinsey consultants profit from this aura of prestige – per head, consultants are reported to bring in $450,000 annually. Among its employees and clients, McKinsey is known simply as "The Firm" (a nickname that predates John Grisham's oeuvre).

BRIGHT BLUE CHIPS

Clients of "The Firm" are the bluest of the blue chips. They include AT&T, Pepsi, IBM, General Electric and General Motors. A consultant at competitor Bain sums up: "The hardest part about competing with McKinsey is that they have these deep relationships with senior management that lead companies to return to McKinsey unquestioned." Besides serving huge global companies, wealthy commercial banks, and vast technology firms, McKinsey also prides itself on offering pro bono assistance to educational, social, environmental, and cultural organizations. The firm is also increasingly working with emerging market companies and family-owned ventures. The bulk of the firm's work is in the private sector, but McKinsey also advises public sector organizations.

THE ULTRA-INTERNATIONAL CONSULTING FIRM

McKinsey consultants become part of a global network and a truly international firm. Despite its far-flung empire, McKinsey adopts a "one firm" approach and makes an effort to maintain a consistent "McKinsey culture" in each of its offices worldwide. (At present, a non-American majority controls the governing committee, 60 percent of revenues come from overseas, and the firm's managing director, Calcutta native Rajat Gupta, is the non-Western person to hold that position.)

LEAD OR LEAVE (OR BOTH)

The McKinsey culture includes an emphasis on upward advancement. The firm has an "up-or-out" policy – consultants must either earn promotion or leave the company. New associates have about six years to make partner; partners then face a similar deadline in their efforts to become directors. On average, only one in 11 consultants who start at McKinsey finishes this journey. Those who leave McKinsey may find themselves in politics (like William Hague, leader of Britain's Tory Party and Roger Ferguson, Governor of the Federal Reserve Board), best-selling authors (the authors of the enormously successful business guide *In Search of Excellence* were former McKinsey consultants), or may even start up rival consultancies (as Tom Steiner did with Mitchell Madison). And many McKinsey consultants wind up with top spots with corporations: the CEOs of IBM, Federal Express and Levi Strauss are all alums of The Firm.

DOING THEIR HOMEWORK

McKinsey prides itself on collecting and interpreting all business theories and information of any possible utility. Firm members are fond of claiming that McKinsey does more research into business issues than the business schools at Wharton, Harvard and Stanford combined. The firm also builds knowledge through conferences, research projects, online databases and intrafirm training and communication. McKinsey also publishes a large amount of booklets, documents, papers and magazines, including the well-regarded *McKinsey Quarterly*. In Washington DC, McKinsey runs the Global Institute which, located just steps from the White House, studies macroeconomic trends. In total, it is estimated that McKinsey has spent as much as $50 million dollars a year on its information gathering.

GETTING HIRED

McKinsey hires only 1 percent of the approximately 75,000 candidates who apply to the firm each year. Successful candidates usually have excellent academic records and degrees from top universities. Although McKinsey was recently slapped with a gender discrimination lawsuit by a former employee, the firm is well known for actively recruiting talented women, minorities, gay men and lesbians.

At the analyst, or undergrad level, McKinsey assigns one campus team per school. Some schools, like the University of Rochester, for example, are not covered; graduates of these schools must pass their resumes to the closest firm office (the New York office in the case of Rochester). MBAs are hired into McKinsey as associates, but 40 percent of the firm's associates don't have business degrees – the firm also recruits law students, PhDs and MDs for associate positions. "We are also looking for people who hold 'APDs' or Advanced Professional Degrees," says one firm insider. "They are associates, not analysts, even if they graduate with a worthless PhD in Renaissance literature or what have you."

The firm's interview process typically involves two rounds on campus, and then a third, final round in the office at which the candidate wants to work. McKinsey will fly final-round candidates cross-country (or cross-ocean), if need be. The final round is normally half a day of inteviews, plus a meal (either lunch or dinner). Most final-round interviews are case interviews. It is McKinsey's intention that all candidates visit the office where they want to work before they get offers. While clearly some offices are larger than others, McKinsey is flexible about placement, believing there is always room for talent.

At business schools, each recruiting team decides which case or cases they want to use in the interviews. The morning of the interview session, school team members normally present their cases to the team leader (a partner) who approves their cases or suggests new ones. These cases are usually based on the interviewer's own recent projects or assignments. The interviewers are told to use the same case all day, so they can gauge how well the candidates perform. "The downside, of course," admits one interviewer, "is that word gets out about the case." McKinsey "doesn't like brainteasers," but will give guesstimates if there is reason to believe that the candidate has a quantitative deficiency.

On many campuses, McKinsey evaluates candidates through a "town hall" process, during which salient information about a candidate is flashed up on a screen. This information includes the candidate's resume, what McKinsey events he or she attended, and other intelligence on the person, including opinions from former business analysts who attend classes with the individual. Normally a consensus quickly develops ("90 percent of the time"). Otherwise, the firm will try to break the tie through one more interview or more extensive questioning of McKinsey alums who know the candidate.

OUR SURVEY SAYS

MOVING UP AND AWAY

McKinsey's high turnover rate is not due to employee dissatisfaction. Though McKinsey consultants are "universally elated" with their "challenging," "rewarding" assignments, they leave because they are actively recruited by corporate America to serve as executives; many McKinsey consultants are hired away by their clients. And of course, there's McKinsey's notorious up-or-out policy; the firm is "vigilant about pushing out those who don't meet its exacting standards." While they're there, McKinsey employees appreciate the "thorough" training they receive as well as the camaraderie of their colleagues, who are "bright, interesting, and fun to be around."

RELATIVELY DOWN TO EARTH

Some consider the culture at McKinsey to be "on the snobbish side." Perhaps because consultants are the most highly paid in the industry: McKinsey consultants with a few years' experience receive more than $200,000 a year. Another consultant opines that "a lot of the people here are pretty square." Still, says one consultant: "Most people are down to earth. Some are very elitist, but those people usually find that in the long run they don't survive. When you visit a client you can't come off as uppity."

ETERNAL VIGILANCE IS THE PRICE MCKINSEY MUST PAY

An integral part of this process is the firm's performance review procedure, insiders tell us. "About 50 percent of your promotional chances depends on your feedback," which involves "page upon page of blunt criticism." If you want to work at McKinsey, you should expect to work long hours. "Hours never go below 60 and at the high end can be 90 to 100 hours a week," reports one insider. While the firm is "proactive" about recruiting minorities and women, the numbers are "hard to find" at the higher levels. All in all, say consultants, they have "a lot of respect" for McKinsey. The firm "offers great promotional prospects," and "when you're ready to move on to another firm or industry, McKinsey gives you a tremendous variety of career prospects."

THE BIRTH OF SPECIALIZATION

"There is definitely a move toward greater industry specialization going on at McKinsey," discloses one insider. "The number of generalists is still high, but we are hiring more and more industry experts. In my department, we've recently taken in a healthcare expert and a market research expert." How does McKinsey decide who qualifies as an "expert" in a particular field? "Our experts are usually PhDs," confirms another insider, "or those with a great deal of experience in a desired industry – especially on the strategic side." What factors account for this change? "I think there are two reasons," replies one thoughtful insider. "First, industry-specific firms like Greenwich Associates are giving us a lot of competition. And second, the other large strategy consulting firms like Andersen are gaining industry-specific expertise that they didn't have five or 10 years ago. To compete, we've needed to become sharper, more focused."

CLASSES ON WHERE TO PUT YOUR HAND

Employees can attend brief training sessions, called "micro-trainings" at McKinsey. "There's one training called Health Care 101," remarks one insider. "It's only a day; and if you want to be better informed, there's always Health Care 102." As far as computer training is concerned, quickie tutorials are easy to come by. "You can go for computer training whenever you want.

All you have to do is call a day ahead of time, say you want to learn advanced Excel, and go the next afternoon."

During their first year at McKinsey, new associates receive ongoing training, including "extensive training on how to behave with clients." Young consultants are drilled on everything from "how to shake hands," "how to present to the client," "the use of graphs and slides," to "where to keep your hands when you sit and when you're presenting." "Remember," McKinsey warns its new hires, "you are always being watched."

To order a 50- to 70-page Vault Reports Employer Profile on McKinsey & Company call 1-888-JOB-VAULT or visit www.VaultReports.com

The full Employer Profile includes detailed information on McKinsey's departments, recent developments and transactions, hiring and interview process, plus what employees really think about culture, pay, work hours and more.

Boston Consulting Group

VAULT REPORTS RANKING 2

Exchange Place, 31st Floor
Boston, MA 02109
(617) 973-1200
Fax: (617) 973-1339
www.bcg.com

THE BOSTON CONSULTING GROUP

LOCATIONS

Boston, MA (HQ)
Atlanta, GA
Chicago, IL
Dallas, TX
Los Angles, CA
New York, NY
Washington, DC
38 offices around the world

DEPARTMENTS

Strategic Consulting

THE STATS

Annual Revenues: $660 million (1997 est.)
No. of Employees: 1,720 (worldwide)
No. of Offices: 46 (worldwide)
A privately-held company
CEO: Carl Stern

KEY COMPETITORS

- Andersen Consulting
- Bain & Company
- Booz•Allen & Hamilton
- McKinsey & Company
- Mercer Management Consulting
- Monitor Company

THE BUZZ
What consultants at other firms are saying about BCG

- "Thinkers, not doers"
- "Friendly, intelligent"
- "Elitist"
- "Technically rigorous"

Boston Consulting Group

UPPERS

- Opportunity to be creative in devising client solutions
- Flat organizational structure
- Emphasis on work/life balance
- Better hours than other top consulting firms

DOWNERS

- Can be initially scary because of lack of frameworks
- Extensive travel
- Overimpressed with flashy work

EMPLOYMENT CONTACT

Associates:
Marianne Jones
National Associate Coordinator

Consultants and experienced hires:
Roxanne Cullinan

The Boston Consulting Group
Exchange Place, 31st Floor
Boston, MA 02109

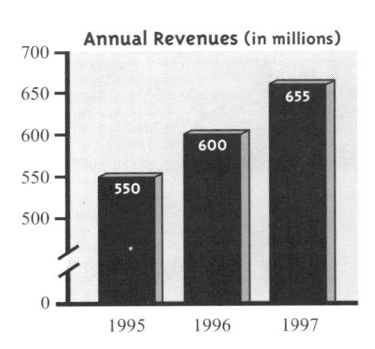

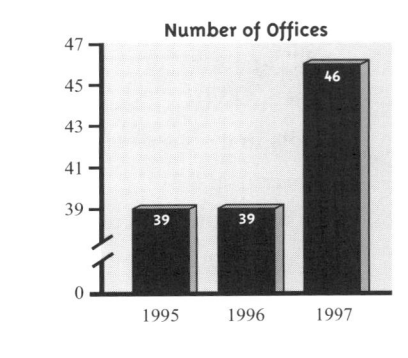

Annual Revenues (in millions)
- 1995: 550
- 1996: 600
- 1997: 655

Number of Offices
- 1995: 39
- 1996: 39
- 1997: 46

HOURS	PAY	PRESTIGE	DRESS	SATISFACTION
BEST = SHORTEST HOURS	BEST = HIGHEST PAY	BEST = MOST PRESTIGIOUS	BEST = MOST CASUAL	BEST = MOST SATISFIED
3	9	10	6	10

Consulting Job Seekers: Receive free e-mailed job postings matching your interests & qualifications! Register at www.VaultReports.com

THE SCOOP

THE INNOVATOR

While The Boston Consulting Group has lagged ever so slightly behind industry leader McKinsey in terms of prestige, the firm has nevertheless been responsible for a number of major management consulting innovations and concepts, such as "time-based competition" and "capability-driven competitive strategies." One of BCG's best-known contributions is the renowned "BCG Matrix" which explains the relationship between a company's profitability and its market share. (However, that framework is "not really used any more," at the firm of its origin according to one BCG consultant. "It's based in a time when there were large industrial conglomerates, and there aren't many of those anymore.") In fact, BCG, and its late founder Bruce Henderson are credited with "being the father of strategic consulting, in every sense of the word," according to a BCG alum, Thomas Doorley. Doorley told the *Boston Herald*: "Historically, the policy decisions were made by a bunch of folk sitting around a table thinking big thoughts. It was [Henderson's] view that it wasn't that easy." Henderson also "had faith in the abilities of young men and women to contribute to solving complex problems," and to marry quantitative data to seat-of-the-pants strategizing. Today, close to 2000 consultants in 46 offices around the globe work at the company Henderson founded.

LATE TO GENERALIZE

BCG organizes its work into industry practices, such as high tech, defense, broadcasting, and media and communication. While BCG serves clients from a wide variety of industries, the firm focuses on clients in the energy, telecommunications, automobiles, financial services, pharmaceuticals, and consumer goods sectors. Consultants can work at the firm for six years (including time as an associate) before electing a specialty.

MOVING ABROAD

In recent years, BCG has expanded its presence in the international market and has a number of major overseas clients, including the Russian government. BCG has been active in Eastern Europe since 1985, advising on acquisitions and restructuring, including projects in the banking industry. By predicting the cost structures and service levels that would be necessary for success in a deregulated environment, the firm has played a major role in preparing companies for deregulation and privatization in the new post-Cold War Europe. BCG has an excellent reputation in Europe; one survey reports that it is one of the top five firms for which European consultants would like to work. The company gets half of its revenues from consulting engagements in Europe, and a third from the Americas (the rest comes from its Asian offices).

AN ASIAN POWERHOUSE

BCG has an unusually strong Asian presence. In fact, the presence is so strong that the firm considers its Asian offices a separate unit (as are its European offices). BCG has staked out a place in Asia since 1966, when prescient Bruce Henderson opened an office in 1966 in Tokyo, becoming the first Western consulting company to enter Japan. BCG has retained this "frontier" feeling, according to one consultant who has worked in the region. "You feel like you're on the edge," that consultant reports. "You work hard to set up your office. You know everyone there." According to BCG, its office in Hong Kong (opened in 1990) signaled the beginning of a truly strong presence in the Asian region. Offices opened since have included Kuala Lumpur, Malaysia (1992), Shanghai (1993), Bangkok (1994), Jakarta (1995), Singapore (1995) and Mumbai, India (1995). In 1998, BCG added a second office in Japan; the firm plans to open an office in Beijing in 1999.

BCG EAST

All those overseas offices aren't just for show. While some consultancies derive most of their business from American firms conducting operations overseas, BCG gets roughly half of its business in Asia from local entites, including private companies, governments and state-run businesses. The firm's clients include five of Asia's biggest non-Japanese firms, three of the top five business conglomerates in Korea, and eight of the biggest local commercial banks in Hong Kong, Indonesia, Malaysia, Thailand and Korea.

GETTING HIRED

BCG's interview format consists of two to three rounds of interviews. For MBAs, the first round is comprised of two interviews, each of which is 45 minutes long; this round consists entirely of case interviews. In the second round, interviewees go through two more case interviews, this time with managers at BCG. In addition, at this second round, each candidate is subjected to three one-on-one interviews with vice presidents at the firm, during which the candidate is tested primarily for interpersonal qualities and fit for the firm. Undergraduate candidates have two rounds on campus and an additional, final round at the office.

Each interview consists of about ten minutes of conversation (meant to suss out personal qualities desirable to consultants), half an hour of case, and five minutes of time in which a candidate may ask questions.

"The cases tend to be very conceptual," says one insider. "They do look to see that you can understand basic concepts about an industry. They do test quantitative skills. There aren't any guesstimates per se, but you do have them within cases – I was asked a few times to estimate the market size for a particular product." Several insiders say the firm "rarely, if ever, asks brainteasers, because that's just not applicable to what we do."

Some candidates report getting a case in everyone of their interviews, though experiences vary by office and individual. "In my second round," reports one consultant, "I met with a partner (called officers at BCG) and a manager and had lunch with two associates. One of my interviews was a case interview and the other was completely personal, a chat session. We talked a lot about my summer experience. They want to see if you are a people person, and maturity is a big thing for them." One person who interviewed with both McKinsey and BCG compares the two. McKinsey's interviews were straightforward, "along the lines of 'How many customers would you need to have this restaurant turn a profit?' There is a definite answer they want." BCG's questions, according to this insider, were more creative and open-ended, "so theirs would be more like 'Tell me all the reasons this restaurant might be losing customers.'" Classmates who have compared notes after first-round interviews often note that they all get the same case interviews at BCG (usually based on a business problem at the firm). This doesn't mean the cases are well-publicized, though. "There are no handouts," notes one interviewee, "so you need to ask questions."

OUR SURVEY SAYS

A BOSTONIAN LOVEFEST

Boston Consulting Group employees think highly of each other and their firm. The "lean organization" places little emphasis on seniority; entry-level employees, therefore, receive "golden opportunities" to contribute their ideas and implement them. The "grueling" hours and "extensive" travel are "taxing," but the firm's prestige and pay scale offer "just rewards." With the pleasure of intellectual activity comes more work. "We tend not to have specific types of analyses done already, so in some sense, we have to reinvent the wheel each time," says one consultant. "This is definitely more creative, and gives better solutions to the client, but it also means much more work for us."

THE DEEP THINKERS

Some recent hires comment that they were at first surprised by the "heavily theoretical" nature of their consulting assignments, but they also comment that they are finding the challenges "even more rewarding" than they expected. Hours "aren't horrible, but not a piece of cake." They are "on average, about 55 hours a week," but "it's hard to define work hours. Generally, weekends are free, but not always." BCG sponsors "around one activity every four or five weeks," with "summertime and fall really big activity times."

PERFORM FOR PAY

The pay at BCG is "very competitive. You won't go hungry, even in New York. The pay in itself is good, but the bonus – which can be substantial, up to 20 percent on top of base pay – makes things even better. A good and bad thing about BCG's pay is that it's based on performance, so how much you get depends on your own self," says one consultant. An associate in the New York office remarks that the "401(k) is good, and the performance bonuses are really substantial." (Actually, the firm has a profit-sharing retirement fund rather than a 401(k); the fund, unlike a 401(k), does not require the employee to make any contributions.)

EVERYONE LOVES BCG, OR AT LEAST REALLY LIKES IT

Employees unanimously confirm BCG's reputation as a pleasant place to work. "BCG is the best firm in the business for quality of life issues," insiders say, although dress in some offices is business formal with casual Fridays. Half of the firm's offices are business casual all week, and the firm plans to move to daily business casual in every office by 2000. "The partners are very fun and very relaxed, and they don't treat you badly. There's a real emphasis on lifestyle versus just doing the work," says one consultant. However, the creativity and emphasis on individuality may mean that management tends to value "smart work way above hard work, which means that those who have a flashier style of working do better than diligent workers." Also remember that job satisfaction is "relative to [consulting], which doesn't have too many [satisfied] people on the whole."

INDEPENDENT DAYS

The frequency of independent work is one reason BCG "wants people who can work alone and make their own decisions," explains one insider. That contact continues: "That is scary for some people and there is always a time in which you are floundering around a bit at first. But the [case leader] will give you help, and frameworks, if you need them." While some adore this flexiblity – one consultant raves that "if you want to work at home for a while, that is rarely a problem" – it means that BCG is "not the best place for someone who likes structure. That's nothing to be ashamed of. Many people function very well with some structure. But BCG favors those who can think in the white space [a trendy new consulting term to replace 'out of the box'] and who can be self-starters."

To order a 50- to 70-page Vault Reports Employer Profile on Boston Consulting Group call 1-888-JOB-VAULT or visit www.VaultReports.com

The full Employer Profile includes detailed information on BCG's departments, recent developments and transactions, hiring and interview process, plus what employees really think about culture, pay, work hours and more.

Bain & Company

RANKING 3

Two Copley Place
Boston, MA 02116
(617) 572-2000
Fax: (617) 572-2427
www.bain.com

LOCATIONS

Boston, MA (HQ)
Atlanta, GA
Chicago, IL
Dallas, TX
Los Angeles, CA
San Francisco, CA

DEPARTMENTS

Strategy Consulting

THE STATS

Annual Revenues: $480 million (1997 est.)
No. of Employees: 2,000 (worldwide)
No. of Professionals: 1,500 (worldwide)
No. of Offices: 25 (worldwide), 6 (U.S.)
A privately-held company
CEO: Orit Gadiesh
Worldwide Managing Director:
Thomas Tierney

KEY COMPETITORS

- Andersen Consulting
- Booz·Allen & Hamilton
- Boston Consulting Group
- McKinsey & Company
- Mercer Management Consulting
- Monitor Company

THE BUZZ
What consultants at other firms are saying about Bain

- "Schmoozy"
- "Prentenious, flamboyant"
- "Snotty and secretive"
- "On the heels of McKinsey"

Vault Reports Guide to the Top Consulting Firms

Bain & Company

UPPERS
- Not as much travel as other consulting firms
- "TLC" in training
- Flex-time, parental leave and sabbaticals
- Convivial culture

DOWNERS
- Very long hours
- Lack of industry specialization

EMPLOYMENT CONTACT

Human Resources
Bain & Company
Two Copley Place
Boston, MA 02116

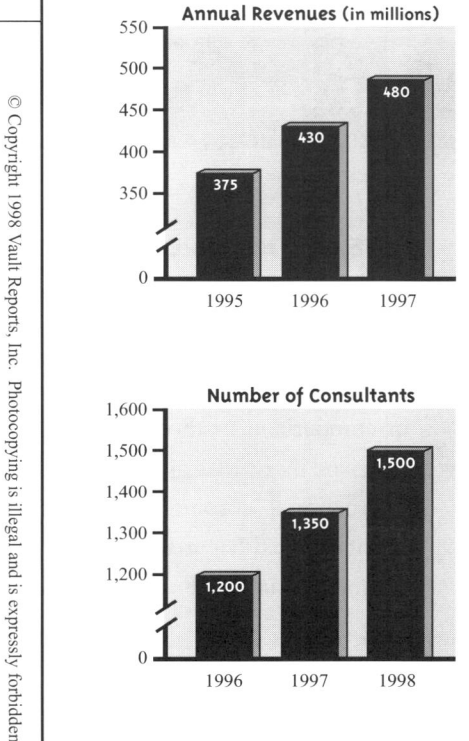

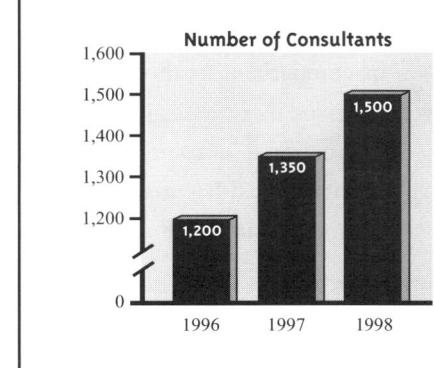

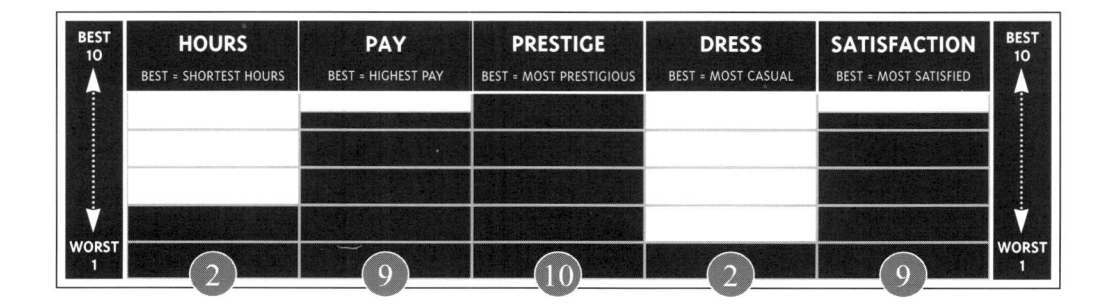

Annual Revenues (in millions)
- 1995: 375
- 1996: 430
- 1997: 480

Number of Consultants
- 1996: 1,200
- 1997: 1,350
- 1998: 1,500

© Copyright 1998 Vault Reports, Inc. Photocopying is illegal and is expressly forbidden.

	HOURS (BEST = SHORTEST HOURS)	PAY (BEST = HIGHEST PAY)	PRESTIGE (BEST = MOST PRESTIGIOUS)	DRESS (BEST = MOST CASUAL)	SATISFACTION (BEST = MOST SATISFIED)
Rating	2	9	10	2	9

Consulting Job Seekers: Receive free e-mailed job postings matching your interests & qualifications! Register at www.VaultReports.com

www.vaultreports.com

Bain & Company

THE SCOOP

ONE OF THE THREE LEADING STRATEGY FIRMS

Bain & Company is among the world leaders in international strategy consulting. Founded in 1973 with a handful of employees, Bain now boasts a consulting staff of 1500 and has served clients in over 80 countries on five continents. The firm has 25 offices in 18 countries, though, in comparison to those of main competitors McKinsey and The Boston Consulting Group, many of its offices are still relatively young. Its client base consists primarily of diversified, international corporations in all sectors of business and industry, among them financial services, health care, and manufacturing. Bain also has a new leveraged buyout practice (developed in San Francisco in 1994, and expanded into a firm-wide practice in 1998).

SPECIALISTS? WE DON'T NEED ANY!

Unlike many of its consulting competitors, which are moving toward increased industry specialization, Bain remains a pure generalist, strategy shop. It must be working – the company projects 10 to 15 percent growth in revenues in 1998 and in 1999 as well. It hasn't always been thus. Bain ran into trouble in the mid-1980s when one of its employees working for Guinness in London was implicated in a share-dealing scandal. Around the same time, a disastrous ESOP (Employee Stock Ownership Plan) overloaded the company with annual payments. Falling business forced the firm to lay off over 20 percent of its workforce, and Bain nearly went bankrupt in 1991.

A VERY IMPRESSIVE REPUTATION AGAIN

Since then, Bain has not only recovered its prestige, but enjoys a high reputation for confidentiality and integrity even in England. Since a management buyout in 1991, the company's revenues have risen year after year. While it shares its headquarters building with Bain Capital, a venture capital firm founded by William Bain in 1984, the two firms have no official connection. However, Bain Capital does exhibit a "preference" for Bain when it needs to hire a consulting firm for its due diligence work, and the two companies are said to use a similar "results-based" operative framework. Bain consultants routinely make the (short) move to Bain Capital; the consulting firm even circulates "help wanted" e-mails for its VC cousin.

BAIN LOVE

Bain is a very close-knit firm. Its consultants are affectionately called "Bainies," and the firm has what some call a collegiate and close-knit culture. "What are you going to do Monday morning at 8 a.m?" is a catchphrase at this consultancy, which concentrates on producing immediately implementable and valuable results for its clients. Orit Gadiesh (or "OG"), the brilliant, flamboyant (and purple-haired) chair of Bain & Company, insists that it's better to have an 80 percent solution that is immediately implementable than a perfect, 100 percent solution that is purely theoretical.

GETTING HIRED

Bain hired approximately 200 MBAs in 1998, and plans to hire about 200 more MBAs for the class of 1999, with the same number of undergraduate hires. The hiring process starts with a first round that occurs on campus or at a local hotel. This round consists of two separate interivews. One is a "fit" interview "that's meant to tell if you are a dynamic, friendly, hyper-smart person who would fit well into the Bain culture, but is mainly going over your resume;" the other is a case interview. These preliminary interviews are short – 20 or 30 minutes each.

The candidates Bain deems worthy of a second interview are interviewed either on campus or at a nearby Bain office. This second round consists of three 40-minute interviews. One of these interviews is a more intense non-case "fit" interview, while the other two are case interviews.

Bain caters to its most desired candidates. At some of its larger core schools – such as Harvard, Wharton, Kellogg, Stanford and Chicago – Bain will make a campus rep available to answer questions. A consultant is available to fly in and answer any questions recruits have about the firm.

OUR SURVEY SAYS

THE GOOD FAITH FIRM

Consultants say that the firm makes a "good faith" effort to put them on assignments in which they are interested and also offers them the flexibility they need to balance their work schedules with the demands of their personal lives. Insiders say that "the level of the assignments is top-notch." "Excellent researchers" on case teams also help solve client problems. We hear that "the hours fluctuate a lot, from 50 to 80 hours a week, and sometimes strange hours."

Bain gives all of its employees – including recent hires – "as much responsibility as they can handle." The "intense," "upbeat" corporate culture emphasizes teamwork "constantly," insiders say, comparing the firm to "an elite fraternity or sorority – Beta Alpha Iota Nu." Even chairman Orit Gadiesh spends about 70 percent of her time on client work.

SUPERPOPULAR BAIN

Plenty of applicants want to join in the fun. The firm "has been known to get 100 resumes a day." Junior consultants interact "frequently" with senior employees, especially at Bain's numerous social events. A special perk at Bain is the "Bain Band," a semiprofessional musical ensemble composed of Bain employees that plays at special events. "Suits are required" at this prestigious firm, "except for Fridays. For a few years, people violated the dress code regularly, until the company cracked down." As for diversity, the firm's record is fairly clean. "Although the breakdown of men to women is about 70/30, I felt women were well-accepted in the organization," says a female former consultant. "And of course, the chairman is a woman, Orit Gadiesh." While minorities are "treated as equals," "at the end of the day, there were few minorities in the company."

IF BAIN CAN MAKE IT THERE...

At the present time, Bain has no office in New York. Some insiders claim the reasons for this are twofold. "First of all, Bain thinks it's more efficient to have fewer and larger offices, and second, most of the partners with families don't want to move to New York," we are told. The firm, however, says it is now actively evaluating the possibility of opening a New York office – not because Bain has any difficulty serving its New York clientele from Boston, but because many potential recruits have expressed a desire to live and work in the city.

ROAD WARRIORS

The amount of travel seems to vary from consultant to consultant and from office to office. One insider remarks, "I worked for Bain for a year and a half. I never traveled internationally and my domestic travel was maybe once a month." Another insider has a different tale to tell: "I traveled constantly. At least three days per week." Another remarks, "I worked on a Japanese case for six months, but spent only six weeks in the country. The same with the France project. I worked almost entirely out of the domestic office; it was only the last two and a half weeks of the project that I flew to Paris." Generally, the firm is "good about transferring its personnel from one office to another, especially if it truly wants you. For example, if Bain needed a healthcare expert in Sydney, it would set you up with a really nice housing situation. On the other hand, [when changing offices] financial gradation depends on how badly you want it versus how badly the client needs you."

POPULAR OFFICES

According to insiders, Bain's more popular offices include San Francisco, London ("you can be abroad, but still speak English"), Paris ("because, well, it's Paris"), Sydney, and Johannesburg ("it's an exciting time to be in South Africa"). Foreign language proficiency, although not a requirement of the company, "is common among Bainies. Many people have studied or lived abroad."

Bain offices are well-equipped, insiders say. "There are some secretaries and a lot of research staff. You can do your own research or sometimes you give your requirements to the support staff," says one consultant. "They'll either give you the stuff the next day or that evening, depending on how much of a rush it is. You can get hundreds of pages sometimes." Reports another insider, "every team has a team assistant, who handles the administrative details. There's also a word processing bay, where you drop stuff off after you write it out. The library is very modern; it has laserdiscs and CD-ROMS, the whole bit."

To order a 50- to 70-page Vault Reports Employer Profile on Bain & Company call 1-888-JOB-VAULT or visit www.VaultReports.com

The full Employer Profile includes detailed information on Bain's departments, recent developments and transactions, hiring and interview process, plus what employees really think about culture, pay, work hours and more.

"For a few years, people violated the dress code regularly, until the company cracked down."

– *Bain insider*

Monitor Company

VAULT REPORTS RANKING 4

25 First Street
Cambridge, MA 02141
(617) 252-2000
Fax: (617) 252-2100
www.monitor.com

MONITOR COMPANY

LOCATIONS

Cambridge, MA (HQ)
Los Angeles, CA
New York, NY
Athens, Greece
Istanbul, Turkey
Manila, Phillipines
Moscow, Russia
Munich, Germany
New Delhi, India
Sao Paulo, Brazil
Singapore
Stockholm, Sweden
Tel Aviv, Israel
Zurich, Switzerland

DEPARTMENTS

Consulting

THE STATS

Annual Revenues: $186 million (1997)
No. of Employees: 1,200 (worldwide)
No. of Offices: 25 (worldwide)
A privately-held company
CEO: Mark J. Fuller

KEY COMPETITORS

- Bain & Company
- Booz·Allen & Hamilton
- Boston Consulting Group
- McKinsey & Company
- Mercer Management Consulting

THE BUZZ
What consultants at other firms are saying about Monitor

- "High-powered, low promotions"
- "Harvard B-school"
- "Few clients"
- "Unusual strategy boutique"

Vault Reports Guide to the Top Consulting Firms

Monitor Company

UPPERS
- Good social scene
- Loose organizational structure
- Low turnover

DOWNERS
- Lack of support staff
- Long workdays

EMPLOYMENT CONTACT

Human Resources
Monitor Company
25 First Street
Cambridge, MA 02141

recruiting@monitor.com

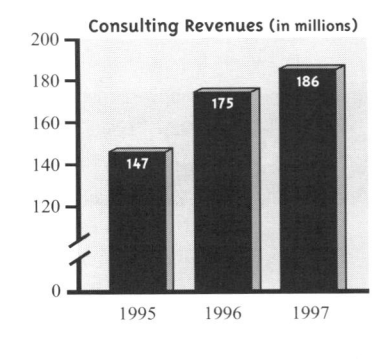

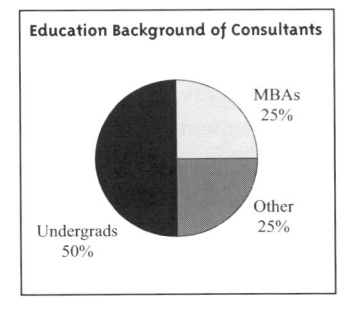

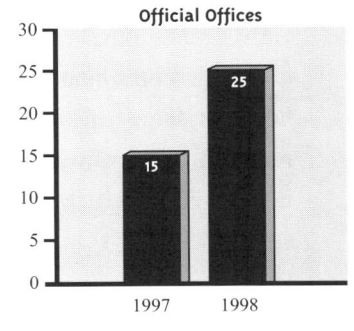

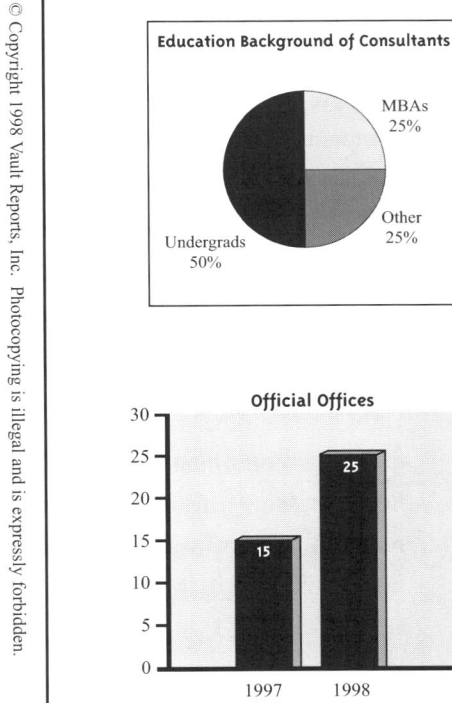

© Copyright 1998 Vault Reports, Inc. Photocopying is illegal and is expressly forbidden.

Consulting Revenues (in millions)
- 1995: 147
- 1996: 175
- 1997: 186

Education Background of Consultants
- MBAs 25%
- Other 25%
- Undergrads 50%

Official Offices
- 1997: 15
- 1998: 25

	HOURS	PAY	PRESTIGE	DRESS	SATISFACTION
	BEST = SHORTEST HOURS	BEST = HIGHEST PAY	BEST = MOST PRESTIGIOUS	BEST = MOST CASUAL	BEST = MOST SATISFIED
	1	9	10	7	9

BEST 10 / WORST 1

Consulting Job Seekers: Receive free e-mailed job postings matching your interests & qualifications! Register at www.VaultReports.com

www.vaultreports.com

THE SCOOP

MONITORING THE WORLD

If those business school professors are so smart, why aren't they putting their words into practice? Michael Porter, charismatic Harvard Business School professor did just that in 1983, when he became a founding father of Monitor Company, a growing consulting firm now charged with the mission of applying Porter's pearls of wisdom to the thorny troubles of companies worldwide. Monitor opened its first office in 1983 and has opened at least one new office every year since. Through 25 offices spread across the globe, the firm offers strategic management consulting services to Fortune 500 companies, international firms, government agencies, and major nonprofit organizations.

UNDIVIDED

Unlike some other management consulting firms, the Monitor Company does not group and divide its consultants by industry. Instead, it fully integrates its practices. The firm does, however, have "affiliate" organizations that provide support in particular areas such as market research and software support. One of Monitor's key strategies is a "horizontal" web of networked expertise and experience rather than what it views to be the vertical monolithic structure of most consulting firms.

BRINGING THE FIVE FORCES WORLDWIDE

Monitor has taken a strong lead in places like South Africa, where it was the first global management consulting company to make a long-term commitment, and the former Soviet Union, where Monitor has been active since the dawn of perestroika. Wherever it operates, Monitor emphasizes profit reinvestment to provide its consultants with state-of-the-art resources.

Though he's reportedly rarely seen around the firm, and was never the CEO of the firm, Monitor is pervaded by the spirit of founding principal and Harvard Business School professor Michael Porter. Porter's book *Competitive Strategy* and successive business-oriented tomes have inspired and led generations of Monitor consultants. The books are guides to the interaction between industry structure and competitive strategy and the logic of the variables affecting a company's competitive situation.

THE ACADEMICS

Monitor still draws inspiration from Porter, but some consultants say "we don't use his stuff as much as we used to." Monitor retains the academic slant of its founding, encouraging a university-like atmosphere, casual dress, and rafts of theories, including "Productive Reasoning," an intervention technique for handling client executives who are nervous about working on the future of their company with outsiders (i.e., Monitor consultants). Monitor also encourages pro bono work through its nonprofit Monitor Institute. In January 1998 consultants from Monitor started a venture capital fund, Monitor Clipper Partners, that is much like competitor Bain's Bain Capital.

GETTING HIRED

Monitor hires consultants at both the college graduate and MBA level, and also considers graduates from other advanced degree programs. While the title is the same, the starting pay and responsibility differs based on the new hire's level of schooling. On average, Monitor hires over 50 new MBAs each year.

Monitor recruits on certain business school campuses during the months of October and November. For those going through on-campus recruiting, the first two interview rounds are held on-campus, at a local hotel, or at a nearby office. The second interview is a case interview – with a twist, insiders tell us. In a typical case interview at other firms, the case interviewer will spring a short case question upon the applicant, who then must quickly come up with pertinent questions and observations. But at Monitor, you'll be given a fairly detailed written case to read (about four or five pages, including exhibits).

The final round is at the desired Monitor office, and is even odder – involving a "group case" for which candidates must collaborate with other applicants. Job offers are typically made the same day as the last interview or no more than 24 hours afterwards by phone. Monitor welcomes hiring inquiries from persons not attending school or at schools not directly targeted by Monitor.

Monitor courts not only undergrad and MBA students but PhD and other advanced degree candidates for its summer consultant program. The program is designed to approximate the work experience of a full-time consultant as closely as possible. Monitor provides training, feedback and mentoring, and places summer consultants on case teams. Summer interns are reuired to work for 10 weeks, but may begin their stints with the firm at any convenient time.

OUR SURVEY SAYS

BUILDING THE MONITOR PYRAMID

Monitor stresses that its organizational structure – a "deep and wide pyramid" – differs from that of other firms in the industry. Its employees report that this organizational structure enables new hires to receive significant responsibilities quickly. Consultants enjoy an "unusual degree of independence" and "continuous, on-the-job learning." Insiders say that Monitor has "no titles or structure" and that consultants "can move at their own pace – either rapidly or slowly."

KINDLY MONITOR FOLK

"Throughout the interview process, people are being evaluated for intelligence and ability," says one insider, "but they are also being judged as good or bad people for Monitor." What is good for Monitor? Monitor is reportedly "a little friendlier, laid back, and personable." "There is uniformity in peoples' attitudes here," reports one content insider. "No one's aggressive or hyper-competitive. And there is no 'up-or-out' policy – of course people help each other out." Another insider proclaims: "Everyone here is fairly humble. It is quite a mature environment. People at Monitor are more sure of themselves people at other firms." This relaxed atmosphere is reflected in the firm's dress code, which is casual except for client meetings – so casual, that one employee at the company's headquarters comments that the Cambridge office "tends to be a tad more formal – khakis instead of jeans."

The firm's consultants maintain that they have more "highly developed interpersonal skills than consultants from BCG, who are often more eccentric." Also, says one insider: "They have a strong sense of civic responsibility – lots of informal pro bono work, especially with community organizations and development work. The original founders were very civic-minded." The firm is is community-minded when it comes to each other, too. Explains one insider: "It's a young group of people and we enjoy each other's company." In fact, one consultant estimates that "about 10 percent of the consultants at Monitor are dating each other."

LOW TURNOVER – DESPITE LOTS OF HOURS

In this "meritocratic" atmosphere, consultants often have the opportunity to travel overseas or to work closely with the CEOs of major corporations. Insiders also say that "Monitor has a very low turnover rate in the ranks because we use a much more thorough screening process." Employees work the "grueling hours" typical of management consulting; one insider reports hearing of a consultant work back-to-back 120-hour weeks.

Big bonuses

Monitor consultants also like the company's generous bonus system: year-end bonuses typically run up to 60 percent of base salary – larger than those given by most industry rivals – and can be as high as 100 percent of base salary. In keeping with the academic slant of the firm, consultants aren't afforded their own assistants. In fact, Monitor "recently downsized its research staff, on the theory that consultants should be able to do their own research more efficiently. We kept one guy to take care of the copy machines and stuff like that." But Monitor consultants aren't eager to graduate. "I thoroughly enjoy the work," says one consultant, "and find that I continue to learn on a daily basis."

To order a 50- to 70-page Vault Reports Employer Profile on Monitor Company call 1-888-JOB-VAULT or visit www.VaultReports.com

The full Employer Profile includes detailed information on Monitor's departments, recent developments and transactions, hiring and interview process, plus what employees really think about culture, pay, work hours and more.

"People at Monitor are more sure of themselves than people at other firms."

– *Monitor insider*

Consulting Job Seekers: Receive free e-mailed job postings matching your interests & qualifications! Register at www.vaultreports.com

VAULT REPORTS™
www.vaultreports.com

Booz·Allen & Hamilton

VAULT REPORTS RANKING: 5

101 Park Avenue
New York, NY 10178
(212) 697-1900
www.bah.com

LOCATIONS

New York, NY (HQ)
Atlanta, GA • Bethesda, MD • Chicago, IL • Cleveland, OH • Dallas, TX • Houston, TX • Los Angeles, CA • McLean, VA • Monterrey, CA • San Francisco, CA and offices in 31 foreign countries

DEPARTMENTS

Communications, Media & Technology
Consumer & Engineered Products
Energy & Chemicals
Financial & Health Services
Information Technology
Operations

THE STATS

Annual Revenues: $1.3 billion (1997)
No. of Employees: 8,500
No. of Offices: 90 (worldwide)
A privately-held company
Chairman: William F. Stasior

KEY COMPETITORS

- Andersen Consulting
- A.T. Kearney
- Bain & Company
- Boston Consulting Group
- McKinsey & Company
- Mercer Management Consulting
- Monitor Company

THE BUZZ
What consultants at other firms are saying about Booz

- "Dropped to second rate"
- "Everything done to you"
- "Lots of government work"
- "Low-ballers, established"

Vault Reports Guide to the Top Consulting Firms
Booz·Allen & Hamilton

UPPERS
- Great intranet
- Generous travel budget
- Individual autonomy
- "Friday in the office" policy

DOWNERS
- Early industry specialization
- Sometimes overly political

EMPLOYMENT CONTACT

Director of Recruiting
Booz·Allen & Hamilton
101 Park Avenue
New York, NY 10178

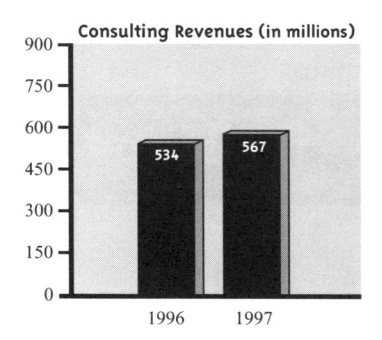

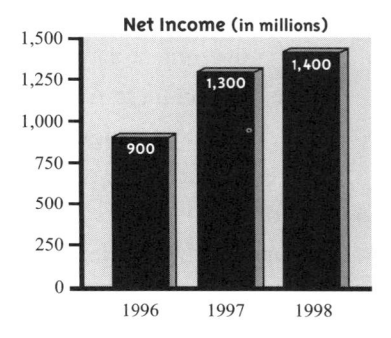

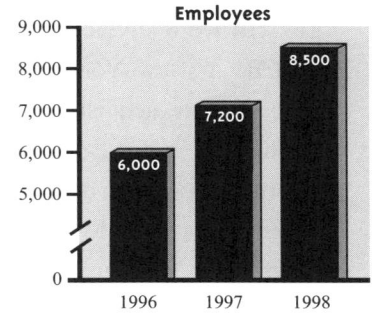

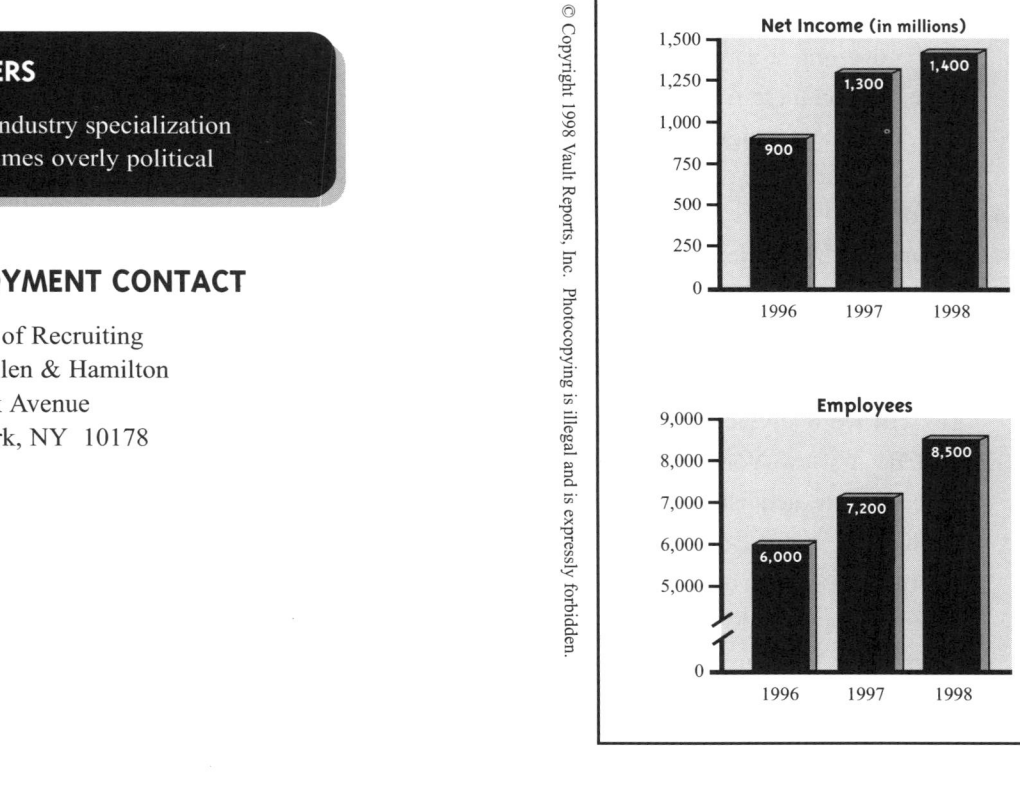

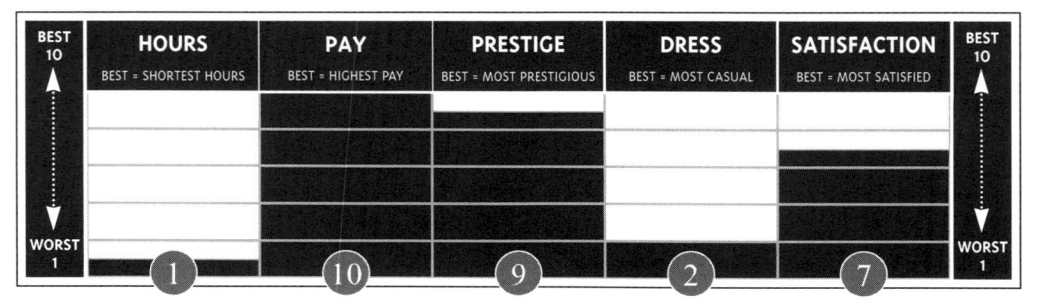

Consulting Revenues (in millions)
- 1996: 534
- 1997: 567

Net Income (in millions)
- 1996: 900
- 1997: 1,300
- 1998: 1,400

Employees
- 1996: 6,000
- 1997: 7,200
- 1998: 8,500

© Copyright 1998 Vault Reports, Inc. Photocopying is illegal and is expressly forbidden.

	HOURS BEST = SHORTEST HOURS	PAY BEST = HIGHEST PAY	PRESTIGE BEST = MOST PRESTIGIOUS	DRESS BEST = MOST CASUAL	SATISFACTION BEST = MOST SATISFIED	
	1	10	9	2	7	

Consulting Job Seekers: Receive free e-mailed job postings matching your interests & qualifications! Register at www.VaultReports.com

VAULT REPORTS™
www.vaultreports.com

THE SCOOP

THE CONSULTING PIONEER

Edwin Booz founded his firm shortly after graduating from Northwestern University in 1914. From the beginning, Booz' consulting firm, one of the first such companies, worked closely with government agencies, consulting with the country's War Department in 1917. Booz was joined by partners Allen and Hamilton during the 1930s. In 1940, the firm worked with the U.S. Government again in preparation for World War II. Since then, Booz•Allen & Hamilton has emerged as one of the world's most prestigious management consulting firms. Booz•Allen continues to work closely with government agencies, but has also expanded its reach to include companies in a variety of industries, from telecom to energy.

THE SPLIT

Booz•Allen is divvied into two major operations. The Worldwide Commercial Business unit (WCB) in New York does corporate strategy, renewal, productivity improvement, growth management, acquisitions, and business restructuring, mainly for international corporations. Within the WCB, Booz•Allen is divided into several industry groups: Energy, Chemicals & Pharmaceuticals; Consumer and Engineered Products; Financial and Health Services; and Communications, Media, and Technology. WCB also includes three functional groups: Operations Management, Information Technology, and Strategic Leadership. The WCB divisions offer classic management consulting services.

The Worldwide Technology Business, based in DC suburb McLean, VA, caters to government clients in the nation's capital and in other nation-states, consulting on defense, national security, environment and energy, transportation and space, telecommunications, civil programs, international projects, and management sciences. MBAs are normally not hired for the WTB; its consultants are normally engineers who work on a different pay scale and hiring schedule.

Strong implementers

With an emphasis on creating change rather than merely prescribing it, the firm reports spending about a third to a half of its time in the implementation process. Before implementation, Booz•Allen often involves the client in the consulting process and frequently integrates executives of a client into the consulting team. In 1993, the firm adopted its "Vision 2000" plan, which reorganized the firm into its current practice areas and restated Booz's original goal of becoming "the absolute best management and technology consulting firm."

The vision

As part of Vision 2000, Booz pared down its number of clients from 1200 to 300; Booz•Allen garners 80 percent of its revenues from 20 percent of its clients. Part of what the company believes will help make it the best is encouraging innovation. Here, Booz•Allen's strong reputation in information technology systems comes into play. The firm's Knowledge On-Line (KOL) database system – which pools the knowledge Booz consultants pick up while on assignment – is often called the best of its kind. The shared system keeps consultants from repeating each other's work, and provides info on an assortment of topics, including resumes, databases and histories of employees.

Knowledge everywhere

KOL is now used widely by Booz•Allen consultants in both the Worldwide Commercial Business and Worldwide Technology Business branches. The first division estimates that about 62 percent of WCB staff members access KOL once a month or more (security concerns prevent WTB consultants, who typically work with government agencies, from accessing KOL on assignments). The database is set up to promote sharing of information; consultants often spend a considerable amount of time entering their findings into KOL. Booz•Allen achieves this informational exchange partially through an appeal to ego: consultants who contribute the database have their names prominently displayed, their entries are linked to their resumes, and it's simple to search for any given consultant's contributions to the database. In addition, the firm encourages contributions through its feedback process – a third of a consultant's evaluation is based in part on contributions to KOL.

Hard and exciting changes

Change is never easy, even for those at the top. Booz•Allen COO Brian Dickie resigned from the firm in April 1998, apparently unhappy over the course the firm had chosen. Booz•Allen insiders say that the new president, Dan Lewis, is working with Stasior on a modification of the Vision 2000 plan. One associate says that while only partners are privy to the exact details, the entire plan is being reconsidered under the aegis of Lewis – steps from closing offices to restructuring the industries yet again are being bruited about. "One thing that I keep hearing about is that we're going to invest very heavily in India – Mumbai," says one insider.

GETTING HIRED

Booz•Allen is somewhat unusual among consulting firms in that it is divided into distinct industry practice and functional groups. This organizational structure affects the firm's hiring process, which consists of two rounds, the first on campus, the second at Booz offices. Interviewees must know which industry practice or functional group is of interest to them, as the second round of interview is exclusively with senior associates (recent college graduates are termed consultants at Booz, while MBA-level employees at Booz are called associates; above them are senior associates), principals (the next level after senior associate) and partners in the industry group of interest. Insiders say that the industry or operational group selection should be "pretty straightforward."

"Don't try to psych out the interviewers," advices one consultant. "It's a bad idea to choose one group thinking it will be easier to get in, and then try to switch to another." While experience in a particular industry is a "boon," it's not necessary. "We hire people who are simply smart as well," says one insider. If you have your heart set on a particular office, beware – not all practices reside at all offices. Hiring for the Worldwide Technology Business arm, which works largely with government contractors, is handled separately and largely targets those with advanced engineering and computer science degrees.

OUR SURVEY SAYS

THE INDEPENDENTS

Booz•Allen's culture encourages "fiercely independent" thinking without "hand-holding" or a "rah-rah team atmosphere." Employees say that this "sink or swim" environment forces them to learn on the job and to test their "mettle" against "a series of increasingly difficult challenges." Some employees object that Booz's flexibility means there is no career management. Insiders also say that Booz•Allen's policy of integrating its consultants into with the client's management into teams at the client's headquarters results in "constant travel" that can take its toll on consultants' lifestyles. We hear that the workplace can "be very political" and that a "sponsor" in upper management is crucial for advancement. This tough attitude is said to impact negatively on women and minorities.

THE UPSIDE OF BOOZ

This is not to say that Booz•Allen is a completely grim, dog-eat-dog sort of workplace. For one, working at Booz is "great for anyone who has a social conscience." The firm permits some pro bono work, and employees say that "unlike most management consulting places, Booz can understand employees who have a conscience and want to help people." The pay is "awesome," with MBAs earning upwards of $120,000 annually (not including bonuses). The best perk of working for Booz•Allen, according to employees, is "the unbelievable opportunities to travel around the world and enjoy yourself in style." One consultant says: "Things I did because of my job there: flew the Concord, went to Lillehammer for the winter

Olympics, took a cruise from Miami to the Bahamas, gambled in Monte Carlo, opera at Covent Garden, dinner in the Eiffel Tower, a summer afternoon at a topless beach in Nice, and the list goes on."

HOURS (AND HOURS)

Insiders report that "good hours on a project are 55 to 60 hours a week. Bad is 100 hours a week. You will have bad weeks." One associate reports "getting put on hellacious projects that are six weeks long and take 80 to 100 hours a week. After that, though, you will normally get a better project." Some of our contacts tie long hours to specific practices. "All the partners in the weaker practices are always trying to get a foot in the door," explains one insider. "What this effectively means is that Booz will want to overdeliver in result and undercut in price. That is good for Booz•Allen, but bad for the people on the projects, who have to work like dogs." "If you want halfway decent hours," advises another insider, "go to Booz in the practices in which it is strong. That's media, aerospace, oil and gas. Otherwise forget your weekends."

THE SATISFACTION RATE

Job satisfaction at Booz is generally "quite high." Employees remark that they are "proud to be working for a top name consulting firm" that "works with the big names in American and international business." Some employees also take pride in working for a firm "with a conscience and social commitment." One consultant points out, however, that "the satisfaction is higher if you are in a stronger industry group." While one insider finds the atmosphere at Booz-Allen "macho and political," others are happy with "the high quality of work and the opportunity to create a skill set in a specific industry."

OFFICE LIFE

Booz•Allen consultants and associates in New York share offices with two others at their level. In other offices, such as Dallas, "you get your own office." The firm's WCB New York headquarters was featured in "*The Associate*, a not-very-good Whoopi Goldberg film." That office, the firm's largest, "is organized by industry practice group. Because of that, you tend to know mostly people in your group." In the smaller offices "you get introduced to people in different groups."

To order a 50- to 70-page Vault Reports Employer Profile on Booz·Allen & Hamilton call 1-888-JOB-VAULT or visit www.VaultReports.com

The full Employer Profile includes detailed information on Booz·Allen's departments, recent developments and transactions, hiring and interview process, plus what employees really think about culture, pay, work hours and more.

Mercer Management Consulting

RANKING 6

1166 Avenue of the Americas
New York, NY 10036
(212) 345-3400
www.mercermc.com

MERCER *Management Consulting*

LOCATIONS

New York, NY (HQ)
Boston, MA • Chicago, IL • Cleveland, OH • Pittsburgh, PA • San Francisco, CA • Washington, DC • Buenos Aires, Argentina • Hong Kong • Lisbon, Portugal • London, United Kingdom • Madrid, Spain • Montreal, Canada • Munich, Germany • Paris, France • Toronto, Canada • Zurich, Switzerland

DEPARTMENTS

Consulting

THE STATS

Annual Revenues: $1.3 billion (1997)
No. of Employees: 1,200 (worldwide)
No. of Offices: 17 (worldwide)
Subsidiary of Marsh McLennan
CEO: Peter Coster

KEY COMPETITORS

- A.T. Kearney
- Bain & Company
- Boston Consulting Group
- McKinsey & Company
- Monitor Company

THE BUZZ
What consultants at other firms are saying about Mercer

- "Evolving"
- "Work ridiculous hours"
- "Octopus-like"
- "Ruthless"

Vault Reports Guide to the Top Consulting Firms
Mercer Management Consulting

UPPERS
- Extensive vacation
- Great insurance benefits
- Two-way feedback system
- Great support staff

DOWNERS
- Long hours
- Demanding assignments
- Still integrating with CDI

Consulting Revenues (in billions)
(Mercer Consulting Group)

Year	Revenue
1996	1.2
1997	1.3

MMC Consultants
(compared to Mercer Consulting Group)

Mercer Management Consulting: 1,200
(Total: 9,000 Mercer Consulting Group)

© Copyright 1998 Vault Reports, Inc. Photocopying is illegal and is expressly forbidden.

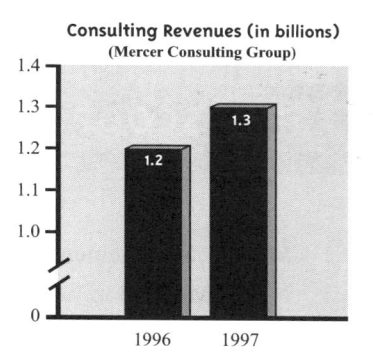

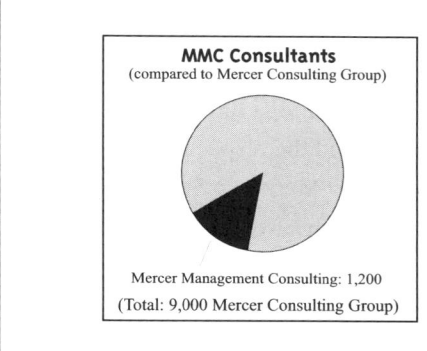

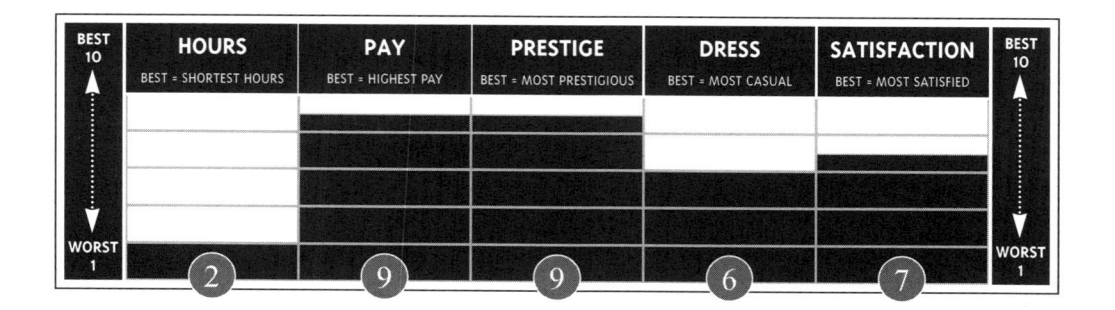

EMPLOYMENT CONTACT

MBAs:
Cathy Baker

Undergraduates:
Nathan Blain

2300 N Street, NW
Washington, DC 20037
(202) 778-7000
Fax: (202) 293-1371
recruiting@mercermc.com

	HOURS (BEST = SHORTEST HOURS)	PAY (BEST = HIGHEST PAY)	PRESTIGE (BEST = MOST PRESTIGIOUS)	DRESS (BEST = MOST CASUAL)	SATISFACTION (BEST = MOST SATISFIED)
Rating	2	9	9	6	7

Consulting Job Seekers: Receive free e-mailed job postings matching your interests & qualifications! Register at www.VaultReports.com

www.vaultreports.com

Mercer Management Consulting

THE SCOOP

Mercer Management Consulting is the sparkling consulting subsidiary of insurance titan Marsh McLennan, which also owns William Mercer (an employee benefits consultancy), the National Economic Research Association (microeconomic consulting) and Lippincott & Margulies (identity strategy). Mercer Management Consulting, which focuses on strategy management advice, was formed in 1990 through the merger of Temple, Barker & Sloane and Strategic Planning Associates. Since its founding, the firm has grown aggressively. Recent additions to Mercer Management include new offices in Europe, the Pacific Rim and Canada, and the respected 120-consultant firm Corporate Decisions, Inc. (CDI), which was snapped up by Mercer in September 1997. Mercer Management Consulting now has 1200 consultants; the firm earned $300 million in revenues in 1997.

THE LEGACY OF CDI

CDI liked to pride itself on helping companies adjust to business conditions like downsizing, re-engineering, and global competition. It also predicted the impact of these changes on given industries. At the time of the merger, Mercer was eager to incorporate CDI's concepts into its own consulting framework. The firm believed its own considerable reputation and clout would enable CDI strategy theory to reach more people. One former consultant with CDI, now a Mercer consultant, describes the merger thusly: "CDI focused on the Fortune 500 and 100, while Mercer had a greater diversity of clients. Mercer does more 'down-the-line' strategy (that is, operations and implementation)."

A HAPPY PARTNERSHIP

Strategy shop CDI has bolstered Mercer's strategic strengths, while Mercer gave CDI the bodies it needed to fill all its engagements and increased savvy in operational and implementation work. While CDI case teams were at first kept intact directly following the merger, and "crossteam strategizing didn't happen right away," the two groups of consultants have now moved together. Mercer is currently debating whether or not to have its consultants work on two engagements at once (a common CDI practice, and one used at other prestigious consulting firms, such as the Boston Consulting Group).

STILL GROWING TO BE GREAT

In other growth-related efforts, Mercer Management Consulting recently added new offices in Buenos Aires, Lisbon, Cleveland, and Pittsburgh to its already expansive international network. The Buenos Aires office is especially noteworthy, since it marks the firm's first office in South America and emphasizes the firm's policy of tackling emerging markets. (In 1996 Mercer opened its first office in Asia by establishing a base in Hong Kong.) The office in Lisbon joins London, Madrid, Munich, Paris, and Zurich on the list of Mercer's European offices. The less exotic offices in Cleveland and Pittsburgh supplement the firm's "natural geographical expansion" in the continental U.S.

GETTING HIRED

Mercer hires recent college graduates for its research analyst positions, and MBAs for its consultant positions. Most non-MBA students in graduate programs will be put in research analyst positions at first, though quantitative PhDs, for example, will also be considered for associate positions. At the undergraduate level, Mercer recruits at Dartmouth, Harvard, Northwestern, Princeton, the University of Pennsylvania, Stanford, and Williams. In search of MBAs, the firm travels to HBS, Kellogg, Sloan, Stanford GSB, Wharton, Tuck, and Michigan. Applicants from Canada, England, France, Munich, and Spain should check the Mercer web site or www.mercermc.com for a list of recruitment-targeted schools in these areas. Mercer hires 30 to 40 summer MBA interns each year (about 30 in the U.S. and about 12 in Europe), and hires only at its core business schools: "Go through the normal recruiting process," advise successful summer consultants. "Mercer doesn't have many back doors."

Mercer conducts a range of interviews including case interviews, group exercises, and resume discussions. Occasionally, the firm will ask an applicant to prepare a presentation, although he or she will always be given advance notice, insiders say. Group exercises, which are conducted with other potential Mercer employees, are also reportedly utilized. Mercer urges interviewees daunted by the prospect of the case interview to relax – the firm is "not looking for a specific answer," but is "trying to gain some insight into your thought processes." An insider recommends that interviewees avoid "looking like you're suffering too much. Problem solving is what you're applying to do, after all."

Mercer runs applicants through five or six interviews in either two or three rounds. In each round, there is generally one personality interview, insiders say. The remainder of interviews are case-related. "Success on the case interviews is absolutely critical," reports one contact. Mercer interviewers reportedly shy away from guesstimates along the lines of "how many golf balls could you fit into a 747?" However, the occasional old-school or devil's-advocate type of interviewer has been known to pull one from his sleeve. Prior to an interview, candidates should learn "Porters Five Forces" and the "3 Cs – cost, customers, competition." One insider reports: "Not only should you know them for the interview, but we actually use them to structure problems at Mercer." Another insider believes that interviewers are looking for candidates to think out loud: "To explain your thought processes clearly – that is a necessary condition rather than a sufficient one-or a 'suff.' You must take a logical, holistic, and innovative approach to the case. Also, ask questions and plenty of them – especially if you're an undergraduate."

Associates join Mercer as part of the Central Resource Group, which gives them the opportunity to work on a variety of issues, functional areas and industries across any or all Mercer practices.

OUR SURVEY SAYS

TOTAL DEVELOPMENT

Insiders say that Mercer "believes in developing each and every employee." Consultants say that Mercer is "a total meritocracy." However, one employee says that while Mercer "has a history of not being very bureaucratic, that may change now that the firm is growing." As part of the firm's commitment to professional development, Mercer uses a two-way feedback system in which both junior and senior employees evaluate each other. Recent hires also benefit from "extensive contact" with more experienced consultants.

THE BENEFITS OF OWNERSHIP

A firm that is looking for its consultants to have longer tenures than those at many of its competitors, Mercer "does not equate personal sacrifice with good consulting" and works to minimize the time its consultants spend away from home. Mercer consultants also benefit from parent Marsh MacLennan. "The insurance package is very impressive – Mercer is owned by Marsh MacLennan, which is in insurance," one employee smartly notices. Other impressive perks include free sports tickets, subsidies at gyms, a "very lucrative" stock option plan; pay, however, is only average for Mercer's prestige class.

DRESS DOWN, BUT DON'T RELAX

Mercer consultants can relax their dress, as "there's no fixed dress code" at the firm – it's normally "khakis and sweaters or open collars." Despite the minimization of time away from home, hours, however, are less blissful. Consultants say that "burnout is a serious problem." To lighten the load, "there is always a secretary to help you." Case teams also have people "called case team assistants, who are basically college graduates from less prestigious schools than most Mercer consultants. They do the research coordination and data entry, basically scut work. Sometimes they get promoted to research analyst, but not very often."

ROCKING SOCIAL LIFE

Insiders rave about Mercer's social life. "Rocking!" says one consultant. "Every Friday there's a TGIF, and there are frequent weekend parties." One consultant happily reports that "a bunch of people from the office get a ski house together every winter," while another describes her co-workers as "very congenial." Mercer insiders says that the level of social activity differs from office to office. "Actually, some offices are a little more social than others," reports one Mercer employee. "On the research analyst level, everyone is always social, but in some offices, like DC, even partners will come out and party." Reports a former Mercer consultant: "On case teams, we always got together one night a week. We would rent a room in a sports bar, or maybe have a nice dinner together."

A NERVY OUTSIDER

Mercer consultants concur in placing Mercer toward the top of the heap in prestige. "Oh, Mercer's right up there with McKinsey and Bain and BCG. If they're Harvard and Yale and Princeton, then maybe Mercer is like Stanford or Chicago. A nervy outsider." Another insider thinks Mercer "is maybe a little behind that pack [Bain, BCG and McKinsey] but not by much, and as far as getting into business school Mercer is just as good." Contends that contact: "I would put Mercer at number four on the list. McKinsey, then BCG and Bain, then us."

To order a 50- to 70-page Vault Reports Employer Profile on Mercer Management Consulting call 1-888-JOB-VAULT or visit www.VaultReports.com

The full Employer Profile includes detailed information on Mercer's departments, recent developments and transactions, hiring and interview process, plus what employees really think about culture, pay, work hours and more.

"Burnout is a serious problem."

– *Mercer insider*

Consulting Job Seekers: Receive free e-mailed job postings matching your interests & qualifications! Register at www.vaultreports.com

Andersen Consulting

VAULT REPORTS RANKING 7

1345 Avenue of the Americas
New York, NY 10105
(212) 708-4000
Fax: (212) 245-4751
www.ac.com

LOCATIONS

New York, NY (HQ)
The firm has 137 offices in 46 countries

DEPARTMENTS

Management Consulting
Technology Consulting

THE STATS

Annual Revenues: $6.6 billion (1997)
No. of Employees: 44,800 (worldwide)
No. of Offices: 137 (worldwide)
A privately-held company
CEO: George Sheehan

KEY COMPETITORS

- Arthur Andersen
- A.T. Kearney
- Booz·Allen & Hamilton
- Deloitte Consulting
- Ernst & Young Consulting
- KPMG Consulting

THE BUZZ
What consultants at other firms are saying about Andersen

- "Lots of bickering and turnover"
- "All systems?"
- "Structured, social"
- "2000-pound gorilla"

Vault Reports Guide to the Top Consulting Firms

Andersen Consulting

UPPERS
- Extensive job training
- Free tickets to sporting and cultural events
- Very social firm
- Concierge on call

DOWNERS
- Long work days
- Frequent travel
- Instability with Andersen Worldwide fission

EMPLOYMENT CONTACT

Human Resources
Andersen Consulting
1345 Avenue of the Americas
New York, NY 10105

Fax: (212) 708-3630

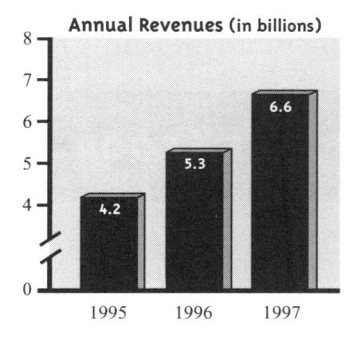

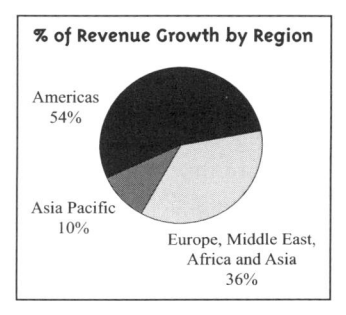

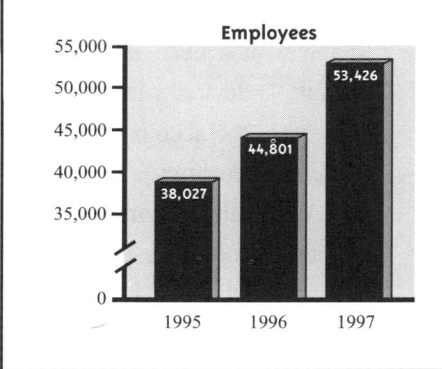

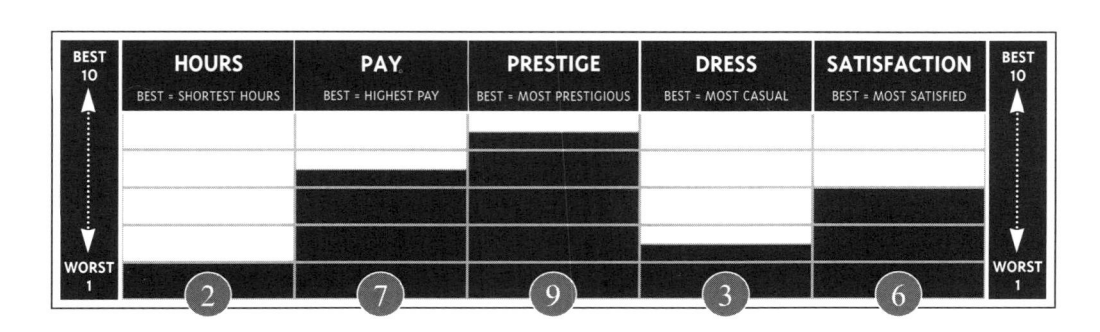

© Copyright 1998 Vault Reports, Inc. Photocopying is illegal and is expressly forbidden.

Annual Revenues (in billions)
- 1995: 4.2
- 1996: 5.3
- 1997: 6.6

% of Revenue Growth by Region
- Americas 54%
- Asia Pacific 10%
- Europe, Middle East, Africa and Asia 36%

Employees
- 1995: 38,027
- 1996: 44,801
- 1997: 53,426

	HOURS	PAY	PRESTIGE	DRESS	SATISFACTION	
BEST 10 → WORST 1	BEST = SHORTEST HOURS	BEST = HIGHEST PAY	BEST = MOST PRESTIGIOUS	BEST = MOST CASUAL	BEST = MOST SATISFIED	BEST 10 → WORST 1
	2	7	9	3	6	

Consulting Job Seekers: Receive free e-mailed job postings matching your interests & qualifications! Register at www.VaultReports.com

www.vaultreports.com

THE SCOOP

THE NEW KID IN THE BIG FIVE BLOC

The younger of the two progeny of Andersen Worldwide (the other being Arthur Andersen), Andersen Consulting is the world's largest management consulting firm. With more than 44,500 consultants and nearly 60,000 employees, Andersen Consulting can draw from a vast array of industrial and technical expertise. Consultants in its four competencies (change management, process, strategic services, and technology) work together to design strategies for more than half of the Fortune 500 in America, as well as many of the other top corporations worldwide.

THE SOURCE OF WOE

Despite its success, Andersen Consulting, led by strong-willed managing director George Shaheen, has been unhappy at an inequitable division between Andersen Consulting and Arthur Andersen. Under the terms of a 1989 agreement that split the two firms, Arthur Andersen, the accounting and financial services division, holds a two-thirds majority vote on Andersen Worldwide's board of directors. Arthur Andersen is also entitled to a percentage of the Andersen Consulting's, despite the fact that Andersen Consulting has become more profitable and faster-growing. Even more galling to Andersen consultants, Arthur Andersen has been setting up its own business and technology consulting services to boost its growth, thus actually competing with Andersen Consulting.

THE SPLIT COMMENCES

In December 1997, Andersen Consulting boldly sought to split off from Andersen Worldwide; George Shaheen announced his intention to take the dispute between the two firms to arbitration at the International Chamber of Commerce in Paris. Under Andersen Worldwide regulations, Andersen Consulting would have to pay compensation of 1.5 times net annual revenues – about $11.5 billion – in order to walk free, but AC plans to argue that Arthur

Andersen had nullified the agreement through its internally competitive actions. In January 1998, Arthur Andersen announced that it would seek a $10 billion payment from Andersen Consulting, and also force AC to surrender the invaluable Andersen name. Arbitration proceedings are expected to drag out for some time.

MEANWHILE…

Andersen Consulting has more than 59,000 employees and offices in 46 different countries. Andersen Consulting works with over 5000 client organizations worldwide, and is growing at the quick-quick rate of 20 percent annually. Revenue in 1997 for Andersen Consulting was $6.63 billion, compared to $5.3 billion in 1996. Revenue was up by 68 percent in the energy competency, 56 percent in insurance and 45 percent in high tech. In 1997, revenue grew by 29 percent to $3.7 billion in the Americas, 29 percent in the Americas (outside the U.S.), 23 percent in Europe/Middle East/Africa/India, and by 16 percent in Asia.

ASIAN CURRENCY CRISIS? NO PROB

The currency gyrations in Asia and subsequent world market turmoil have thus far been only a minor setback; they simply caused Andersen to grow by 25 percent in 1997, as opposed to 29 percent in 1996. In the United States alone, the largest home country for Andersen Consulting, with 51 offices in 27 states and 25,000 consultants, revenues in 1997 hit $3.4 billion. Andersen Consulting estimates that in recent years, its revenues have been growing 25 percent a year in the United States. The firm works with 75 percent of Fortune's Global 200 largest companies, and "all but one of the 30 most profitable." The split with Arthur Andersen is not projected to cause serious problems with Andersen Consulting's clientele – the firm estimates that "fewer than 5 percent" of Andersen Consulting clients also use Arthur Andersen's audit or tax services. (So much for Andersen Worldwide synergy!)

HERE'S THE REAL STARTER

A major source of growth for Andersen Consulting has been its Business Process Management (BPM) unit. BPM works with clients over a period of years, actually taking over key departments like logistics, human resources, information technology and finance. By outsourcing these non-core groups, clients save money. Andersen's careful cost management has made BPM quite popular – the unit accounted for nearly $1 billion of revenues in 1997.

THE METHODOLOGY TAKES HOLD

Andersen Consulting is no garden of Eden for nonconformists. The nickname "Andersen Android," like all stereotypes, has some basis in fact. It's no surprise that Andersen, except perhaps for its wriggly cohort of strategic consultants, is a regimented firm, a fact highlighted by the firm's astounding emphasis on training – in 1997, the firm spent an astonishing $430 million on training its consultants.

Since 1997, Andersen has been promoting its Business Integration Model, a system of interconnected client services that will be the basis for 21st century Andersen. (The BIM gospel is preached from the mount – that is, Andersen's main training facility, a former college campus in St. Charles, Illinois.) The goal is to mold Andersen consultants into team players who use a uniform process to achieve a common goal. Though dull and unspectacular, the system allows Andersen to offer standardized solutions and permit consultants from disparate office and backgrounds to work well together (important for a firm with more than 59,000 employees). George Shaheen, chairman of Andersen, points out that this approach also means "we don't have to start from scratch each time."

GETTING HIRED

Andersen has a very high profile on campuses, but even if you've read this entry, don't ignore Andersen's workshops and recruiting events – attending them can be a competitive advantage for candidates. "Andersen is desperately trying to get top-tier people into the company," says one candidate. "They even flew over people from the London office just to take people to a baseball game. It was ridiculous. Because of the time difference it was about 3 in the morning for them by the time they arrived. The partner I was talking to was falling asleep."

Candidates have two interviews on campus. The first is with one person, the second with two people (normally partners or experienced managers, though you will also interview with a peer). After making it through these screening rounds, there is a day at the nearest office. There are apparently minor differences between offices and campuses; some candidates have had a second round with three managers or partners at an Andersen office. While candidates do have the option to fly out to visit the office of their interest, "it isn't necessary to interview where you want to work, except in the case of San Francisco [a very popular office location]."

Contacts say Andersen makes its big push "at sell weekend, which is very structured." Reports one insider: "The first day is in the office and features a series of meetings with the various industry groups. They provide much more specific information than you get in the recruitment brochures. There is also the opportunity to speak one-on-one with peers, and you go out to wining and dining things and to a show." Apparently, no one ever mentions Arthur Andersen.

OUR SURVEY SAYS

THE PLACE TO BE

Many consultants opine that "Andersen Consulting is the place for exciting opportunities and highly visible clients." One employee explains that the firm "is entrepreneurial in the sense that employees can control their own career paths." Consultants travel so frequently that their "home lives often fall into shambles," but they are "rewarded with good salaries." Andersen Consulting also offers a plethora of perks – "free flights, great social events, relaxed expense policies, expensed dinners at great restaurants." One outstanding perk – a "concierge service that runs errands for a subsidized rate of $5 an hour. They'll feed your cat, take your car in for service, whatever you need."

SEE YOU IN THE OFFICE ON FRIDAY?

Andersen has a "Friday in the office policy" under which the firm makes an effort to fly back its consultants to their home offices on Thursday night. Says one former consultant about Fridays: "I was usually back in the office. Fridays are mostly for administrative stuff – internal development, evaluations, training." Weekend work is "rare but does happen." A business process management consultant agrees with that time assessment. "I work about 55 hours a week and bill 60. The policy is that your work hours are 8:30 to 5:30 and if you go over that you get overtime." Every service line except for strategy gets overtime. "Strategy will bill up to 10 hours a day, but after that they don't bother."

THANKS FOR THE COMP TIME

But while strategic consultants don't get overtime, they may get "comp time. What happens is that you work like a dog for six months and then you're done. Your manager says, 'It's Wednesday, take Thursday and Friday off.' It's separate from your vacation time, and just gets billed to some random black hole account." In times of crisis, however, the Friday in the office policy shifts. Says one insider: "Despite the Friday in the office policy, I have often stayed at the client site five days a week with no trip home. I have heard of some consultants who worked through the weekend at the client with no trip home."

TOUGH HOURS

"While Andersen Consulting employees are reportedly "a fun-loving, hard-working, thinking group of people" and the scope of work is "global," the hours are "crazy" and the firm itself is "not as prestigious as other consulting firms yet." "The work can be great," says one employee, "but it wears you down after a while. It's tough on personal relationships because you travel so much. You can start to feel like a number sometimes." We hear that "rank is everything. Things aren't as meritocratic as you might expect." One consultant warns that "you need to be flexible and be able to handle a lot of stress."

MOTHER ANDERSEN

On the whole, however, Andersen Consulting is said to be a "very cohesive, very friendly firm." 'There is a distinctive Andersen-speak," says one consultant, "and maybe it does sound like android language to others, I don't know." "Leaving Andersen Consulting is like getting a divorce," says a former consultant. "The company has one of the strongest cultures I have ever seen. You have to be bright, and it helps to be cheerful. Most of all, you have to be driven by an extremely strong desire to succeed and be willing to buckle under and do what it takes."

To order a 50- to 70-page Vault Reports Employer Profile on Andersen Consulting call 1-888-JOB-VAULT or visit www.VaultReports.com

The full Employer Profile includes detailed information on Andersen's departments, recent developments and transactions, hiring and interview process, plus what employees really think about culture, pay, work hours and more.

A.T. Kearney

VAULT REPORTS RANKING 8

222 West Adams Street
Chicago, IL 60606
(312) 223-6030
www.atkearney.com

ATKEARNEY

LOCATIONS

Chicago, IL (HQ)
Cleveland, OH • Houston, TX • Los Angeles, CA • Miami, FL • Minneapolis, MN • New York, NY • Phoenix, AZ • San Francisco, CA • Stamford, CT • Washington, DC • Amsterdam, Holland • Barcelona, Spain • Berlin, Germany • Brussels, Belgium • Copenhagen, Denmark • Dusseldorf, Germany • London, England • Mexico City, Mexico • Madrid, Spain • Melbourne, Australia • Milan, Italy • Munich, Germany • Moscow, Russia • Paris, France • Singapore • Tokyo, Japan • Toronto, Canada

DEPARTMENTS

Consulting
Financial Institutions

THE STATS

Annual Revenues: $1.1 billion (1997)
No. of Employees: 4,700
No. of Offices: 63
A privately-held company
CEO: Fred G. Steingraber

KEY COMPETITORS

- American Management Systems
- Andersen Consulting
- Booz•Allen & Hamilton
- McKinsey & Company
- Mercer Management Consulting

THE BUZZ
What consultants at other firms are saying about A.T. Kearney

- "Great analytics but churn and burn culture"
- "McKinsey wannabes"
- "Bright, strong in the Midwest"
- "Link with EDS makes me nervous"

Vault Reports Guide to the Top Consulting Firms

A.T. Kearney

UPPERS
- No up-or-out pressure
- Good firm camraderie
- No stereotypical Kearney consultants

DOWNERS
- Strict dress code
- EDS merger knocks down prestige in strategy consulting

EMPLOYMENT CONTACT

Corporate Recruiting
A.T. Kearney
222 West Adams Street
Chicago, IL 60606

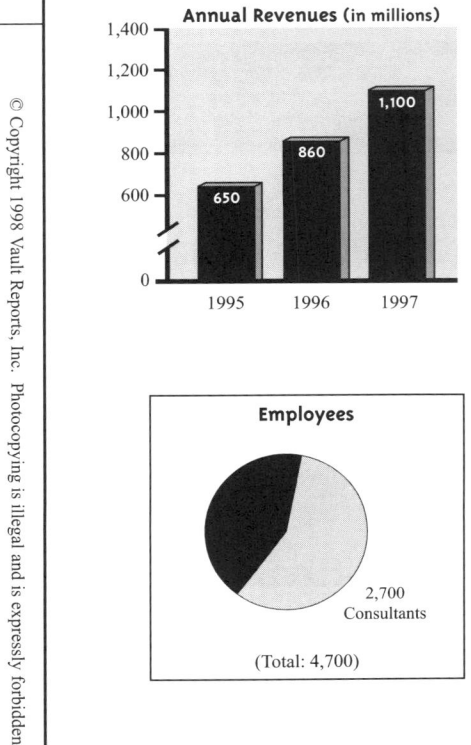

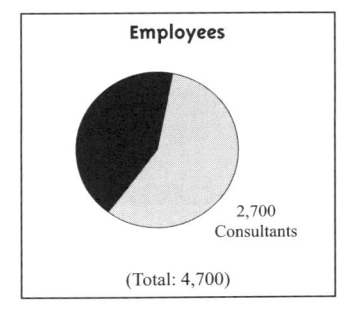

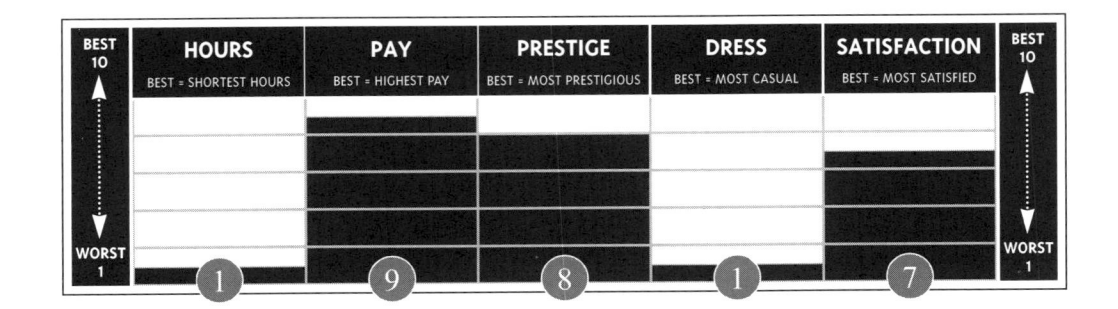

Annual Revenues (in millions)
- 1995: 650
- 1996: 860
- 1997: 1,100

Employees
2,700 Consultants
(Total: 4,700)

© Copyright 1998 Vault Reports, Inc. Photocopying is illegal and is expressly forbidden.

	HOURS (BEST = SHORTEST HOURS)	PAY (BEST = HIGHEST PAY)	PRESTIGE (BEST = MOST PRESTIGIOUS)	DRESS (BEST = MOST CASUAL)	SATISFACTION (BEST = MOST SATISFIED)
	1	9	8	1	7

Consulting Job Seekers: Receive free e-mailed job postings matching your interests & qualifications! Register at www.VaultReports.com

www.vaultreports.com

Vault Reports Guide to the Top Consulting Firms
A.T. Kearney

THE SCOOP

SPLITTING OFF FROM MCKINSEY – IT WORKED!

An employee of McKinsey & Co. in the 1930s, Andrew Thomas Kearney split off from that firm in 1939 to start an eponymous firm in Chicago. Solid results with early engagements, including an extensive study of U.S. Steel and a longtime relationship with the supermarket chain Kroger helped put A.T. Kearney on the map. Steady expansion exploded in the 1970s, when then-CEO Ken Block instituted the "Go for Growth" program, doubling the firm's size by 1980.

THE CLEVER CANARY

Under the tenure of current CEO Fred Steingraber, A.T. Kearney has entered 26 new countries and doubled revenues every three years. In 1998, A.T. Kearney ranked as the 12th-largest consulting firm in the world, with operations in 30 countries. A.T. Kearney has been called "the canary that swallowed the cat." In 1995, the 70-year-old consulting firm was acquired by EDS, the gigantic Texas-based computer and information systems giant founded by the ever-interesting Ross Perot. EDS was seeking to shore up its money-losing consulting services; A.T. Kearney CEO Fred Steingraber was attracted to EDS' piles of money and experience in information technology and its implementation – a growing business area for consultancies. EDS merged its consulting service division under A.T. Kearney's name and direction.

THE INFORMATION TECHNOLOGY SUCCESS STORY

The marriage between EDS and A.T. Kearney has been a resounding success. A.T. Kearney achieved revenues of $870 million in 1996, and hit $1.1 billion in 1997. Today, Kearney maintains offices across the globe and earns more than two-thirds of its revenues outside the U.S. While Kearney claims expertise in all types of industries, it has particular experience in aerospace, financial institutions, health care, and retail. Unlike some of its competitors, Kearney believes in sticking around to help its clients implement the firm's consulting advice – implementation has become increasingly important to clients. As a result, Kearney's clients are both satisfied and loyal: More than 75 percent of the firm's business comes from past clients. The firm generally targets companies with at least $2 billion in annual revenue.

IT EVERYWHERE

A.T. Kearney is also expanding its IT specialties overseas. The firm has formulated its own business model designed to help Indian banks develop and integrate IT solutions in a more efficient way. Already, a large number of publicly owned Indian banks are considering its use. In India's highly deregulated environment, such banks frequently reside at the bottom ranks when it comes to managing information.

PROGNOSIS FOR THE WORLD

In the European market, Kearney is hoping that the introduction of a single European currency will bring a rise in the long-term strength of the U.S. dollar. Specifically, Kearney predicts economic opportunities in Poland, Hungary, Spain, and Portugal. In Latin America, Kearney predicts that "Argentina's expectations for a second consecutive year of real economic growth will be dampened by the recessionary impact of Brazil's austerity package." On a larger scale, the firm foresees Latin America's continued integration as a threat to "U.S. influence in the region." In the Middle East and Africa, Kearney predicts economic discontent arising as a result of a "lack of market reform and scant non-extractive economic activities." However, the firm believes companies can capitalize on the accelerated economic growth of "nations such as Uganda, South Africa, Cote d'Ivoire, and Ghana" as a result of continued restructuring.

GETTING HIRED

Kearney recruits on the campuses of selected colleges and universities for both business analysts (college graduates) and associates (MBAs). Although the majority of its consultants arrive fresh from campus recruitment, the firm also welcomes interested persons who are unaffiliated with academic institutions. Insiders report that these applicants are more likely to have extensive and intense pre-interview phone screenings, however. Kearney also hires a fair number of new associates and managers through headhunters.

Kearney is a place for the intelligent and the ambitious, but it is also for the persistent. One insider reports that he was able to make his way to the first round after failing to sign up for on-campus interviews, but "making an informed and dramatic plea" for a much coveted "wildcard spot." Those who are dead-set on working for Kearney shouldn't lost heart. Another insider reports that, despite a "relatively shoddy resume," he was able to stake claim on a job offer by "nailing his interviews."

Kearney's interview process typically includes two rounds, with two interviews in the first round and three in the second, insiders tell us. Interviews are generally 30 to 50 minutes each and include a smattering of case studies, "fit" questions, guesstimates, and on rare occasions, brainteasers. In the past, case interviews and "fit" interviews (which are designed to see if an applicant's personality complements or contradicts firm culture) were equal in number. Our contacts tell us however, that more recently the balance has swung in favor of case interviews. Both associates and analysts are given case study questions, although typically, only associates are given brainteasers.

Insiders report that A.T. Kearney interviewers are "kind" and "supportive." Although the interview questions – especially the case studies – are themselves often tough, the interviewers don't try to bully or intimidate. One insider reports: "The Kearney consultants who interviewed me had a minimal amount of attitude. They were bright, friendly, and very likeable." Other insiders report that their overwhelmingly positive impressions of interviewers led them to pick Kearney over other firms.

The firm has instituted diversity programs to increase diversity in its consulting workforce. The percentage of minority hires was upped in 1998 to 36 percent, although the percentage of women rose to a less-than-impressive 29 percent on the MBA level. In terms of diversity recruitment, Kearney makes a point of attending a variety of minority and women's events such as the Women in Leadership Conference.

Business analysts typically work at A.T. Kearney for two or three years. Exceptional business analysts may be promoted to associate positions during their time at A.T. Kearney. Analysts who have satisfactorily completed the analyst program are frequently invited to obtain an MBA at Kearney's expense; after that point, they are required to work at the firm for a minimum of three years. This program is extremely popular, with 80 percent of a recent class attending business school on Kearney's checkbook.

MBAs generally remain at the associate level for two to three years, before moving on to a managerial level. After about another three years, managers become principals. The next step up is senior partner. Unlike some of its competitors (most notably McKinsey), Kearney does not follow an "up-or-out" policy.

OUR SURVEY SAYS

LIFESTYLE CONSCIOUS A.T. KEARNEY

Perhaps even more than other consulting firms, A.T. Kearney considers management consulting a "lifestyle," not just a career. As a result, Kearney employees work "long days and even longer weeks." In addition, Kearney employees report plenty of travel – over 65 percent of Kearney employees have worked on engagements outside their home offices. As part of its "zealous" commitment to quality, Kearney maintains a close eye on employee performance. The firm conducts periodic evaluations to assess the quality of each employee's work.

INTENSE WORK AND SOCIAL ACTIVITY

Despite an environment that one employee describes as "intense," A.T. Kearney employees get along well with each other, with "plenty of socializing" among project team members. "There are a lot of extracurricular activities," says one consultant. "I pick the ones I want to go to and don't go to the rest, otherwise I'd be doing company stuff seven days a week." Another consultant says: "I find the camaraderie here very appealing, because this industry is somewhat cutthroat and it's good to have that human touch."

THE ISSUE OF DIVERSITY

Kearney is said to employ "a mix of people including new MBAs, undergrads, and industry experts (especially from the operations and the high-tech industry)." Insiders consistently report that there is "no pressure to conform to any fit type of image." Indeed, unlike the drone-in-a-suit stereotypes that permeate other firms, "you will rarely hear about 'the typical Kearney person.'"

Despite one insider's assertion that there is "no A.T. Kearney prototype," not everybody agrees that the firm's diversity is up to par. "Kearney is not doing anything extraordinary in the diversity department," concedes one. "Kearney's better than most, which is not to say that it's good. About a third of the people I entered with were women. But I didn't see that many non-Caucasians, especially at the top levels. That's probably a function of the fact that this emphasis on diversity is a fairly new thing. Diversity hiring has only been in effect for four to five years and it will probably take another four to five years before we see a difference at the top." Another insider praises Kearney for at least making the effort: "The firm's efforts are genuine, I'm sure. Kearney was a presence at a recent NAACP conference I attended." Nevertheless, Kearney may have "some work to do." Another insider asserts, that "the minority numbers here are considerably less than in my business school class."

FLEXIBLE PROMOTIONS – BUT NOT SO IN DRESS CODE

Many consulting firms have a rigid promotion process. Not so at A.T. Kearney. One consultant praises the lack of an "up-or-out" policy. "That kind of policy creates a lot of insecurity. It's survival of the fittest, and I don't know how much teamwork a culture like that would encourage. Kearney doesn't have that policy and it makes it a nicer place to work." Still, don't expect to enjoy the company of your colleagues in a polo shirt and khakis. "Fred Steingraber, the CEO, hates casual dress days and refuses to have them around the office," reports one employee.

THUMBS UP TO "THE DOLLARS"

"As far as perks are concerned, insiders give kudos to Kearney's "nice, strong salary." One insider claims that "the dollars" [pay] are "higher than average," as well as "a notch above BCG and Bain." In addition, Kearney is reportedly trusting and "very relaxed" about its billing arrangements. "I've worked at other firms where there is a daily allowance or per diem maximum," reports one insider. "There's nothing like that at Kearney. Moreover, nobody asks any questions." Such laxity can lead to the occasional abuse of power – and it does. "People take advantage of the system because it's easy," says one insider, "I know people who put personal dinners on the firm. You can, say, eat an $8 dinner, but write $25 in your travel and expense report since anything under $25 doesn't have to be accounted for."

To order a 50- to 70-page Vault Reports Employer Profile on A.T. Kearney call 1-888-JOB-VAULT or visit www.VaultReports.com

The full Employer Profile includes detailed information on A.T. Kearney's departments, recent developments and transactions, hiring and interview process, plus what employees really think about culture, pay, work hours and more.

Mitchell Madison Group

VAULT REPORTS RANKING: 9

520 Madison Avenue
New York, NY 10022
(212) 372-9000
Fax: (212) 372-9000
www.mmgnet.com

LOCATIONS

New York, NY (HQ)
Boston, MA • Chicago, IL • Los Angeles, CA • San Francisco, CA • Frankfurt, Germany • London, United Kingdom • Madrid, Spain • Melbourne, Australia • Montreal, Canada • Munich, Germany • Paris, France • Rotterdam, The Netherlands • Sydney, Australia • Toronto, Canada • Zurich, Switzerland

DEPARTMENTS

Consulting

THE STATS

Annual Revenues: $200 million (1997)
No. of Professionals: 650 (worldwide)
No. of Partners: 86 (worldwide)
No. of Offices: 16 (worldwide)
A privately-held company
Managing Partner: Thomas D. Steiner

KEY COMPETITORS

- Bain & Company
- First Manhattan Consulting Group
- Greenwich Associates
- McKinsey & Company
- Mercer Management Consulting
- Monitor Company

THE BUZZ
What consultants at other firms are saying about Mitchell Madison

- "Aggressively growing"
- "Mostly financial"
- "Up and coming"
- "Not worth their billing rates"

Vault Reports Guide to the Top Consulting Firms

Mitchell Madison Group

UPPERS
- Loose management structure
- Growing firm

DOWNERS
- Long hours, even for consulting
- Frequent travel
- Abrupt management decisions

EMPLOYMENT CONTACT

Carol Labi
Recruiting Manager
Mitchell Madison Group
520 Madison Avenue
New York, NY 10022

recruiting@mmgnet.com

© Copyright 1998 Vault Reports, Inc. Photocopying is illegal and is expressly forbidden.

FUNCTIONAL AREAS

Business Strategy
Change Management
Corporate Restructuring
Database driven Customer Segmentation and Marketing
Distribution Management
Electronic Commerce
Information Systems and Technology Management
Mergers and Acquisitions
Organizational Effectiveness and Capability Building
Payment Systems
Reengineering/Restructuring
Risk Management
Sourcing and Outsourcing
Trading

HOURS	PAY	PRESTIGE	DRESS	SATISFACTION
BEST = SHORTEST HOURS	BEST = HIGHEST PAY	BEST = MOST PRESTIGIOUS	BEST = MOST CASUAL	BEST = MOST SATISFIED
1	9	8	4	7

(Scale: BEST 10 — WORST 1)

Consulting Job Seekers: Receive free e-mailed job postings matching your interests & qualifications! Register at www.VaultReports.com

www.vaultreports.com

THE SCOOP

THE LITTLE SPINOFF THAT COULD

Mitchell Madison Group was founded in 1994 by a group of former McKinsey consultants, led by a former director, Tom Steiner. Steiner was frustrated at McKinsey's frequent shedding of talented personnel and calcifying management structure, and wanted to approach consulting by focusing on the role of technological innovation. He left McKinsey in 1991, bringing along many McKinsey associates and analysts, to set up a financial services group for rival A.T. Kearney. After A.T. Kearney was acquired by EDS in 1994, Steiner opted to leap from the newly enlarged company to set up his own consultancy, Mitchell Madison. The new firm was named after two streets – Mitchell Street in Long Island, where Steiner, sitting in a bar, had first cooked up the notion to leave McKinsey, and Madison Avenue, the location of the firm's first office (and still the site of its headquarters today).

WEED-LIKE GROWTH

The famous McKinsey connections came in handy for the new firm, which had plenty of business as soon as it was formed. Starting with perhaps 50 employees in 1994, Mitchell Madison now has upwards of 650 professionals; the firm ultimately plans to have at least 1000 consultants. Mitchell Madison currently boasts a client list that includes prominent financial institutions and insurance companies. Mitchell Madison has also been instrumental in helping companies in the following industries: consumer electronics, financial services, health care, IT, manufacturing, media, oil/gas, pharmaceuticals, real estate, retailing, telecommunications, transportation & travel, and utilities.

YOUNG COMPANY WITH BIG CLIENTS

Though Mitchell Madison is a relative tyke among consulting firms, it works with heavy hitters. Mitchell Madison claims its clients "are of global stature: to date we have served no client (irrespective of industry) smaller in size than a Fortune 50 or its local industry equivalent." The company presently has 16 offices; it is exploring the possibility of opening its first office in Asia. The firm participates in a range of pro bono engagements as well. In 1997, 25 Mitchell Madison women participated in the seventh annual New York Race for the Cure, a 3.1-mile race in Central Park dedicated to breast cancer research.

GETTING HIRED

Mitchell Madison recruits from 16 undergraduate and 16 graduate institutions. It hosts a number of recruiting events at each of these prestigious schools; information on these event, as well as the low-down on the number of Mitchell Madison alumni from each school, is available on the firm's web site, located at www.mmgnet.com. The site also sports contact information for recruiting managers from the U.S. (at both the undergraduate and graduate levels), Europe, Canada, South Africa, and Australia. Recruiting information can gained by calling the recruiting hotline or (212) 372-9100.

Mitchell Madison looks for employees who are willing and able to take a long-term interest in building the firm. The firm conducts campus recruiting but also encourages applicants to submit resumes via regular mail, e-mail, or fax. Career paths at Mitchell Madison are less structured than they are at more established consulting firms. Most undergraduate hires start as business analysts and are expected to combine "many of the responsibilities of a full-time associate with more formal professional development activities." Associates join the firm directly from business school or other graduate degree programs. They can expect to develop "a robust set of traditional problem solving and client management skills." Mitchell Madison also accepts summer associates, who are generally students midway through business school.

The firm encourages multilingual candidates and individuals with strong, yet non-traditional academic and professional credentials (in other words, the firm is looking for industry hires too).

OUR SURVEY SAYS

THE YOUNG AND FLAT FIRM

A young and quickly growing firm, Mitchell Madison has an "entrepreneurial corporate culture" that "encourages freedom of expression," approves of a "variety of lifestyles," and "values diversity." MMG's management structure is one of "a strong egalitarianism," insiders report. The firm's founders and partners are "readily" accessible to junior employees and administrative staff; consultants say they "work closely with partners on visible and important aspects of assignments."

RIDE 'EM COWBOYS

While the "unstructured" atmosphere offers new employees "immediate independence," some say that its "chaotic" nature can become "occasionally frustrating." "Our clients often describe us as cowboys," one consultant remarks. We hear that "the upside to working at [Mitchell Madison] is that it's easy for someone at any level to make their mark. The downside is that when you need some support, there's not much there." The "rawness" of company culture means that "sometimes decisions are made at the last minute, which can make life difficult."

HOURS THAT CAN GO UNTIL DAWN

Hours are varied, but usually long at Mitchell Madison. Says one consultant: "There are times when you leave at 6 or 7, and other times when you work until 3 in the morning and all you can think about is the smell of fresh air." On the bright side, "MMG is refreshing in that it is pretty much devoid of face time. If you don't have any work, you don't have to come in, you can come in at 11 or noon, even."

HOPPING SOCIAL LIFE

The social life is described as extremely active at this young firm. "When there is a Mitchell Madison party," says one consultant, "everyone comes, from business analysts to managers. It's super." Others concur that "there are always e-mails going around the firm inviting people to parties." For lunch, MMGers at headquarters can try out one of the "hundreds" of delis around Madison Avenue, or have a fancier lunch at local posh eateries "21" or "Michael's."

SHORT-TERM TRAINING WHEELS

Insiders say "all newbies are taught how to use Access, our database system, and Excel. Those programs are very important." However, training isn't a major emphasis at Mitchell Madison. One consultant explains: "There are a few weeks of training, but training is really de-emphasized. Mitchell Madison wants people who can produce right away. The initial week of training is just basically how to use the computers, and then off you go." Although initial training may be sparse, new recruits undergo more training six months into their tenure. Material covered in this training session includes: accounting, presentation, chart drafting, finance, client interviewing. "But by then," insiders say. "It's really too late. You already have a handle on most of that stuff."

BUILDING A NEW FIRM

If you want to get in on the fun, say consultants, you should know that "the firm looks for extraordinarily smart people who have the ambition, the ability and the self-discipline to give 200 percent when only 100 percent would suffice. Our consultants are experts in fields you've never heard of. They are mavericks and builders and it is a true joy to work with them."

Mitchell Madison Group

To order a 50- to 70-page Vault Reports Employer Profile on Mitchell Madison Group call 1-888-JOB-VAULT or visit www.VaultReports.com

The full Employer Profile includes detailed information on MMG's departments, recent developments and transactions, hiring and interview process, plus what employees really think about culture, pay, work hours and more.

"There are a few weeks of training, but training is really de-emphasized. Mitchell Madison wants people who can produce right away."

– *Mitchell Madison insider*

Marakon Associates

RANKING 10

300 Atlantic Street
Stamford, CT 06901
(800) 695-4428
Fax: (203) 961-1460
www.marakon.com

LOCATIONS

Stamford, CT (HQ)
Chicago, IL
New York, NY
London, England

DEPARTMENTS

Consulting

THE STATS

Annual Revenues: $60 million (1997)
No. of Employees: 200 (worldwide)
No. of Offices: 4 (worldwide)
A privately-held company
CEO: Peter Kontes
Chairman: James McTaggart

KEY COMPETITORS

- Booz•Allen & Hamilton
- Mercer Management Consulting
- Mitchell Madison Group
- Stern Stewart & Company
- Strategic Decisions Group

THE BUZZ
What consultants at other firms are saying about Marakon

- "Good boutique"
- "The real strategists"
- "Culture focused"
- "One product"

Vault Reports Guide to the Top Consulting Firms

Marakon Associates

UPPERS

- Over 200 hours of formal training in the first two years
- Cross-discipline assignments
- Formal and systematic performance evaluations

DOWNERS

- Limited nature of assignments
- Lack of recognition by other consulting firms

EMPLOYMENT CONTACT

Undergraduates:
Becky Dolman

Grads & MBAs:
Melissa Feliberty

Marakon Associates
300 Atlantic St.,
Stamford, CT 06901

(800) 819-2806

SELECTED CLIENTS

BankAmerica
Boots Co.
Champion International
Dow Chemical
Lloyds TSB Group
Nordstrom
Coca-Cola*

*former client

© Copyright 1998 Vault Reports, Inc. Photocopying is illegal and is expressly forbidden.

	HOURS (BEST = SHORTEST HOURS)	PAY (BEST = HIGHEST PAY)	PRESTIGE (BEST = MOST PRESTIGIOUS)	DRESS (BEST = MOST CASUAL)	SATISFACTION (BEST = MOST SATISFIED)
Score	2	8	8	6	7

Consulting Job Seekers: Receive free e-mailed job postings matching your interests & qualifications! Register at www.VaultReports.com

THE SCOOP

THE HEDGEHOGS OF MARAKON

"Marakon is hedgehog heaven," wrote *Fortune* magazine in 1998. Does this mean that Marakon consultants have a prickly disposition and an animalistic drive? Not quite. What it signifies, according to *Fortune*, is Marakon's place among the two different categories of consultant – the fox, which does many things, and the hedgehog, which hunkers down and sticks to a single strategy. Indeed, Marakon's strongest facet is its primary governing objective: to increase shareholder value. As such, all strategy, energy, and creativity is directed toward the end of increasing shareholder value. The company devotes enormous amounts of time and money to analyzing economic profit (or profit that includes a charge for the cost of capital) and plotting ways to increase it.

THE HAPPENSTANCE OF MARAKON STRATEGY

Marakon's creed, "Strategy Happens" (also the title of an essay by Marakon CEO Peter Kontes) indicates the firm's unrelenting quest for answers. Because Marakon is convinced that strategy is the result of a detailed process, it analyzes a client's every analysis and decision – even those made at the lowest levels. (This is somewhat different from the emphasis of most other top strategy firms, which typically concern themselves with strategy and decision-making at the highest levels.)

MARAKON COSTS

The process is a long and expensive one; indeed, Marakon has been known to spend three to four years and to charge $5 to $10 million in consulting fees before completing a project. Nevertheless, Marakon's success rate speaks for itself. Having assisted – and impressed – the likes of Coca-Cola, Dow Chemical, Nordstrom, and BankAmerica, Marakon has proven that a meticulous working method reaps great rewards.

MARAKON MEANS CHOICE

Marakon's method of consulting, which embraces value-based management and capital-market economics, differs from the norm on a number of levels. Unlike many consulting companies, which generally offer one solution to a client's business woes, Marakon attempts to create choices. The firm offers each of its clients at least three strategies for increasing the value of its business – all with the end result of maximizing shareholder value. Typically, Marakon serves U.S. companies listed in the Fortune 100 and large, multinational European businesses.

STRONG GROWTH AND A DIVERSITY OF CLIENTS

Although Marakon serves a diverse set of clients, approximately 25 percent of the firm's business comes from the consumer products industry and another 20 percent each from the retailing and chemical industries. In the past five years, Marakon's active clients have enjoyed returns on shares 3.1 percent higher than their industry peers, and 4.5 percent higher than broad market indexes. Marakon Associates itself boasts an average annual growth rate of 25 percent over the last 10 years.

HOBSON'S CHOICE OF MODELS

Marakon consultants say that the firm is one of the few firms in the industry that holds fast to one sole model (Stern Stewart – with its EVA concept – is another). The majority of consulting firms, insiders say, "operate like supermarkets, where you can go in and get whatever you want." Marakon, on the other hand is proudly focused. The firm requires its clients to submit wholly to its philosophy. Most companies are likely to defer to Marakon's wishes once they consider the enormous amount of work Marakon consultants put into each project.

A LITTLE CONSULTANCY

Yet clients also seek Marakon because of its intimate size. Although Marakon's revenues per consultant ($475,000 in 1997) are on par with industry titans like McKinsey and Bain, the company remains relatively anonymous because of its small size. Whereas McKinsey and Bain employ 4627 and 1500 consultants, respectively, Marakon has only 220 consultants, and only four offices (in Connecticut, New York, Chicago and London). Although Marakon does have plans to open new domestic and international offices in the near future, its present leanness pleases clients, who realize that Marakon's fat fees aren't being spent on posh offices.

GETTING HIRED

Marakon hires approximately 30 new consultants each year, although this number may increase as the firm opens new U.S. and foreign offices. Marakon looks for employees who are "analytically gifted" and who have a credible presence when dealing with the firm's clients. Current employees suggest that applicants consult Marakon's book *The Value Imperative*. Marakon's recruiting web page, located at www.marakon.com/recruiting/recruit.html, describes the firm's campus recruiting schedule and also lists contact addresses for the firm's recruiting team. One former summer associate says Marakon "loves people who are high on capitalism. Better yet, skim through *The Value Imperative*. It's actually a decent read, especially the first half, and it helps frame answers to their cases."

During the interview process, Marakon asks both general discussion and case study questions. During the general discussion interview, the interviewer (usually a senior associate or manager) will give the interviewee the opportunity to ask specific questions about Marakon's policies and business climate. This interview is also an occasion for Marakon to assess the applicants and their potential. The firm encourages candidates to "try to be engaging, but not overly familiar." In other words, resist being chummy and asking inappropriate questions or questions that are personal in nature.

In the case interview, the candidate will be asked business problems or scenarios. The case studies are meant to test an applicant's analytical ability, not his or her "pre-existing knowledge." However, know that Marakon's focus on profitability extends to its interview process. Insiders report case interviews based around "participation and positioning strategies, profitability improvement strategies, and profitability variation" problems.

OUR SURVEY SAYS

THE MARAKON MARATHON WORKWEEK

Marakon consultants work "marathon" weeks that range from 60 to 90 hours and usually spend two to three days each week away from the office. Unlike at some consultancies, where consultants work on cases that can go on for years, at Marakon "you change cases every six to nine months, which is good and bad," says one insider. "Good, because you get a variety of experiences, bad, because you are in a different area of the country every few months."

SHERLOCK MARAKON

Another insider draws a parallel between Marakon and "first-rate detective work." Does a Marakon candidate stand a better chance of getting hired if he dons a Sherlock Holmes hat and brushes up on those math skills he never quite mastered? "Not at all," reports another insider. "Marakon looks for discipline and the ability to learn quickly and thoroughly. Whether a candidate majored in history or economics doesn't matter. Although," he admits sheepishly, "candidates for all positions, but especially the analyst positions, tend to be Ivy Leaguers with excellent transcripts and resumes."

SMALL FIRM, SIZEABLE PERKS

Report Marakon consultants: "You travel four days a week, though the firm does pay for everything." Employees say that the firm's pay scale is "attractive" and "competitive," and that they benefit from their "extensive contact" with the senior management of client companies. Don't expect to get away with too much expense sheet-sheet padding, though. A former employee says "Marakon is still a small firm, so they stay on top of travel and hours worked." However, the firm does offer a profit sharing scheme, and cool quarterly meetings. "First the partners tell the gathered consultants and other employees how the company's doing, and what new projects are coming in. Then in the evening we have an event. Some of these events have included a ball at Claridges [a fancy hotel in London] and an entire weekend in Dublin."

SMALL, INTIMATE, LITTLE-KNOWN

While Marakon may not offer the "universal prestige" of some other consulting companies, it does give consultants a more "realistic" chance of receiving a partnership sooner in their careers than they might receive at a competitor. Those interested in working overseas "might have better luck going to the U.S. office and then asking for an international assignment," insiders say. For the ambitious, employees concur, "the learning curve is steep and interesting."

To order a 10- to 20-page Vault Reports Employer Profile on Marakon Associates call 1-888-JOB-VAULT or visit www.VaultReports.com

The full Employer Profile includes detailed information on Marakon's departments, recent developments and transactions, hiring and interview process, plus what employees really think about culture, pay, work hours and more.

"Marakon is still a small firm, so they stay on top of travel and hours worked."

– *Marakon insider*

Leading Consulting Firms

The Advisory Board

600 New Hampshire Avenue
Washington, DC 20037
(202) 672-5600
Fax: (202) 672-5700
www.advisory.com

LOCATIONS

Washington, DC (HQ)
London

THE STATS

No. of Employees: 800 (U.S)
No. of Offices: 2 (worldwide)
A privately-held company

KEY COMPETITORS

American Practice Management
Boston Consulting Group
Monitor Company

UPPERS

- Swinging Melrose Place-like social life
- Fast-growing culture breeds quick responsibility

DOWNERS

- Inexperienced supervisors
- Limited branch offices
- Pay below other consulting firms

EMPLOYMENT CONTACT

Human Resources
The Advisory Board
600 New Hampshire Avenue
Washington, DC 20037

Fax: (202) 672-5700
jobs@advisory.com

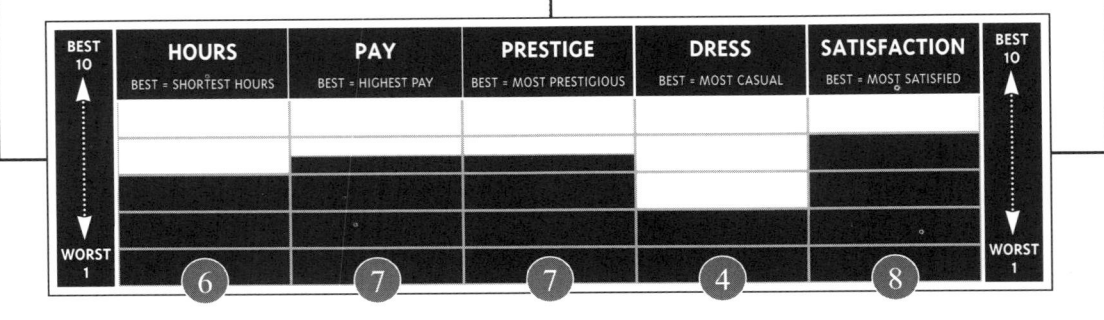

HOURS	PAY	PRESTIGE	DRESS	SATISFACTION
BEST = SHORTEST HOURS	BEST = HIGHEST PAY	BEST = MOST PRESTIGIOUS	BEST = MOST CASUAL	BEST = MOST SATISFIED
6	7	7	4	8

THE SCOOP

THE VERBOSE HEALTH ADVISORS

Located in the famous Watergate complex in Washington DC, The Advisory Board is best described as a cross between a think tank, a publishing company and a consulting firm. The membership-based organization provides customized strategic research and educational services for more than 2400 institutions in North America, Europe and the Pacific region. Through market studies, the firm reveals the best (and worst) management practices extant, aiming to help companies maximize revenues, and increase quality while reducing cost. In addition to its 'think tank' reports (which can be up to 300 pages long), the firm archives information in a series of best practices and quantitative databases that are accessible to all members. Advisory Board researchers get most of their data through primary research – they speak directly with people from member institutions and beyond. One of the firm's strengths is in outlining and critiquing current 'hot topics' – HMOs have been a big one for the firm's healthcare group during the past few years.

RESEARCH YOUR WAY

The Advisory Board was founded in 1979 to conduct customized research projects for Fortune 500 companies. In the 1980s, the firm established its current focus on the financial services and healthcare industries. It expanded in 1993 by adding a Corporate Executive division, which focuses on Fortune 2000 companies from numerous industries. Within the Corporate Executive Board are a number of councils that serve Chief Information Officers and senior-level executives in "corporate leadership" (human resources), corporate strategy, and sales. In the works is a unit that will offer research services to CFOs.

SPLITTING BOARDS

In 1998, the financial and healthcare divisions were officially split – they are now known as the Corporate Advisory Board and the Healthcare Advisory Board, respectively. The former serves 750 of the world's largest corporations, and offers research and executive education in areas including financial services, business banking, financial competition and insurance. The Healthcare Advisory Board concentrates on business strategy, operations, clinical strategy and management. It serves more than 2000 members, including hospitals, insurers, physician practices and medical technology companies. Together, the Corporate and Healthcare Advisory Boards publish approximately 60 major strategy studies and 25,000 customized research briefs a year. They also conduct meetings with members to present more salient research findings and solicit member recommendations for the following year's study topics.

SUBSTANTIAL, SPICY GROWTH

All told, The Advisory Board has grown from 167 employees in 1991 to nearly 800 in 1998. Revenues have also grown substantially – at a compound annual rate of over 50 percent for the past five years. Its consultants (mostly MBAs) are on the road about 25 percent of the time, interviewing industry leaders, academics and other consultants. The Advisory Board Company (or as it's fondly known, ABC) is an egalitarian place – nearly 60 percent of its employees are female. And because its employees, on the average, are so young, many fondly call The Advisory Board "the *Melrose Place* of research firms."

GETTING HIRED

Recent growth at The Advisory Board has put hiring on the rise, and the firm claims new employees can expect speedy merit-based promotions. MBAs are hired as consultants, while BAs are hired for research positions [though they can and are promoted to consulting positions]. The firm looks for applicants with strong analytical skills and well-rounded academic backgrounds. Insiders advise applicants to research the firm before applying, and if you can, "send your resume through someone." Visit the "Employment Opportunities" section of the firm's web site for job listings and descriptions, as well as a recruiting calendar for both the fall and spring. The Advisory Board generally recruits in the Ivy League, but welcomes applications from other schools, and from people already in the workforce. Send or fax resumes to human resources, or e-mail resumes to jobs@advisory.com. Interviewees generally go through a three-round process, with final interviews conducted at headquarters in DC. "There are no case interviews for BAs, per se" one source reveals, "but they do present an example of a research project and ask how you would approach it."

OUR SURVEY SAYS

VIBRANCY ABOUNDS

"Young, vibrant and growing" describes The Advisory Board, where the staff has nearly doubled in size in the past five years, and more than half of employees are recent college grads. Employees report "an enormous amount of opportunity for advancement" at The Advisory Board, and note that managers "really recognize talent." One source reports moving up three times in three years. Another insider notes, however, that "if you're not in it for the long haul, it's also a great place to work for a year or two prior to going to grad school." "A lot of people – particularly undergrads – stay for one year. Some know they are going to medical school, and they work on the healthcare side to familiarize themselves with issues in the industry." In addition, "a fair amount of people leave for law or business school after two or three years." Undergraduates "work on relatively short-term projects. They "do lots of primary research, and work on a broad range of projects" – from the ultra-specific to "broader, more strategic reports." MBAs are hired as consultants, and are staffed on long-term studies that "are extremely intellectually engaging." Either way, our sources agree that "it's a wonderful way to learn about an industry."

YOUTH AND INEXPERIENCE HAVE THEIR DRAWBACKS

The firm's average age of 26 makes for a "young and fun" office, with employees often socializing after work. The company sponsors an in-house happy hour every two weeks. Youth has its downside, though, as one employee reports: "Because the company's so young and has so many opportunities to advance quickly, you will most likely be managed by someone who has no prior experience managing people. This can sometimes cause tension." An insider who came to the Advisory Board after working for a few years remarks that "it was better that I came into the company with some experience under my belt." That source goes on to add: "Not everyone has a totally positive experience, because they are not familiar with the realities of the working world." Advisory Board consultants warn that new employees can face strict, though not impossible deadlines for weekly research reports. "The deadlines cause a lot of people problems," one employee says, "but the expectations are not unreasonable. You have to be able to manage your time well."

MERIT COUNTS

Employees describe their co-workers as "smart, ambitious, and driven." Though "it's not a really competitive place," sources say "people feel pressure to perform because there is so much opportunity and everyone is extremely talented." Sources say women are treated "very fairly." One female employee reports that "opportunities for advancement are totally based on merit, and there are lots of women in positions of authority." Minorities are also treated well, but sources say "there are not that many here."

OFFICIAL HOURS? HA!

Official hours are 8:30 to 5:30, but "most people work longer," reports one source. "It's really your call though," another notes. "How much you work is entirely dependent on your ability to manage your time and finish your work. Some people go home at 5:30 everyday, while others stay late fairly consistently." For researchers, at least, "it's not like investment banking – people don't give you a ton of work at the last minute and expect you to stay there all night." Consultants usually work a bit more; and "just before a study comes out, they work some pretty serious hours." They do travel, "but not like the consultants at McKinsey or Bain." Dress is "professional but not enormously formal," and employees dress down on Fridays unless there are clients in the office. Men do have to wear ties, "but no suits are required."

DECENT CARE AND FEEDING OF CONSULTANTS

The Advisory Board offers "excellent and generous" benefits. Pay is "on par with the industry, if not a bit better." The greedy and ambitious will be pleased to hear that reviews are biannual, providing frequent occasions for promotions and raises. The top salespeople (marketers) may earn up to $500,000, while consultants typically earn $70,000. There are also bonuses, but insiders remark that, unlike at major consulting firms, "they are not really significant relative to total salary." Employees say that "the city itself is full of perks – free museums, free meals and cheap transportation." To add to the fun, "ABC offers overtime meals, for those nights you get caught in the office, full expense reimbursement, MBA training, internal training, career counseling, grad school recommendations, OK benefits, and great co-workers." One employee crows: "You have the ideal conditions required for rapid advancement, huge responsibilities and a true meritocracy. Most of us have fun meeting deadlines, talking with industry leaders (and losers), and enjoying DC." Any downside? "The 401(k) stinks!"

American Management Systems

4050 Legato Road
Fairfax, VA 22033
(703) 267-8000
www.amsinc.com

LOCATIONS

Fairfax, VA (HQ)
Frankfurt, Germany (European HQ)
AL • CA • CO • CT • FL • GA • IL • LA • MD • MA • MN • MS • NH • NJ • NM • NY • NC • OH • PA • RI • TX • VA • WA • Canada • Mexico

THE STATS

Annual Revenues: $872 million (1997)
No. of Employees: 7,100
No. of offices: 55 (worldwide)
Stock Symbol: AMSY (NASDAQ)
CEO: Paul A. Brands

KEY COMPETITORS

Andersen Consulting
Arthur Andersen
A.T. Kearney
Gartner Group

UPPERS

- Flexible hours
- Social place
- Employees sought after by headhunters
- Good on gender issues
- Business continues to grow

DOWNERS

- Prestige slipping?
- Disorganized training
- Dearth of ethnic diversity
- Lower profile than competitors

EMPLOYMENT CONTACT

Human Resources
American Management Systems
4050 Legato Road
Fairfax, VA 22033

Fax: (800) 326-6139
ams_recruiting@mail.amsinc.com

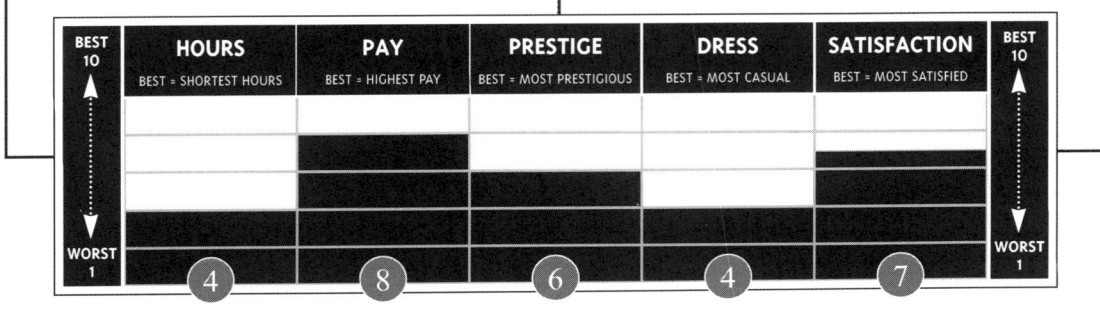

	HOURS BEST = SHORTEST HOURS	PAY BEST = HIGHEST PAY	PRESTIGE BEST = MOST PRESTIGIOUS	DRESS BEST = MOST CASUAL	SATISFACTION BEST = MOST SATISFIED	
	4	8	6	4	7	

© Copyright 1998 Vault Reports, Inc. Photocopying is illegal and expressly forbidden.

THE SCOOP

LINKS TO THE GOVERNMENT

AMS has its roots in Nixon Administration officials, and continues its legacy through the frequent projects it undertakes at the behest of the United States government – though, we trust, without any requests for wiretapping or breaking and entering. The firm was founded in 1970 by five men, including Ivan Selin, Frank Nicolai, Patrick Gross, and Charles Rossotti, a protégé of Nixon Defense Secretary Robert McNamara, and one of McNamara's so-called "whiz kids." The founders raised $300,000 in venture capital from Lehman Brothers, then wrote to 24 former Pentagon peers, offering consulting services "from some of the people who brought you Vietnam and the ABM." Despite this doubtful pedigree, AMS made $15,000 in profits its first year in business, and won its first big contract after another six months, with Burlington Northern Railroad.

SYSTEMS AND OPERATIONS FOCUS

AMS concentrates on systems and operations consulting in a variety of industries and thus faces a wide field of competition. The firm has grown every year since its founding, and still maintains close links with the U.S. government, which is the firm's largest customer and accounts for about 17 percent of revenues. Including local governments, a third of its revenue is provided by government clients. While AMS is the world's 13th-largest consulting organization, it has a way to go to catch up with some of the elephants it competes with, such as Andersen Consulting and Deloitte Consulting.

WHEN WE SAY "BU" WE DON'T MEAN BOSTON UNIVERSITY

AMS is organized into Business Units (BUs) that generally operate independently of each other. The BUs focus on the following target markets: Financial Services Institutions, Telecommunications Firms, Educational Institutions, Healthcare Providers, Insurance Companies, State and Local Governments, Federal Government Agencies, Electric and Gas

Utilities, and "Other Corporate Clients" in a variety of industries. Telecom is by far AMS's largest BU. These groups are sometimes called "silo industries" because of their relatively independent status – each business unit has full profit and loss responsibility for their industry areas. However, business units may coordinate on certain projects as necessary. Additionally, the management team in each unit is responsible for planning, marketing, selling, researching and consulting within its area – though business units may, of course, draw upon corporate resources.

THE AMS TECHNOLOGICAL HIVE

While the firm's BUs may operate independently, they try to share their expertise. AMS features a sprinkling of jewel-like "Knowledge Centers," communities of practitioners who offer a particular expertise in one or more AMS services, or so-called "core disciplines." The firm has Knowledge Centers for Advanced Technologies, Business Process Renewal, Systems Development and Information Technology Management, Organization Development and Change Management, Engagement and project management, and Customer Value Management. All 815 AMS Knowledge Center associates spend about 30 hours per year inputting research or "lessons learned" into the Knowledge Center database. This information is then accessible to any AMS consultant.

GETTING HIRED

AMS' web site, www.amsinc.com, allows job seekers to search job databases, submit their resumes, and use a job match service that will notify the candidate of opportunities that match her or his particular interests. Other online resources that AMS uses are JobTrak, Job Web, and Peterson's Job Choices.

The bulk of AMS recruiting takes place on campus. For the 1998/1999 recruiting season, AMS hopes to hire more than 900 individuals through its on-campus efforts. Of these hires, 70 percent will be recruited from their undergraduate studies, and 30 percent will come to the firm from MBA, MA, MS, and PhD programs. On-campus recruiting is led by 12 to 15 recruiting coordinators who maintain relationships with college and university career centers. These individuals also cultivate relationships with other on-campus connections, such as heads of departments (notably in computer science and other technology-related disciplines), professors, and leaders of computing clubs. Note that AMS' recruiting efforts will usually be focused towards a particular "Business Unit," or functional area. AMS also makes extensive use of job fairs and employers' conferences, and prospective AMSers should keep an eye out for recruiting events like cocktail parties and dinners.

OUR SURVEY SAYS

FLEXIBLE, RELAXED CULTURE

Comments on AMS' corporate culture reveal that the firm values flexibility, and is generally a relaxed place. "It feels like college was just extended a few more years," notes one insider, who adds: "From other companies I have worked with, I was always the young kid. Here, since the majority of people are right out of school, the college mentality continues." "Relaxed," says another contact about the firm's culture. That consultant also notes that the firm is "not overwhelmed by structure, although it could be better managed." One contact notes that "no one tells me when to come and go. I come in at 7 a.m., I come in at 11 a.m. I leave at 2 p.m., I leave at 3 a.m. My time. I am valued as an individual and as an employee." Another contact describes the firm's culture in somewhat political terms: "Slightly to the left of center from a cultural standpoint. Business casual attire and attitudes."

SOMETIMES ERRATIC HOURS

Most AMS consultants say they spend between 50 and 55 hours a week at the office. "Typically, the hours I put in are more on the order of 50 hours per week," says one. While 50 to 55 seem to be the magic numbers, the consensus is that "hours fluctuate with the project work," a common refrain for consultants. "Your schedule will vary with your project," notes one. "Some weeks you may not be very busy, and others you will be very busy – working up to 70 or 75 hours." "In 1998, summer was somewhat slow," reminisces another consultant, "but spring was a killer – 290 hours in March."

HOPPING SOCIAL LIFE

One of the major assets of life at AMS, say insiders, is the hopping social life. The DC area is a fun place for twentysomethings, and AMSers take full advantage. Love in the air? "Numerous AMSers I know are married to another AMSer, if this is an indication of social interaction," says one. Another picks up on the marriage theme: "You would be surprised how many AMSers are married to each other. It's amazing what happens when you cram several hundred single twentysomethings in a building." "Dating within the company is frequent," says yet another. One consultant describes social life at AMS as "very incestuous – in a good way."

STRONG ON GENDER

On gender issues, our contacts give AMS a very favorable rating. "I feel that AMS regards me as a member of the professional staff – not a female member. I have not experienced any kind of discrimination," says one consultant. "AMS is a great place to work as a woman. I have been here for four years and I have only ever worked for women managers," claims another woman.

To order a 50- to 70-page Vault Reports Employer Profile on American Management Systems call 1-888-JOB-VAULT or visit www.VaultReports.com

The full Employer Profile includes detailed information on AMS's departments, recent developments and transactions, hiring and interview process, plus what employees really think about culture, pay, work hours and more.

"Since the majority of people are right out of school, the college mentality continues."

– *AMS insider*

American Practice Management

1675 Broadway
New York, NY 10019
(212) 903-9300
www.csc.com

LOCATIONS

New York, NY (HQ)
Atlanta, GA
Boston, MA
Chicago, IL
San Francisco, CA
Toronto, Canada

THE STATS

Subsidiary of Computer Sciences Corporation

KEY COMPETITORS

ABT Associates
The Advisory Board
Booz·Allen & Hamilton
Ernst & Young Consulting
The Lewin Group

UPPERS

- Excellent leadership
- Fun working environment
- Talented staff

DOWNERS

- Recent merger-induced uncertainty
- Onerous workloads
- Insurmountable hours

EMPLOYMENT CONTACT

Human Resources
American Practice Management
1675 Broadway
New York, NY 10019

HOURS BEST = SHORTEST HOURS	PAY BEST = HIGHEST PAY	PRESTIGE BEST = MOST PRESTIGIOUS	DRESS BEST = MOST CASUAL	SATISFACTION BEST = MOST SATISFIED
6	4	5	3	6

© Copyright 1998 Vault Reports, Inc. Photocopying is illegal and expressly forbidden.

THE SCOOP

A HEALTHY HISTORY

Almost a quarter of a century ago, Arthur H. Spiegel III founded American Practice Management to provide management expertise and business discipline to the healthcare industry. His interest in improving the management of healthcare delivery was based on his own experiences as Deputy Administrator of the New York City Housing and Human Services Administration.

A THRIVING COMPANY

The company presently employs more than 250 consultants in offices in New York (its headquarters), Atlanta, Boston, Chicago, San Francisco, and Toronto. In the last five years, it has achieved a 36 percent growth rate and has plans to conquer new business sectors. APM's typical client base includes hospitals, academic medical centers, integrated delivery networks, physician groups, practice plans, insurers, and health plans. Impressively, APM has served more than 100 of the 250 largest clients in the healthcare industry

CSC MOVES IN

Despite APM's triumphs, the company learned in July 1996 that life in the consulting world is necessarily whirlwind. Information technology and systems consulting titan Computer Sciences Corporation (CSC), bought up APM in July of 1996, thereby causing confusion in newspaper headlines everywhere with acronym overload. The acquisition forever altered APM's management structure. The old management team stayed on, but APM's Chief Executive Officer, Spiegel, now reports to CSC's President and CEO, Van B. Honeycutt.

Vault Reports Guide to the Top Consulting Firms
American Practice Management

THE NOW-MIGHTY FIRM

New parent CSC is a management consulting, information technology, and systems integration firm. A whopper of a company, CSC is home to 45,000 employees in more than 650 offices worldwide. Competitors include major IT consulting firms like Andersen Consulting and Electronic Data Systems.

GETTING HIRED

APM recruits almost exclusively from prestigious universities and business schools. Past favorites have included the Amos Tuck School of Business at Dartmouth, Yale, The Wharton School of the University of Pennsylvania, Harvard Business School, the University of Chicago, and Haas School of Business. In addition to hiring consultants and associates straight from school, APM also seeks nurses and physicians as specialty consultants. APM also offers a limited number of summer associate consultant positions.

APM associate interviews are typically conducted over several rounds. At interviews, candidates should expect three or more back-to-back meetings with consultants and other upper-level managers. Insiders say that APM interviewers posit hypothetical scenarios that require candidates to ask probing and insightful questions.

For example, an interviewee might be asked to respond to the following situation: "There are two hospitals in the Twin Cities. Both hospitals are being consolidated and one must close its Pediatrics wing. Which hospital should be allowed to keep its Pediatrics wing open?" In such a scenario, insiders say, the interviewer is looking for a future associate's ability to uncover detail and elucidate a complicated set of circumstances. Questions to ask with this case might include how much care pediatrics patients usually require, what the precise geographical locale of each hospital is, and how far local patients are willing to travel to receive hospital care.

Although interviewees should brush up on their healthcare industry knowledge before their interviews, not all of APM's cases will involve the industry. One amused summer associate reports geting a case that revolved around a bicycle manufacturer.

OUR SURVEY SAYS

TEAM PLAYERS

APM insiders report a brisk and friendly atmosphere. The firm's dress code is "business," although employees receive a respite from their suits on Friday (which is business casual). The fourth Friday of every month is APM's Office Day, when everyone is expected to attend training sessions about firm activities, community service opportunities, and to take part in employee "caucuses."

DRUDGERY AND OPPORTUNITIES

APM insiders report a mixed bag of drudgery and fantastic opportunities at the firm. One insider describes her co-workers as "open, honest, friendly, social, and driven. They are people who ask really good questions." Yet another calls APM "a place where miscommunication lurks around every corner."

One former consultant addresses the mixed reports. "APM doesn't have a reputation as a great place to work," admits that insider. "I was warned of long hours and a rigid environment. And I heard rumors that the company was making motions to be a 'kinder, gentler' place. Personally, I had a great experience there and never saw the need."

A CHEERFUL, PERIPATETIC CROWD

More than one insider qualifies his superiors as "leaders, people I really respect and admire." Still another consultant praises the ability of APM consultants to have fun in the face of an onerous workload and insurmountable hours. The only universal complaint among our insiders concern the amount of travel APM requires. "It take a toll on you, that's for sure," admits one person. Reports another: "The travel is rigorous. It's hard to have a life when you're gone all the time. Then, when you arrive at your hotel at 8 p.m. one night, you have to ask yourself what there is to do. Watch free HBO?"

THE GOLDEN PRE-CSC YEARS

Insiders report a nostalgia for APM's independent years, before it was acquired by CSC. "It'll probably be years before all the rough spots are smoothed out between CSC and APM," confides one consultant. "There is integration going on, but such integration requires constant negotiation." Another insider's comments make the two companies seem more like star-crossed lovers than money-hungry tycoons. "CSC and APM need to work on their relationship," she admits. "They need a little more give and take. I think they can do it. Both companies have good people working under them."

"It'll probably be years before all the rough spots are smoothed out between CSC and APM."

– *APM insider*

Arthur Andersen

33 West Monroe
Chicago, Il 60603
(312) 580-0033
Fax: (312) 507-5222
www.arthurandersen.com

LOCATIONS

Chicago (HQ)
Domestic offices in 19 states
North American: Calgary • Montreal • Ottawa • Quebec • Toronto • Vancouver • Winnipeg • Guadalajara • Mexico City • Monterrey • Bermuda

THE STATS

Annual Revenues: $5.2 billion (1997)
No. of Employees: 60,000
A privately-held company
CEO: Jim Wadia
Year Founded: 1913

KEY COMPETITORS

American Management Systems
Ernst & Young Consulting
KPMG Consulting
PricewaterhouseCoopers

UPPERS

- Regenerating company
- Excellent training

DOWNERS

- Uncertainty because of split with Andersen Consulting
- Underpaying company

EMPLOYMENT CONTACT

Joel Stern
Arthur Andersen
33 West Monroe Street
Chicago, IL 60603

recruiting@arthurandersen.com

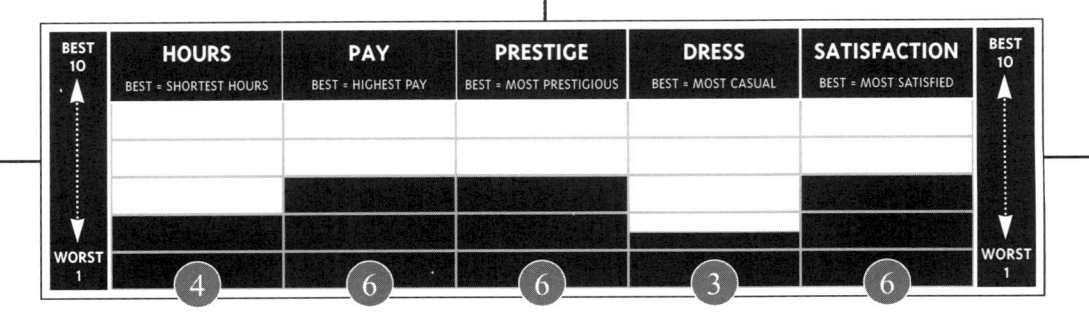

© Copyright 1998 Vault Reports, Inc. Photocopying is illegal and expressly forbidden.

	HOURS BEST = SHORTEST HOURS	PAY BEST = HIGHEST PAY	PRESTIGE BEST = MOST PRESTIGIOUS	DRESS BEST = MOST CASUAL	SATISFACTION BEST = MOST SATISFIED
	4	6	6	3	6

123

THE SCOOP

THE SIBLING RIVALRY

Since 1989, Arthur Andersen has played the stodgier sibling to the sleeker, sexier Andersen Consulting. But now, Arthur Andersen must stand on its own. The firm seems to be headed for an inevitable confrontation with Andersen Consulting – once its subsidiary, then a fully fleshed-out sibling, and now an adversary.

The roots of the split go back to 1952, when Andersen accountants first helped General Electric install an electrical system. Arthur Andersen's consulting subsidiary continued to grow, until, in 1989, the firm was split into two units – Arthur Andersen, which was expected to concentrate on accounting business, and Andersen Consulting, which would do consulting, especially computer consulting. The agreement contained a proviso that the more profitable side would transfer money to the other.

THE BIRTH OF ARTHUR ANDERSEN BUSINESS CONSULTING

However, Arthur Andersen soon found that Andersen Consulting was passing up smaller-niche consulting projects, and mobilized its own business consulting units to take advantage of them. Arthur Andersen became more and more adept at consulting – much to the displeasure of Andersen Consulting. The consulting boom of the 1980s had swollen AC's profits beyond those of Arthur Andersen – and the consulting arm was transferring money to a sibling it viewed as competition. While in 1997 Andersen Consulting was the world's biggest consulting firm (with revenues of $5.7 billion), Arthur Andersen came in as the 14th-largest ($953 million in consulting revenue). In December 1997, Andersen Consulting filed for arbitration, intending to split off from Arthur Andersen. Arthur Andersen has rejoined that Andersen Consulting, under the partnership agreement, must pay $10 billion in penalty fees and a royalty fee for the continued use of the Andersen name. Andersen Consulting claims that, by developing consulting capabilities, Arthur Andersen has voided the 1989 agreement.

Arthur Andersen

AN ONLINE FUTURE

Today, Arthur Andensen, though hardly puny at a size of 60,000 employees and revenues of $5.2 billion in 1997, is surpassed in revenues by its erstwhile subsidiary Andersen Consulting. In the meantime, Arthur Andersen hasn't been idling. Arthur Andersen has also introduced KnowledgeSpace, a gateway to online business information, tools and resources designed to make the Internet more efficient and productive for business users. Online subscribers receive access to many of the formerly proprietary diagnostic tools and insights from Arthur Andersen's "Global Best Practices" knowledge base as well as many other business performance enhancement tools.

GETTING HIRED

If you're looking for the inside scoop on starting an Arthur Andersen career, you won't find it on the willfully obtuse Arthur Andersen "careers" site. Our sources, however, are happy to oblige.

Typically, Arthur Andersen gives one (sometimes two) screening interviews on campus. The firm does two interview rounds on campus for MBAs. The interviews are either with managers, who have been with the firm for five years, or junior partners, who have been there at least seven. Explains one insider: "The interview process is pretty standard, but they run you through the wringer pretty well. You have a first screening interview, which is on campus, or, if you come in somewhere besides on-campus recruiting, with an HR person."

Those lucky enough to snare a callback interview will see them "last all day. You will have three interviews at a minimum, and you will interview with managers on up." The firm reportedly does not make offers quickly; turnaround time is "a week, minimum." Sometimes, "there's another callback interview with a partner, if they're not sure." Insiders say that while junior consultants are involved in the process, "partners have the final say. If you have to pick who to impress, pick a partner."

Arthur Andersen tends to shun hard quant questions, insiders say, preferring to give behavioral interviews to its prospective consultants. Reports one contact: "There are no guesstimates or case interviews, but they will grill you pretty hard about your understanding of the job and why you want to do it."

While Arthur Andersen, like most large companies, has distinct hiring cycles, "the needs lately have happened at random. In some markets, Arthur perceives they are leaving a lot of money on the table, so they are eager to expand the size of the office." MBAs say the firm is assiduously recruiting them for its business consulting practice – "just don't screw up and call them Andersen Consulting by accident."

HARSH TRAVEL

"The travel can be brutal," says an Arthur Andersen business consultant. "In the interviews they'll tell you three days a week, or four max, but that's just bullshit. Consultants at every level are very much virtual. If you're thinking of taking a job [at Arthur Andersen], don't even bother to get your own apartment. Just keep your stuff at your partner's and save what you'd pay in rent – you're going to be living out of a suitcase. From what I've seen, people often fly out Sunday night and don't leave the client site until Friday at 5 – and that's if you're staffed at a city with airport connections."

THANK GOODNESS FOR BROOKS!

"We keep Brooks Brothers in business," says one consultant. "There is very much a dress code in business. But three years ago they finally started doing business casual Fridays." Another insider mentions that "for the summer in some offices, they've made it a business casual summer. Of course, this screws everyone up, because most of us only have one or two outfits to wear – three at the most, so everyone ends up wearing the same stuff. But it was a nice effort, I think."

One significant anti-perk at one office – "there's no brown bagging (lunches). It is deemed 'unprofessional.'" A contact at another office confirms that "brown bagging is discouraged," but adds "this is because we are supposed to go out of the office with each other." While "your supervisor will pay for quite a few of your lunches if you are working at the client," at the home office "most people, if they have to pay, go to fast food places." This means that "your paid lunch expenses can be rather high."

NO BAD BLOOD

The Arthur Andersen/Andersen Consulting split is the topic of some conversation at Arthur Andersen, though less than you might expect. "Certainly all the people at the senior level, the managers, were watching [the long, slow, painful descent toward arbitration] with interest, and everyone else was talking about it a bit." "We knew it could cost the partners a lot of money," comments one insider. "Basically, they would lose about $100,000 a year, which I think for them is nothing much. At our meetings, the [split] would be discussed, and we would get voice mails on recent developments. We knew the partners were concerned, but to be honest, after a while, the rest of us were sick of the topic." One contact credits firm management with "being very classy about the whole situation. We see articles in the *Wall Street Journal* and I think we come off very well." "There is no bad blood between Arthur Andersen consultants and Andersen consultants," says one insider. "All that stuff is at the partner level."

THE SLOWLY CHANGING CONSULTING FIRM

The firm is "very old school, which also means that advocacy of minority and female leadership kept to a minimum." "As a huge firm governed by a smallish elite of profit-sharing partners, AA can be slow to adapt to prevalent trends in the marketplace," advises one contact. "There is definitely a strong sense of hierarchy. While we pick up on trends and sell them on the revenue generating side, on the operations side it seems we seldom practice what we preach."

GOOD STARTING POINT

Despite the gripes, say insiders, "Arthur Andersen is a great place to get a start on your career. You acquire great skills, both technical and interpersonal, and a great name on your resume." "The firm invests a lot in training and education," says another insider, "which means that they value us, and it's something you can take away with you."

> To order a 50- to 70-page Vault Reports Employer Profile on Arthur Andersen call 1-888-JOB-VAULT or visit www.VaultReports.com
>
> The full Employer Profile includes detailed information on Arthur Andersen's departments, recent developments and transactions, hiring and interview process, plus what employees really think about culture, pay, work hours and more.

Arthur D. Little

Acorn Park
Cambridge, MA 02140
(617) 498-5000
Fax: (617) 498-7228
www.adlittle.com

LOCATIONS

Cambridge, MA (HQ)
Other offices across the U.S. • Europe • Latin America • Asia-Pacific

THE STATS

Annual Revenues: $589 million (1997)
No. of Employees: 3,000 (worldwide)
No. of Offices: 52 (worldwide)
A privately-held company
CEO: Charles LaMantia

KEY COMPETITORS

Andersen Consulting
Booz•Allen & Hamilton
Boston Consulting Group
Deloitte Consulting
Ernst & Young Consulting
KPMG Consulting
McKinsey & Company

UPPERS

- Profit sharing
- Weekly orientations and seminars
- Subsidies for daycare services

DOWNERS

- Fewer perks than most consulting firms
- Grungy HQ

EMPLOYMENT CONTACT

Susan G. McDonald
Recruiting Manager
Arthur D. Little
Acorn Park
Cambridge, MA 02140

(617) 498-6070
Fax: (617) 498-7140
careers@adlittle.com

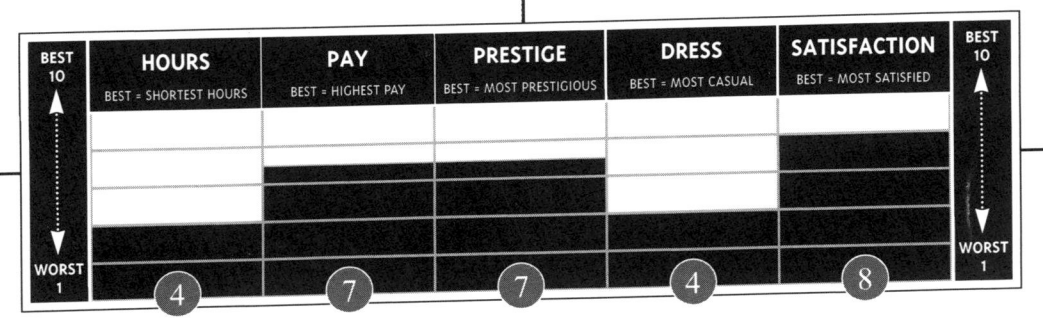

HOURS	PAY	PRESTIGE	DRESS	SATISFACTION
BEST = SHORTEST HOURS	BEST = HIGHEST PAY	BEST = MOST PRESTIGIOUS	BEST = MOST CASUAL	BEST = MOST SATISFIED
4	7	7	4	8

THE SCOOP

THE BATTLE-TESTED VETERAN

Founded in 1886, Arthur D. Little is the oldest consulting firm in the world and still going strong. The firm has more than 3000 staff members in 51 offices worldwide. It aims to distinguish itself from its competitors through the breadth and depth of its experience, and through the caliber of its own employees. ADL has worked with more than 75 percent of Fortune 100 companies worldwide, in such industries as automotive, chemicals, consumer goods and services, energy, financial, health care, public administration, resources, TIME (telecommunications, information technology, media, electronics), transportation, and utilities. Its services range from design and development to safety and risk.

THE TECHNO-CONSULTANTS

ADL's most glorified experts reside in the firm's technology unit, which has sponsored numerous useful advances over the years. These range from the development of the first acetate fibers in the early part of the 20th Century, to a recent fuel-powered energy cell breakthrough, which should make electric cars more feasible. The technology division not only develops innovative products, but sponsors investors and assists them in bringing their creations to market (for half of the proceeds). For example, the U.S. Army asked Arthur D. Little to help it design gloves suited for outdoor wear, rough use, and a wide range of hand sizes.

ADL's consulting teams are laden with high-up personnel, and emphasize a "side-by-side" method of working with clients. With its focus on lasting results, Arthur D. Little keeps clients coming back for more. The firm gets 80 percent of its business from repeat customers. It has boasted 16 percent annual revenue growth over the last several years, as well as an average stock increase of 17 percent per year. Because all ADL consultants are shareholders, they are personally invested in the maintenance of this impressive record of achievement.

THE EDUCATORS

ADL consultants publish frequently on topics in the fields of management consulting, technology and production innovation, and environmental, heath, and safety consulting. Excerpts and summaries of the firm's quarterly publication, *Prism*, are available at the Arthur D. Little "Cybrary," which can be downloaded off the firm's web site at www.arthurdlittle.com. In addition, the firm offers a rainbow of educational programs. The Arthur D. Little School of Management, the only graduate program offered by a consulting firm, offers a one-year Master of Science in Management (MSM) Program, as well as a series of other courses in business management.

GETTING HIRED

Painfully perky painter's motif aside, the "careers" section of ADL's web site is both thorough and informative. Like most consultancies, Arthur D. Little recruits at prestigious schools at both the MBA and undergrad level. It sports its yearly recruiting schedule on its web site, complete with exact dates and resume deadlines. At the undergraduate level, ADL makes presentations at the University of Michigan, MIT, Northwestern University, Princeton University, Tufts, Cornell, and the University of Pennsylvania. The dates and times, which shift each year, can also be found on the firm's web site.

"Arthur D. Little has a very positive attitude about MBAs," says one insider. "Traditionally, most of their consultants came out of the industry, but direct hire from top MBA schools is an increasingly significant source of talent." The firm expects to hire between 70 to 80 MBAs for full-time positions in 1998-99. Applicants will go through a "very long, very intense" phone interview before being invited to the recruiting weekends at the firm's offices, where they will have two more interviews. In some cases, ADL gives presentation interviews, for which interviewees prepare and make brief presentations on a case study that Arthur D. Little provides. Presentation interviews are typically given to management consultants with some experience.

In general, the interviews aren't "tricky" – ADL is very concerned with past experience. The case interviews are reportedly more like "mini-cases," and focus on recent industry experience. There are no "mind games," according to one recent hire. Offers are made by the end of the weekend for U.S. offices.

OUR SURVEY SAYS

BRINGING UP CONSULTANTS

New hires at Arthur D. Little are paired with senior consultants to encourage "quick on-the-job learning." Consultants "rapidly" move into positions of "vast responsibility" and are required to travel extensively as part of the firm's "major commitment" to its clients, though you should be prepared to "direct your own career path." Insiders comment that Arthur D. Little offers its consultants "flexibility in terms of the type of work that they do" as well as a work schedule that, while demanding, "is slightly lighter than other management consulting firms."

OPEN VISTAS, FEW PERKS

The minimalist or "stripped-down" feel of Arthur D. Little continues in the realm of perks. Don't expect lavish frills at sensible ADL. "It's not that perky. We travel coach domestically and business class overseas," says one consultant. Fortunately, "the company pays full-fare coach, so most of us can at least grab an upgrade with all our frequent flier miles." On the bright side, another insider notes that "we have free coffee and soda in our office." Other contacts stress that "Arthur D. Little might look more closely at little frills than some other consulting firms, but the benefits and pension plans are great. This is a down-to-earth place."

COMFORTABLE PAY AND ENVIRONMENT

As for pay, ADL's offerings are "not too shabby," though "performance bonuses are given out in a kind of stealthy way." Insiders report that "Arthur D. Little still has a small company feel," and that management "is very approachable in a way that goes beyond the usual 'open door' rhetoric." Employees say that their "friendly" colleagues make the office atmosphere "egalitarian" and "lively and interactive." In general, people stay a long time at Arthur D. Little because "they earn a piece of the firm, and they feel comfortable" there.

HEADQUARTERS: SHABBY CHIC?

Although Arthur D. Little boasts about its Cambridge headquarters, the firm may be overstating the case. "ADL is proud that its Cambridge headquarters was the first corporate campus," say insiders, "but the physical buildings are not nice at all." Another insider goes so far as to describe them as "frumpy." In a burst of raw honesty, the consultant remarks: "There is a credit union and a cafeteria, but in general the place looks like an underfunded community college. So maybe that's the campus part."

To order a 50- to 70-page Vault Reports Employer Profile on Arthur D. Little call 1-888-JOB-VAULT or visit www.VaultReports.com

The full Employer Profile includes detailed information on Arthur D. Little's departments, recent developments and transactions, hiring and interview process, plus what employees really think about culture, pay, work hours and more.

"There is a credit union and a cafeteria, but in general the place looks like an underfunded community college."

– *AD Little insider*

Buck Consultants

Two Pennsylvania Plaza
New York, NY 10121-0047
(212) 330-1000
Fax: (212) 695-4184
www.buckconsultants.com

LOCATIONS

New York, NY (HQ)
Atlanta • Boston • Chicago • Cincinnati • Cleveland • Dallas • Los Angeles • Philadelphia • Seattle • 50 other offices worldwide

THE STATS

No. of Offices: 60 (worldwide)
Subsidiary of Mellon Bank Corporation
CEO: Joseph A. LoCicero

KEY COMPETITORS

Andersen Consulting
Hewitt Associates
Towers Perrin
Watson Wyatt Worldwide

UPPERS

- Flexible and short hours
- Possible stock boom from takeover

DOWNERS

- Corporate restructuring
- Limited specialties
- Unimpressive pay

EMPLOYMENT CONTACT

Human Resources
Buck Consultants
Two Pennsylvania Plaza
New York, NY 10121-0047

info@buckconsultants.com

© Copyright 1998 Vault Reports, Inc. Photocopying is illegal and expressly forbidden.

HOURS BEST = SHORTEST HOURS	PAY BEST = HIGHEST PAY	PRESTIGE BEST = MOST PRESTIGIOUS	DRESS BEST = MOST CASUAL	SATISFACTION BEST = MOST SATISFIED
8	6	4	2	8

THE SCOOP

CONSULTING THE EMPLOYEES

Buck Consultants, Inc. is an employee benefit, actuarial and compensation consulting firm whose clients range from large multinational utilities and industrial corporations to small businesses and non-profit organizations. Buck's employee benefit plans cover more than 10 million active and retired employees and have assets totaling over $400 billion. Earlier this year, Mellon Bank Corporation acquired Buck Consultants, and Buck will heretofore operate as a Mellon subsidiary while retaining its operational identity. According to the December 1996 agreement, Buck shareholders will have the option to receive Mellon common stock or cash.

THE BUCK EVOLUTION

George B. Buck, Consulting Actuary, was established in New York City in 1916 as an individual proprietorship that worked with states and large cities in establishing funded retirement systems. Buck Consultants, Inc. evolved from its entrepreneurial beginnings in 1970, when it became a closely-held, employee-owned corporation. In the last 80 years, Buck has pioneered new approaches to retirement plans, trusts for corporate employees, and global employee stock ownership plans. Through its partnership with the giant Pittsburgh-based Mellon Bank, Buck Consultants looks forward to gleaning the benefits of the company's $1.3 trillion assets and to becoming a leader in the booming business of corporate benefits outsourcing.

GETTING HIRED

Interested applicants should send a resume by fax or mail to Buck's New York headquarters. Since Buck has over 60 offices nationwide, applicants should indicate their geographic preferences. Cover letters should indicate a special interest in compensation and benefit consulting (and not, say, strategic consulting).

OUR SURVEY SAYS

THE SCARY MERGER – SEEMS OK

There was "some apprehension" among Buck Consulting's employees regarding the merger with Mellon Bank, but it "hasn't affected us – yet," and employees report "business as usual" at the firm. Employees at Buck are "constantly challenged" and one remarks that "employee benefits consulting is unexpectedly interesting."

A GOOD WORK ENVIRONMENT

The hours are "more manageable" at Buck than at other consulting firms – "37 hours a week," – and "even those hours are flexible." Employees work in "management teams," which is "ideal, because it builds camaraderie" and "nurtures friendships." The dress code is "business casual with casual Fridays." There are "several women supervisors" at Buck, and the male-female ratio is "about 50/40" which "beats most firms." The salary is "not terribly high" but the "bright people" and "conscientious management" at Buck "are more important than a few cents' less pay."

"Employee benefits consulting is unexpectedly interesting."

– *Buck insider*

Cambridge Technology Partners

304 Vassar Street
Cambridge, MA 02139
(617) 374-9800
Fax: (617) 374-8300
www.ctp.com

LOCATIONS

Cambridge, MA (HQ)
Atlanta • Chicago • Dallas • Detroit, MI • Lansing, MI • Los Angeles • New York, NY • San Francisco • Locations throughout Europe

THE STATS

Annual Revenues: $438.3 million (1997)
No. of Employees: 4,300
No. of Offices: 35
Stock Symbol: CATP (NASDAQ)
CEO: James K. Sims

KEY COMPETITORS

Andersen Consulting
Computer Sciences Corporation
Electronic Data Systems
Gemini Consulting
Renaissance Worldwide
Sapient

UPPERS

- Laid-back "high-tech" environment
- Stock options
- Two-week training session with party atmosphere

DOWNERS

- Fixed time standard can mean high-stakes pressure
- Slow travel reimbursement

EMPLOYMENT CONTACT

Human Resources
Cambridge Technology Partners
304 Vassar Street
Cambridge, MA 02139

Fax: (925) 824-0328
ersjobs@ctp.com

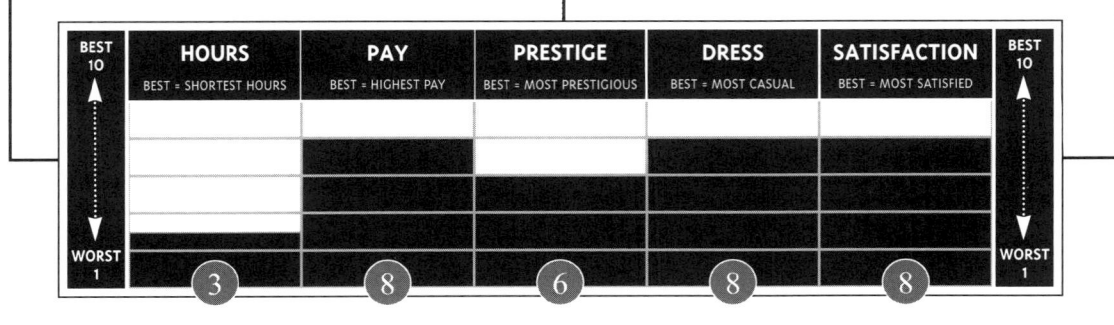

HOURS BEST = SHORTEST HOURS	PAY BEST = HIGHEST PAY	PRESTIGE BEST = MOST PRESTIGIOUS	DRESS BEST = MOST CASUAL	SATISFACTION BEST = MOST SATISFIED
3	8	6	8	8

THE SCOOP

WHEN AND WHERE YOU WANT IT

Cambridge Technology Partners (CTP) sticks to a "fixed price, fixed time" standard, the only high-tech consulting firm to give customers an up-front guarantee of how much a job will cost and how long it will take. In addition to helping Fortune 1000 companies design new, more efficient computer networks, Cambridge works with companies in building intranets and helps them with Internet and electronic-commerce technology.

A YOUTHFUL POWERHOUSE

The firm was jointly established in 1991 by Safeguard Scientifics, Radnor Venture Partners, and Cambridge Technology Group. Under the leadership of cofounder James Sims, the company went public in 1991. In 1994, the firm acquired Sweden-based IOS Group, an information technology and software development corporation. Continuing to expand, it acquired the Systems Consulting Group and Axiom Management Consulting the following year. In a $36 million deal, Cambridge acquired software consulting firm Ramos & Associates in 1996. With a yearly growth rate of more than 50 percent, Cambridge Technology Partners has expanded outside its historic home, Cambridge, Massachusetts, by leaps and bounds. The firm now has facilities across the U.S. and Europe, as well as in Brazil and Mexico. The firm recently opened an office in Tokyo.

THE STRATEGY PET

CTP also has a smallish management consulting division called Cambridge Management Consulting (CMC), which also guarantees a fixed time and fixed price for its services (most transpiring in the space of six to 12 months). CMC's willingness to name its price up front, to share with its clients the risk of change, and to guarantee on-time project delivery in an accelerated time frame all form the policy and special consulting offering that CMC calls "Rapid Business Renewal."

A TECH STRATEGY NICHE

Founded in 1988, CMC today has 180 consultants and is headquartered in San Francisco. Borrowing from its technology-savvy parent, CMC has found its niche in the field of technology business solutions, especially electronic commerce. Its varied list of clients includes Sun Microsystems, 3Com, Citibank, J.P. Morgan, Saab, Enron, the City of Sacramento, Federal Express, AT&T, Burger King and Nike. CMC recommends that those interested in the potential of the electronic commerce market read *Net Gain: Expanding Markets through Virtual Communities* by John Hagel III and Arthur Armstrong.

GETTING HIRED

Visit the "Job Opportunities" section of Cambridge's web site for the low-down on job openings. With positions in many different locations, send or e-mail resumes to the addresses listed at the web site. Both CTP and CMC maintain lists of current openings and qualifications. CTP's job openings, which range from marketing managers to project leaders to Windows NT instructors, is at http://www.ctp.com/html/HR/html/position_descriptions.html.

CMC looks for entrepreneurial, creative college graduates for its entry-level analyst positions, and an MBA and other career experience for more advanced consultant slots. CMC claims to value dedication, ambition and motivation as highly as academic achievement and real-world experience, though some kind of computer background is still a big plus.

OUR SURVEY SAYS

CONVIVIAL CULTURE

At this "highly social" tech-focused company, employees turn in top ratings for company culture. "The culture is probably the best part of the company," one employee says, "a very laid-back environment dominates throughout the entire company. Everyone just has a good time." With an average age of less than 30, the fun starts with new employee orientation at the firm's headquarters, which one employee describes as, "two weeks of partying in Boston!" The company sponsors regional activities each quarter including "clam bakes, beach events, and happy hours." One employee notes: "The culture is very employee-centric, and people find it very hard to leave Cambridge because of it." Another employee enjoys his Cambridge co-workers so much, he raves: "Though work hours can get very hectic at times, the people are so great that you don't even notice the time."

THE TRAVEL AND TIME LIMITS GRATE

In fact, work hours at Cambridge are a sore spot for many. Consultants note that the company's "fixed price, fixed time" mantra can put undue pressure on them. One insider complains: "People around here don't always do a great job of estimating projects. It usually requires a massive effort on someone's part to accomplish anything on time." In addition to long hours, many consultants dislike the extensive travel Cambridge requires of its professionals. One employee complains about the reimbursement process at Cambridge, saying: "I travel a lot, so expense reports are a part of my life. Cambridge is not good at processing these things, it takes about four weeks to get one back."

CASUAL DRESS, SERIOUS PERKS

With the exception of client meetings, dress at the firm tends to be "business casual," with "Dockers and collared shirts for guys," though some offices take the dress down philosophy even further. One contact reports: "My home office allows shorts, T-shirts and sandals during the summer, five days a week." Insiders say minorities have "excellent opportunities" at Cambridge. Though one employee notes that "men definitely outnumber women, probably 70 percent to 30 percent," another reports that "there are many women in very key high-level positions. For example, Lee Dingle is a Vice President in charge of our Electronic Commerce Domain." Consultants agree that the firm's pay is very good, and enjoy perks including free meals, a free membership in the Hyatt health club, 90 percent payment for part-time education, and a "pleasing year-end bonus." Opportunities for travel are reportedly good, with one consultant reporting trips to Australia and Japan. To sum up, says one consultant, "interesting things are always happening at CTP."

"The culture is very employee-centric, and people find it very hard to leave Cambridge because of it."

– *Cambridge insider*

Charles River Associates

200 Clarendon Street, T-33
Boston, MA 02116-5092
(617) 425-3000
Fax: (617) 425-3132

LOCATIONS

Boston, MA (HQ)
Los Angeles, CA
Palo Alto, CA
Toronto
Washington, DC

THE STATS

Annual Revenues: $448 million (1997)
No. of Professionals: 145
No. of Offices: 3
Stock Symbol: CRAI (NASDAQ)
President: Jim Burrows

KEY COMPETITORS

Booz•Allen & Hamilton
Boston Consulting Group
Mercer Management Consulting
Monitor Company

UPPERS

- Cheap food in cafeteria
- Brilliant co-workers
- Unusual specialties

DOWNERS

- Long work days
- Poor training
- Small raises
- Entry-level employees have minimal contact with clients

EMPLOYMENT CONTACT

Cynthia Butler
Human Resources Director
Charles River Associates
200 Clarendon Street, T-33
Boston, MA 02116-5092

Fax: (617) 425-3112
cdb@crai.com

HOURS BEST = SHORTEST HOURS	PAY BEST = HIGHEST PAY	PRESTIGE BEST = MOST PRESTIGIOUS	DRESS BEST = MOST CASUAL	SATISFACTION BEST = MOST SATISFIED
2	7	6	5	8

THE SCOOP

THE NONTRADITIONAL CONSULTING FIRM

Founded in 1965, Charles River Associates (CRA) offers more than just traditional management consulting solutions. In addition to business strategy, market analysis and M&A work, the firm has made a name for itself advising law firms and corporations involved in intellectual property issues, environmental disputes, and antitrust litigation – not the typical clientele for a consulting firm! Charles River also offers consulting services for companies dealing with securities, bankruptcy, legal and regulatory economics, and technology assessment. The firm is comprised of two consulting groups: litigation and regulation, and business consulting. The former accounts for about two-thirds of its revenues, while the business side accounts for the other third. Its consultants are typically MBAs and PhDs with specialties in finance, economics, technology, energy policy, metals, minerals and materials. Charles River consultants are often called upon to testify as expert witnesses in a variety of cases before the Federal Trade Commission and the Department of Justice.

A GRAB BAG OF CLIENTS

The firm serves a diverse group of clients – including major law firms, domestic and foreign corporations, public and private utilities, and government agencies around the world. Its consultants have developed special expertise in the chemicals, transportation, energy, telecommunications, and health care industries. Through a joint program with Market Design, Inc. – a California-based firm that offers software and consulting services for the design and implementation of electronic auction markets – Charles River offers auction consulting services to clients in telecommunications, energy, mineral rights and other industries. Clients of the joint venture include the Federal Trade Commission and the Mexican Federal Telecommunications Commission.

SELF-PROPELLED

CRA officers and directors completed a buyout of the firm in March 1995, with each officer gaining an equity interest in the firm. The officers cashed in when the firm went public in May 1998. The firm has benefited largely from its proficient rainmakers – 33 percent of its 1997 revenues came in through five of its consultants; 10 of its engagements accounted for 23 percent of earnings. In June 1998, CRA opened new offices in Toronto and Los Angeles. A few months later, the firm announced that the acquisition of the Tilden Group, a California-based consulting firm specializing in economic analysis for litigation, public policy design, and business strategy development.

GETTING HIRED

To fill its research assistant positions, Charles River recruits undergraduates from top colleges and universities, and encourages applications from finance, economics, or engineering majors from any school. Nearly half of CRA's professional-level employees hold advanced degrees – the firm hires candidates with Masters degrees in economics, engineering and computer technology as associates. Higher-level professionals, insiders say, "are economists with PhDs – many of them are former college professors who didn't get tenure, or wanted more money." CRA does not actively recruit MBAs.

The recruitment process usually consists of interviews on campus followed by "second-round interviews in the office with five or six people." Other candidates may screened by phone, then invited to the firm to meet with managers. Insiders say "you'll meet with the people who would be your managers, as well as with people in the position you're applying for." The firm looks for candidates with "strong quantitative and communications skills." Case questions "are not a standard part of the interviewing process," reports a contact, though "some people use them from time to time."

OUR SURVEY SAYS

A LOVE OF RISK

Consultants at Charles River Associates "revel" in the firm's "entrepreneurial culture," which encourages "risk-taking," "independent thinking," and "an aggressive attitude." "This is not a typical job in marketing or finance," one former CRA consultant explains, "though it can have elements of both." Another source adds that the firm is suited to "someone interested in economics or in manufacturing companies." Recent hires like the fact that CRA "is one of the few places where you can use things you learned in school in a professional setting." "The type of analysis we deal with is more sophisticated than what they do in regular management consulting or I-banking," boasts one contact.

SINK? SWIM?

One big complaint, however, is that "there's no formal training program." As one source describes it, "from day one they just hand you projects and it's sink or swim." Though some like the challenge, the fact is "there are times when you'll have no idea how to approach a problem." Sources say managers "are as helpful as they can be, but if it's a really busy time, there may not be someone with time to explain things to you." For this reason, some research assistants say working at CRA "is sometimes really frustrating." Some insiders assert that "[research assistants] have minimal contact with the client," and note that the company does very little as far as "career development for employees without graduate degrees." However, one contact tells us assistants "have a good track record as far as people getting into good schools." Undergraduates spend an average of three years at CRA.

PARTYING FOR ECONOMISTS

There are "a good number of women and minorities in the firm," says an employee, "and there are several female VPs." That insider adds that young employees are "pretty social – we go out together every few weeks or so." "Our managers," on the other hand, "are economists – generally not the most fun people in the world." Insiders say "the holiday parties and company picnics are truly boring affairs." On the positive side, "there's lots of brainpower here – some of the people are geniuses." Unfortunately, some "are not too great at managing people."

Consultants at the firm wear "business casual for the most part." "You can get away with not wearing a suit, plus there's casual day on Fridays." Consultants in Boston say "our office is in a great location, and add that "we have cheap food in the cafeteria." Hours "vary quite a bit, but the median is somewhere in the 55 to 60 range." As at most consulting firms, "there are periods where you will work 100 hours or more per week for several weeks." Travel is "not bad for research associates. But it gets more intense as you move up the ranks." We hear that "starting salaries are adequate to above average," but sources also tell us that "pay raises are never higher than 10 percent per year."

"There are periods where you will work 100 hours or more per week for several weeks."

– *Charles River insider*

Computer Sciences Corporation

2100 East Grand Avenue
El Segundo, CA 90245
(310) 615-0311
www.csc.com

LOCATIONS

El Segundo, CA (HQ)
Washington, DC
As well as hundreds of offices across the nation and the globe

THE STATS

Annual Revenues: $6.6 billion (1998)
No. of Employees: 45,000
No. of Offices: 600
Stock Symbol: CSC (NYSE)
CEO: Van B. Honeycutt

KEY COMPETITORS

Andersen Consulting
Booz·Allen & Hamilton
Deloitte Consulting
Electronic Data Systems
IBM

UPPERS

- Generous maternity leave
- Staff development programs
- Consultants choose assignments

DOWNERS

- Long workdays
- Grueling travel
- Gigantic organization can be disorienting

EMPLOYMENT CONTACT

Human Resources
Computer Sciences Corporation
2100 East Grand Avenue
El Segundo, CA 90245

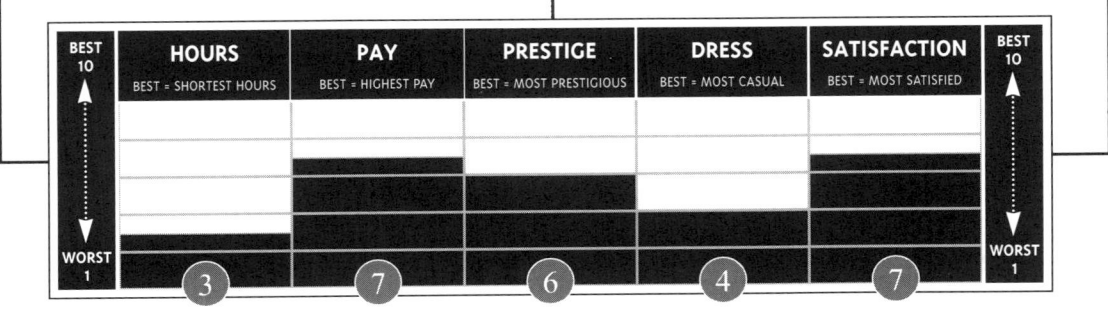

HOURS (BEST = SHORTEST HOURS)	PAY (BEST = HIGHEST PAY)	PRESTIGE (BEST = MOST PRESTIGIOUS)	DRESS (BEST = MOST CASUAL)	SATISFACTION (BEST = MOST SATISFIED)
3	7	6	4	7

© Copyright 1998 Vault Reports, Inc. Photocopying is illegal and expressly forbidden.

THE SCOOP

THE HUGE COMPUCONSULTANCY

Computer Sciences Corporation provides management and information technology consulting, systems integration, and outsourcing services to governments and companies worldwide. It works in a variety of sectors, most notably aerospace, chemical, oil & gas, credit services, financial services, and heathcare. CSC also considers the U.S. Government one of its primary business targets.

PRONE TO MERGERS

CSC makes frequent and impressive acquisitions; in 1997 it merged with American Practice Management (APM), one of the largest independent strategic consulting companies in North America. APM's thorough knowledge of the heathcare industry was no doubt a factor in the acquisition, as CSC hopes to gain both field expertise and geographic presence through its mergers. The firm's 1997 merger with DataCentralen, an important information solutions and technology provider in Denmark, marks an attempt to extend its dealings in Scandinavia. Above and beyond its merger, acquisition, and networking skills, CSC is also adept at creating original business tools – and at adding to the already overcrowded dictionary of consulting jargon. The firm recently developed a methodology known as "CSC Fusion," which is, in essence, a set of tools that can identify, prioritize, align, and merge business and IT strategies.

GROWTH DESPITE SCANDAL

Over the past five years, CSC has seen its revenues grow at least 25 percent annually, although the firm was shaken by a scandal in 1995, when the company was discovered to have purchased tens of thousands of copies of a book written by two CSC consultants, to ensure that the book made bestseller lists. The firm was not interested in profits from the book, called *The Discipline of Market Leaders*, but sought to make the impression that its theories were widely sought after, thereby increasing CSC's business. In response, several firms canceled their engagements with CSC, and the two authors of the book left the firm. Despite the uproar, CSC has managed to survive, and some would say, to flourish. It recently signed landmark, multi-billion-dollar contracts with J.P. Morgan and DuPont. CSC's acquisition list has grown to include Continuum, Planmetrics, DAN Computer Management, and The Pinnacle Group, and its number of offices has increased to 600 worldwide.

GETTING HIRED

In 1997, CSC hired over 1000 college students. It actively seeks quality undergraduates and business students. For recent hires interested in IT, the company offers several training programs. It also has special training programs for industry hires and MBA recruits. CSC travels to over 100 college campuses each year; its visiting/presentation schedule can be found on the firm's web site, or at careers.csc.com. Note that interested persons must register with CSC prior to submitting their resumes. Because of its large size, CSC is able to offer an assortment of tailored positions, including full-time, part-time, co-op, research, and associate-level opportunities. The CSC web site also contains information on positions that are available outside of the recruiting circuit. Because the positions are as nonstandard and varied as CSC's scope of technical and consulting services, individual employment requirements vary. The site lists specific contact addresses for each job and location.

OUR SURVEY SAYS

STRONG PAY, LONG WEEKS

Insiders report that the typical CSC consultant endures "grueling" travel schedules and "marathon" workdays. Employees are usually in their "home" office Monday and Friday and at the client's site Tuesday through Thursday. However, the firm compensates employees for this "exacting" schedule in other ways. Not only do employees benefit from a "robust" pay scale, consultants usually have the chance to select their own roles and projects. CSC must be doing something right; almost universally, insiders say that "everybody wants to stay" because of the "abundance of interesting projects and the leeway given with them."

GENUINE FLEXIBILITY

CSC is also said to be "genuinely flexible" in allowing employees to transfer to another of its 600 worldwide locations. The "creative" and "fun" culture keeps employee satisfaction high: turnover rate is less than 15 percent – well below the industry average. Insiders also praise "the somewhat more relaxed promotion schedule." One insider remarks: "There is no up-or-out policy, which is cause for a lower stress average." The dress "varies between offices." While Chicago employees sport business casual all the time, the Cambridge office is "somewhere between business casual and business business." Of course, the bottom sartorial line is ultimately drawn by the client. One insider stresses, "you wear whatever they wear – like in Simon Says."

Dean & Company

Fairfax Square
8065 Leeburg Pike, Suite 500
Vienna, VA 22182-2738
www.deanco.com

LOCATIONS

Washington, DC

THE STATS

No. of Employees: 60

KEY COMPETITORS

Greenwich Associates
Integral
Mars & Company
Parthenon Group
Pittiglio Rabin Todd & McGrath

UPPERS

- Industry expertise in a multitude of areas
- Consultant development programs
- In-office golfing

DOWNERS

- Young culture sometimes means lack of business experience
- Harsh career review process
- Small size can be stifling

EMPLOYMENT CONTACT

Richard P. Rohloff
Director of Recruiting, MBA Level
Dean & Company
Fairfax Square
8065 Leeburg Pike, Suite 500
Vienna, VA 22182-2738

recruiting@deanco.com

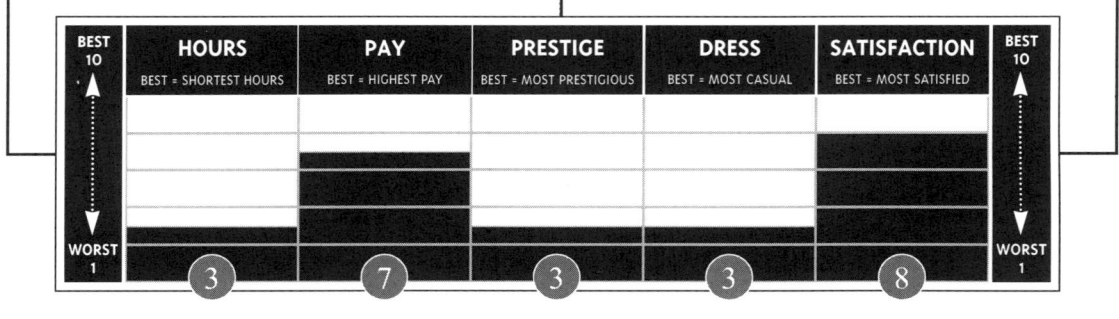

HOURS	PAY	PRESTIGE	DRESS	SATISFACTION
BEST = SHORTEST HOURS	BEST = HIGHEST PAY	BEST = MOST PRESTIGIOUS	BEST = MOST CASUAL	BEST = MOST SATISFIED
3	7	3	3	8

THE SCOOP

LITTLE BUT FAST GROWING

Located in the Washington DC area, Dean & Company is a management consulting firm that works with national and international corporate clients (generally among the Fortune 100). Although the firm has experienced rapid expansion and is growing at an average rate of 40 percent a year, Dean still snugly fits in the "small firm" category. At last count, its total number of consultants hovers below 100. Dean & Company was founded in 1993 by Dean Wilde and Dean Silverman. Silverman, the firm's current president, was once an Executive Vice President of consulting firm Strategic Planning Associations (SPA) and a member of its governing policy committee. Wilde, the firm's chairman, was also an Executive Vice President of SPA (which was acquired by Mercer Management Consulting in 1990).

THE DEAN SPEEDOMETER

Dean believes that it employs a "simple, flexible and non-hierarchical structure." A management committee consisting of the firm's four senior partners controls major policy and strategy questions, while the managers control day-to-day case work. The remaining management and administrative functions are widely delegated among the analysts, associates, and other professionals. Dean claims to have a "speedometer" – rather than an "odometer" – approach to promoting its faculty. In other words, career progression depends more upon demonstrated progress than on time-in-grade. To this end, Dean employs a rigorous career review process and keeps a careful check on the output of its workers.

RECENT SUCCESSES

Dean provides support to CEOs and senior management in select companies in the following areas: business development and expansion, shareholder value expansion, business unit strategy development, competitive analysis and positioning, market segmentation, new product development, restructuring and turnarounds, and business process reengineering. The firm targets the communications, financial services, and computing and software industries, among others. Recent engagements have included the restructuring of distribution in a financial services firm and strategy development for a print publisher about to enter the electronic media field.

GETTING HIRED

Due to Dean's small size, the firm plans to hire only 10 to 20 full-time consultants in 1998 (including both associate and analyst level). The company recruits candidates from top business schools, both on-campus and on an ad hoc basis. During the fall, Dean makes on-campus presentations at a small group of schools, while soliciting interest on a broader scale through advertising. Interviews are typically conducted over the course of the fall and winter, generally on-campus and consistent with the guidelines of various placement offices.

During the on-campus round, the applicant will meet with three to five people from the firm, including at least one partner, insiders say. The format for all interviews revolves around a case "problem" which is outlined by the interviewers. Dean stresses that these cases are not tests, but rather opportunities to demonstrate logical thinking, clear communication, and creative insight. Of course, a correct answer to a case study won't hurt one's chances of being hired.

After the on-campus round, successful candidates are invited to the office for a "familiarization visit." Such a visit generally occurs in the spring and includes one-on-one discussions, presentations on firm strategy and recent assignments, and group social gatherings. During the 1997-1998 recruiting season, Dean visited the following graduate schools for its MBA recruiting: Chicago Graduate School of Business, Colgate Darden Graduate School of Business, Harvard Business School, MIT Sloan School of Management, and Wharton School of Business. At the undergrad level, Dean recruits at Carnegie Mellon University, Dartmouth College, Harvard University, MIT, the University of Pennsylvania, Princeton University, University of Virginia, and Yale University.

Hoping to diversify its pool of associates, Dean has recently ventured outside of business school perimeters and is looking at individuals who hold graduate degrees in other fields. The firm is also on the prowl for individuals who are already in the workplace – either in other consulting firms or in industry-specific companies. For a select number of outstanding business school candidates, Dean has designed a summer program. Summer associates participate as full case team members, working on actual casework and attending the company's social activities.

OUR SURVEY SAYS

SWIFT PROMOTIONS

There's one thing good about Dean's intense review process – promotion comes quickly at Dean & Company. One insider notes, "I started as an analyst and was promoted to associate only six months later. Case reviews come every three months, formal career reviews every six months, and promotional reviews every six months too."

A DIFFICULT COMPANY TO ENTER

Although climbing the ranks is a relatively rapid process at Dean, another consultant warns that entrance into the company is the hardest part. "We are a small company, so of course we encourage internal promotion. Nevertheless, getting into this place can be tough. We tend to pick people with technical degrees. Our approach to consulting is extremely quantitative; there is lots of digging into numbers and data assessment. The people coming to us straight out of undergrad tend to be math majors or people with highly developed quantitative skills." How rough are the interviews? "The first round is always the most telltale," reports another insider. "There's a quick and brutal weeding-out process. After that, candidates stand a pretty good chance." Those who bemoan their low standardized test scores should beware of Dean. "The company looks at your SAT scores, no matter how old you are. Typically, however, our analysts are only 22 or 23."

SMART AND FUN CO-WORKERS

At the same time, consultants report that the Dean employees are among "the smartest people I've ever worked with. Among the analyst pool, people are fun and laid back. It's a young culture." The relationships across corporate levels are also solid. "My relationship with the managers is quite informal," says one insider. "Again, I think it's because of our small size." Little perks are numerous. "We get free bagels in the morning. There are tons of social events organized by the firm such as pool/billiard outings and Friday happy hours," says one consultant.

GOLFING AT DEAN

Another insider raves about the firm's annual in-office golf tournament. "It's like a miniature golf tournament in the office, complete with a totally elaborate floor design. The analysts – and there are a number of engineers among them – design the whole thing. From a structural and creative standpoint, it gets more impressive every year." Insiders do have a few quibbles about Dean's recruitment record. Reports one concerned insider: "The company does a lot better hiring at the analyst level. The analysts learn by doing and work up the ranks. The associates, on the other hand, have to speed up the learning process before they can become managers." Are there other downsides to Dean? "We have the typical small firm problems," sighs another insider. "There is a limited number of cases and not a huge breadth of options."

"There's a quick and brutal weeding-out process. After that, candidates stand a pretty good chance."

– *Dean & Co. insider*

Deloitte Consulting

1633 Broadway
New York, NY 10010
(212) 492-4000
www.dttus.com

LOCATIONS

New York, NY (HQ)
CA • GA • IL • MA • MI • MN • MO • NJ • OH • PA • TX • WA • Washington, DC
Numerous offices overseas

THE STATS

Annual Revenues: $2.3 billion (1997)
No. of Employees: 2,900
A privately-held company
CEO: J. Michael Cook

KEY COMPETITORS

Andersen Consulting
A.T. Kearney
Booz•Allen & Hamilton
Ernst & Young Consulting
KPMG Consulting
PricewaterhouseCoopers

UPPERS

- Unpretentious atmosphere
- Saturday childcare in some locations
- Women's initiative has improved opportunities for women

DOWNERS

- Poor treatment by some partners
- Strategy consulting deemphasized

EMPLOYMENT CONTACT

Human Resources
Deloitte Consulting
1633 Broadway
New York, NY 10010

HOURS (BEST = SHORTEST HOURS)	PAY (BEST = HIGHEST PAY)	PRESTIGE (BEST = MOST PRESTIGIOUS)	DRESS (BEST = MOST CASUAL)	SATISFACTION (BEST = MOST SATISFIED)
3	8	8	2	7

THE SCOOP

GLOBAL RELATIONSHIP BUILDERS

Deloitte & Touche (D&T), one of the Big Five professional services firms, is the American branch of Deloitte Touche Tohmatsu, a global leader in professional services with 59,000 employees in 126 countries. The firm's consulting arm, Deloitte Consulting, which has 2900 employees in the U.S., and ranks as one of the largest consulting practices in the industry, exploits the firm's expertise in international business and its global resources. Deloitte Consulting complements its parent company's other competencies, and emphasizes the building of long and lasting relationships with its clients; more than 75 percent of its business comes from repeat customers.

LEADERS IN CONSULTING

D&T's consulting group has grown rapidly in recent years, doubling its revenues from 1995 to 1997. The firm is considered a leader in certain fields such as systems integration consulting. Relationships with software and systems companies like Oracle, AutoTester and SAS Management only enhance Deloitte Consulting's techno-savvy. A recent *ComputerWorld* survey ranked Deloitte Consulting highest among all management consulting firms for systems consulting; its customer relationships and efficiency were praised by respondents. In 1997, about half of Deloitte & Touche's revenues came from Deloitte Consulting; half of that was IT consulting revenue. The firm expects that its consulting revenues will break $3 billion in 1999.

ESTABLISHING A REP

In 1998, D&T set aside $25 million in an aggressive advertising campaign designed to differentiate it and its consulting arm from the rest of the Big Five. The ads target Andersen as "distracted by infighting," and portray PricewaterhouseCoopers and KPMG as part of an undifferentiated mass. The firm already has a reputation as a nicer place to work than the other

Big Five – the firm earned the No. 14 spot in *Fortune* magazine's 1998 100 Best Companies to Work For list, and was the only Big Five firm to make the list.

GETTING HIRED

For the most part at Deloitte Consulting, "there are very few technical questions asked during the interview process. There isn't much emphasis on grilling recruits to determine their technical abilities because the recruits' academic records should speak for themselves." Applicants to the more technically-oriented areas are warned to be ready for an occasional question testing their aptitude, though it will not necessarily be the determining factor in hiring decisions. There may also be "a little written test – something quantitative that's quick and dirty." More commonly though, "most of the questions asked are 'What would you like to do? Where you see yourself down the road? What previous experience do you have?'" In other words, Deloitte "spends a lot of time on fit." For example, for MBAs, "they do the fit interview first and the case interviews second. Everyone else does them the other way around."

"Quantitative analytical capabilities" are, as usual, of paramount importance for consultants, since "the client throws books and books of data at you, and it's your job to sift through them." Other valued assets include "oral and written communications skills, especially in a presentation format," and "a history of leadership." In fact, sources warn that without leadership experience, it may be difficult to obtain an interview. Volunteer activities are suggested as a suitable means by which to acquire such experience. While Deloitte "wants someone who is well rounded more than [someone] in the top 5 percent of their class," grades do hold sway to a degree. The prestige of a candidate's school also matters. In fact, the pay scale is "pretty much the same for the top six to eight [business schools], but after that it is different," to the tune of 20 to 30 thousand dollars in initial pay.

Most people who have been through the consulting interview process describe it as "fairly long and stressful," but "not as rigorous as investment banking interviews." Deloitte "lets you know shortly [afterwards] by giving a phone call and sending a basket of goodies."

OUR SURVEY SAYS

WORKING AND LIVING IN HARMONY

Deloitte Consulting likes to emphasize that "experience teaches better than training." The lack of ego is also refreshing, say employees: "People don't go around bragging about where they went to school. The jerk is the exception." While most consultants acknowledge that "we aren't a McKinsey or Andersen," they feel "we are well known." Even though consultants work "intensely demanding schedules," they say that the firm has an "extremely flexible" approach to the ways in which employees structure their time. Deloitte, one employee comments, "respects personal commitments and fosters a better life-work balance than many of its competitors." Contributing to this balance is Deloitte's "3-4-5" policy: Employees spend three nights on the road, fly back on the fourth day, and spend their fifth day at the home office, ensuring a weekend at home (or at least, in the home city).

BUREAUCRACY AND MANAGEMENT

Despite this enticing flexibility, "sooner or later, the bureaucracy gets to you," insiders report. One consultant complains that "Deloitte's corporate culture is great, but I don't know where it comes from, because the partners are not a great lot at all. I've worked for a few who are decent, but overall they don't know what you're doing as far as human resources go." Turnover is about 19 percent a year, and "only a few people stay a decade."

HARD-WORKING, CONSERVATIVELY-DRESSING WOMEN WANTED

Workweeks can be "ominously long," and the dress code is "suits, suits, suits all around," except for Fridays, "which are business casual, though not beach bum casual." However, Deloitte Consulting is making a valiant effort in the field of gender diversity. Its "Women's Initiative" has "immensely improved" career prospects for women, as "Deloitte Consulting has become very sensitive to gender and life-style issues." Ethnic diversity is less impressive; one employee comments that "until Deloitte comes up with a Minority Initiative like its Women's Initiative, nothing is going to change."

> **To order a 50- to 70-page Vault Reports Employer Profile on Deloitte & Touche call 1-888-JOB-VAULT or visit www.VaultReports.com**
>
> The full Employer Profile includes detailed information on D&T's departments, recent developments and transactions, hiring and interview process, plus what employees really think about culture, pay, work hours and more.

"People don't go around bragging about where they went to school. The jerk is the exception."

– *Deloitte Consulting insider*

DFI/Aeronomics

650 Castro Street, Suite 300
Mountain View, CA 94041
(415) 960-2600
Fax: (415) 960-3656
www.dfi.com
www.talus.net

LOCATIONS

Mountain View, CA (HQ)
Atlanta, GA
Washington, DC
London, England
Sydney, Australia
Vancouver, BC

THE STATS

No. of Employees: 280
A privately-held company
President and CEO: Robert Phillips

UPPERS

- Increased staff size
- Ambitious agenda

DOWNERS

- Merger may bring employment instability
- Recent changes at top echelon
- Insipid company name

EMPLOYMENT CONTACT

Emily Zemke
Human Resources Specialist
DFI/Aeronomics Inc.
650 Castro Street, Suite 300
Mountain View, CA 94041

jobinfo@talus.net

HOURS (BEST = SHORTEST HOURS)	PAY (BEST = HIGHEST PAY)	PRESTIGE (BEST = MOST PRESTIGIOUS)	DRESS (BEST = MOST CASUAL)	SATISFACTION (BEST = MOST SATISFIED)
4	7	2	3	7

THE SCOOP

A MERGER TAKES WING

Not very long ago, Decision Focus Incorporated was a small consulting company specializing in revenue management ("making sure that companies sell the right product to the right customer at the right time for the right price). Then Robert L. Phillips, DFI's president and CEO, met Robert G. Cross, the Chairman and CEO of Aeronomics, a software engineering firm. Following the new fashion of corporate combining, the two companies consummated their relationship in 1997 with a merger agreement.

NUMEROUS CHANGES IN THE AIR

Now DFI/Aeronomics Incorporated (the company's new name pending a more inspired choice) has a roster of approximately 280 employees and 300 clients worldwide. Not much has remained the same, including the corporate hierarchy. Cross is now Chairman of the new company, while Phillips is president and CEO. Before the merger, DFI and Aeronomics were each successful in revenue management. By combining their capabilities, the two firms hope to develop innovative and original strategies which will boost them to the top of the field.

INTENDED CONCENTRATIONS

The new company hopes to follow where DFI left off. The consultancy will advise companies in the airlines, freight transportation, travel & leisure, broadcasting, and electric power industries. It intends to provide quantitative analysis of proposed policies and regulations to government agencies, industry groups, and private companies. Clients will include companies in the oil and gas, manufacturing, telecommunications, and health care industries.

GETTING HIRED

DFI/Aeronomics's hiring process is extremely stringent. DFI actively recruits from only the best engineering schools (notably Stanford and Cornell) and business schools (favorites here are MIT, Berkeley, and Harvard). DFI stresses that candidates must be enthusiastic about using computers and leveraging information technology.

Invited applicants can expect two sweeping rounds of interviews with six to eight people. Those applying for consultant positions should have an advanced degree (MS, PhD, or MBA) in a quantitative or information technology field. Aspiring research associates need a BS and exceptional quantitative skills. All candidates should be well versed in management science (optimization, decision sciences, probabilistic modeling, economics), software development and information technology (C++, RDBMS, SAS, Windows, UNIX, GUI, among others), and business process development.

OUR SURVEY SAYS

THE KINGDOM OF NUMBERS

Numbers, numbers, numbers. Across the board, our insiders at DFI/Aeronomics Incorporated cite a need for constant and accurate quantitative crunching. "We tend to look for people with fairly extensive skills in applied math or industrial operations. You should be good with software, math, or both." What does one do with all these digits? "We specialize in helping big industrial companies automate their quantitative decision making," remarks another consultant. "For instance, we work with rental car companies to forecast demand and appropriately adjust inventory."

SCARCITY

Of course, to be able to use one's mathematical wizardry, one must first show it off in an interview. "Getting in is tough. The final interview requires a technical presentation and also a case interview that is conducted here in our office," reports one insider. "In general, we try to get a good feel for your technical skills." Those hoping for interview should be warned that the stakes are higher at the Bachelors degree level. "DFI doesn't hire very many people straight out of college," states one insider. "But," that insider states charitably, "the few that I know have found [the workplace] very rewarding."

Diamond Technology Partners

875 North Michigan Ave, Suite 3000
Chicago, IL 60611
(312) 255-5000
Fax: (312) 255-6000
www.diamtech.com

LOCATIONS

Chicago IL (HQ)
Cleveland, OH
Austin, TX
Opportunities to live in various U.S. locations

THE STATS

Annual Revenues: $58.4 million (1998)
No. of Employees: 223
Stock Symbol: DTPI (NASDAQ)
Chairman and CEO: Mel Bergstein

KEY COMPETITORS

American Management Systems
Andersen Consulting
A.T. Kearney
Electronic Data Systems
Gartner Group
Gemini Consulting
IBM

UPPERS

- Lots of upward mobility
- Opportunity to work from home
- Generous vacation package
- Stock Options

DOWNERS

- Constant travel demands
- Not the place for those looking for structure

EMPLOYMENT CONTACT

Human Resources
Diamond Technology Partners
875 North Michigan Ave, Suite 3000
Chicago, IL 60611

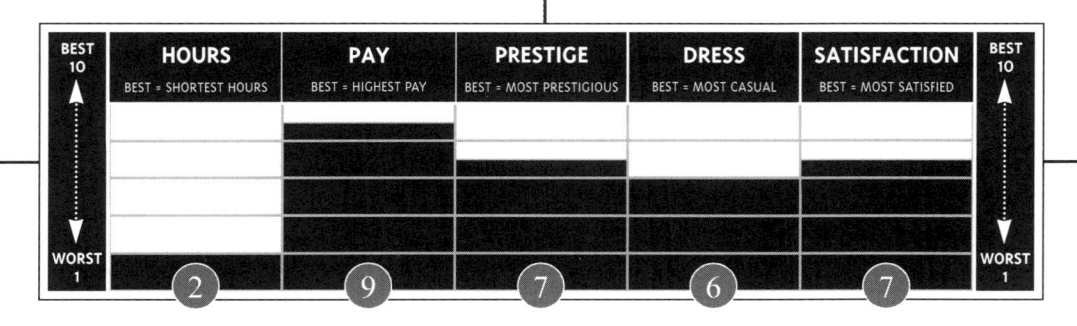

HOURS (BEST = SHORTEST HOURS)	PAY (BEST = HIGHEST PAY)	PRESTIGE (BEST = MOST PRESTIGIOUS)	DRESS (BEST = MOST CASUAL)	SATISFACTION (BEST = MOST SATISFIED)
2	9	7	6	7

THE SCOOP

TECHNOLOGY IS OUR MIDDLE NAME!

Technology is Diamond Partners' middle name, underscoring the firm's commitment to the integration of traditional business strategy techniques and cutting-edge technological solutions – what the firm calls "technosynthesis." Founded in 1994, the young company is still run by its founders. Diamond's clients come from a variety of industries including insurance, manufacturing, telecommunications, and agriculture. Its areas of expertise range from strategy and structure to program management.

SMALL TEAMS, NOT SMALL TIME

Diamond emphasizes a small-team, collaborative approach instead of bringing in large groups of programmers and technical specialists. Because Diamond is not committed to any particular technology, it believes it can be more fair than its competitors in assessing the needs of its clients. A petite consulting firm, with about 200 professionals, Diamond Technology does three kinds of glibly named work: Strategy, Technology and Speed. Strategy is traditional financial business strategy and overall direction, technology means guiding the development of new tech systems (for example, databases or pricing systems). Speed is what's normally called operations – improving internal processes.

THE ROAD WARRIORS

Travel at Diamond is a constant phenomenon – most successful employees must adapt to living out of a suitcase. Many speak highly of this "road warrior" lifestyle, while others say that the rigors of wandering take a toll on their mental and physical health. (One major advantage for some is that Diamond consultants can live wherever they want in the country, as long as they are at the client four days a week.) Nevertheless, from a general perspective, employees report that Diamond's culture is open, full of insight, and more intellectually challenging than that of comparable consulting firms.

PUBLICLY ACCOUNTABLE

One fact makes Diamond stand out from the consulting crowd – unlike most of its peers, the company is publicly traded, having completed an IPO in February of 1997. All of its partners and employees are shareholders, meaning that each person's compensation (stock and options) is directly tied to the success of the company.

A RECIPE FOR SUCCESS?

The Diamond formula seems to be working. Revenues have grown approximately 40 percent a year since Diamond's inception. In 1998, revenues increased to a record of $58.4 million, a 55 percent increase over the previous year. Net income for the year rose to $6 million, yielding a whopping 900 percent increase from the previous year. In recent business activities, the company expanded business activities in Japan and the Far East by signing a representation agreement with Diamond Pro-Shop Nomura Company Ltd. in Tokyo. It looks like the world needs a tech firm that can do consulting well. (Or is it vice versa?)

GETTING HIRED

Diamond's primary recruiting efforts involve snatching people directly from top graduate MBA and MS programs. Once accepted for an interview, individuals can expect to undergo two or three rounds of interviews with five to six of the company's consultants and partners. Currently experiencing an unprecedented growth spurt, Diamond expects to increase its recruiting and total number of new hires. Those with prior management consulting experience stand as much of a chance of landing Diamond jobs as those who received their degrees from elite business schools, insiders say.

Like many other consulting firms, Diamond sometimes uses cases and guesstimates in its interviews (i.e., the applicant is presented with a business scenario and asked to "solve" it, or to estimate some outlandish figure). For example, one employee recalls being asked to estimate the number of tennis balls that could fit into the Fuji blimp. Although cases and guesstimates vary, Diamond has a reputation for rigorous interviewing. Suffice it to say, applicants should do their homework before walking through Diamond's front door. Current starting pay for MBAs is $90,000 plus stock options.

OUR SURVEY SAYS

"On the road," by Diamond

To be employed at Diamond, one must learn to accept a vagrant lifestyle. Indeed, work-related travel is relentless. "I view the travel as a perk," chirps one enthusiastic consultant. "Unlike 'normal' jobs, I commute to work only once per week instead of five times per week. Of course, I do not mind living out of a suitcase." That contact continues: "Acknowledging that travel is constant, Diamond provides us with airline club memberships and first class upgrades." Another insider reveals, "Diamond provides us with lots of travel-worthy equipment. Things like Lotus Notes and dial up network access facilitate an effective work environment anywhere there is a phone line."

No need to give at the office

Other consultants see Diamond as a "virtual firm," or one "where people are allowed to live anywhere they want to live." Employees are not required to live in Chicago, the unofficial site of Diamond's "main office," or in Cleveland, which is "considerably smaller."

THE TRAINING PROCESS

Insiders praise Diamond's training program for incoming employees. "For analysts, there is usually three weeks of initial training, followed by an apprenticeship with a consultant. The apprenticeship is a period of coaching and mentoring. New employees can also expect a minimum of twelve days of in-house training." Nevertheless, insiders warn that Diamond employees "must learn on the job. This is a small firm; there is no three-month period of solid training. People who lack iniative or who need structure should stay away."

NEEDED: MORE FOCUS

Insiders generally speak highly of Diamond's environment of fluid advancement. "Diamond is a very, very mobile organization, upward and otherwise. There is increasing focus on merit-based advancement." Nevertheless, another insider insists that not everyone is a gem when it comes to promotions. "The [company's] focus has slipped a bit recently – meaning that some people are advancing despite relatively poor performance."

As far as Diamond's status as a public company, the reviews are all thumbs up. "We are an anomaly in the consulting industry because everyone in the firm has stock and/or stock options in the firm," explains one insider. Is everything shared at Diamond? "Information is also shared," discloses another insider. (Well, it is a public company.) "Every week the employees hear about recent company news." All in all, Diamond insiders seem hell-bent on spreading the good news of their company. "I would – and have – recommended Diamond to several friends. I've worked for Diamond for over a year after graduating from business school. So far, my experience has been great."

"Things like Lotus Notes and dialup network access facilitate an effective work environment anywhere there is a phone line."

– *Diamond insider*

Edgar, Dunn & Company

115 Perimeter Center Place
Suite 385
Atlanta, GA 30346
www.edgardunn.com

LOCATIONS

Atlanta, GA (HQ)
San Francisco, CA
London, England
Sydney, Australia

THE STATS

A privately-held company

KEY COMPETITORS

Dean & Company
Greenwich Associates
Kurt Salmon Associates

UPPERS

- Entry-level consultants have plenty of responsibility
- Rapid upward mobility
- "Inverted pyramid" hierarchy
- Congenial atmosphere

DOWNERS

- Minimal training program for incoming consultants
- Overdose of travel time
- Dearth of internal administrative resources

EMPLOYMENT CONTACT

Rona Simmons
Edgar, Dunn & Company
Suite 385
115 Perimeter Center Place
Atlanta, GA 30346

rsimmons@atl.edgardunn.com.

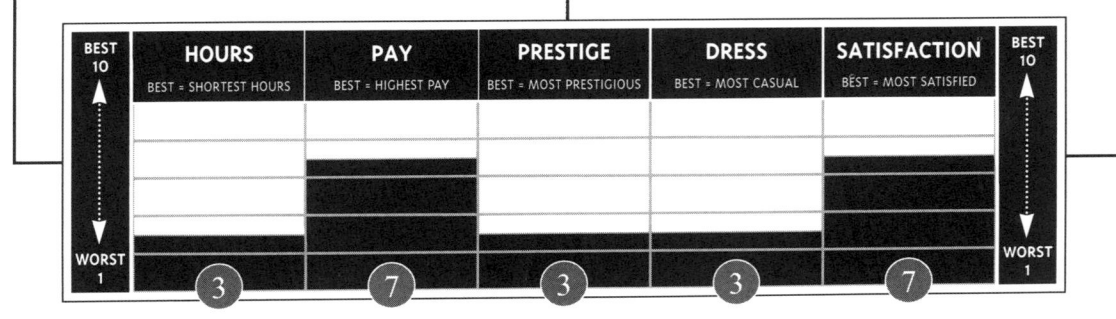

HOURS BEST = SHORTEST HOURS	PAY BEST = HIGHEST PAY	PRESTIGE BEST = MOST PRESTIGIOUS	DRESS BEST = MOST CASUAL	SATISFACTION BEST = MOST SATISFIED
3	7	3	3	7

THE SCOOP

EDGAR'S TARGETS

Edgar, Dunn & Company (EDC) is a general management consulting firm with offices in San Francisco, Atlanta, London, and Sydney. Although it works in and around a variety of industries, EDC's more recent engagements have primarily been financial services, electronic commerce, energy services, and brand/market strategy projects. In recent financial services client news, EDC has assisted commercial and retail banks, savings institutions, payment card associations and leasing companies. On the electronic commerce front, the firm has worked on projects ranging from corporate web sites to smart card applications. EDC recently counseled a Fortune 500 company on how to introduce its proprietary coal product to various markets as part of its growing energy services operations. Finally, in brand/market strategy, the firm has worked on consumer products, sporting events, and health care.

THE TURTLE CONSULTANCY — SLOW AND STEADY

Although the breadth of EDC's interests is large, its own size is rather small. The firm reportedly hires only two or three college grads per office annually. While a preference for math whizzes and MBA graduates may account for EDC's pickiness, the firm's growth rate is purposefully "slow and steady." Indeed, EDC wants to retain its "small firm" ways, although some of the incoming consultants wish the firm would expand and conquer at a more ferocious pace. On an altruistic front, the company is pleased to announce its involvement in a pro bono effort with the Metro Atlanta Chamber of Commerce. EDC is presently working on a three- to five-year plan with the Arts & Business Council of Atlanta designed to strengthen bonds between the arts and business communities.

GETTING HIRED

EDC recruits at both the undergraduate and MBA levels. Employees fresh out of undergrad are considered "entry-level consultants." They learn about a variety of industries and receive a thorough grounding in business and critical strategic issues. Although entry-level consultants often play second fiddle to regular consultants, their responsibilities are approximately the same. Entry-level consultants conduct primary and secondary research, interview clients and client affiliates, develop qualitative and quantitative analyses, interpreted data, and create financial/economic models.

Those who have completed their MBAs lose the "entry-level" tag to their consulting title. In addition to performing standard research and analysis, they present recommendations to client management and interpret more complex data. EDC recruits candidates from a few prestigious schools through on-campus interviewing. However, the firm encourages any interested students who do not attend the firm's targeted schools to forward their cover letters and resumes to the appropriate contact. Both e-mail and standard mail applications are accepted.

"EDC hires people in two ways: through campus recruiting and through industry/network hires," reports one insider. As more and more consulting firms try their hand at recruiting specialists who are already in the workforce, EDC is following suit. "We hire a lot of experts in growing industries. We want people with solid knowledge bases," one insider admits. Because the company is so small, "we really don't hire many undergrads – maybe one or two a year [at each office]." Regardless of entering level, recruits will interview "two or three times. The number of interviews depends upon the experience level of the candidate." How should a candidate prepare herself? "Interviewees should prepare to do a case study, but there won't necessarily be one," says one contact. "The interview is more about culture and company fit." This sentiment is echoed in the remark of another insider: "The interviews are often soft. An EDC flaw, if it has a flaw at all, is that the interviewers are too nice."

AN INTIMATE RELATIONSHIP WITH PARTNERS

Once inside the company's golden gates, employees may feel a kinship with the partners as well as with fellow consultants. "It's the plus of being at a small firm. The pyramid is inverted – meaning that the partner to consultant ratio is very low, 1:2 or 1:3," explains one source. At EDC, all people are consultants, and some consultants are partners." Another insider considers this feeling of solidarity to be the reason behind his own loyalty: "Edgar Dunn is a destination, not a stopping point."

AREAS OF EXPERTISE – DIVERSITY NOT AMONG THEM

EDC declares itself to be a general consulting firm, but it "has a lot of expertise in certain areas like financial services and electronic commerce." Historically, the firm has done work with a variety of industries, including "banking, insurance, utilities, consumer products, sports marketing, and travel/tourism." Diverse as its client base may be, internal diversity is not of EDC's strong points. "I haven't seen any employees of African American descent," admits one insider. Another reports: "The firm is maybe 25 percent female. I stress the 'maybe.'"

SELF-PROPELLED

Other common complaints include the firm's paltry internal administrative resources and the lack of a graphics department. ("No one creates beautiful, multicolored computer demonstrations. We have to do that ourselves.") Finally, the firm's very size is a factor which troubles a few: "The new people want huge growth – they want the company to explode. But the partners are letting EDC evolve in a slow and controlled way." Despite these gripes, many insiders say EDC is a step above the larger, more glamorous firms. "Everything at EDC is about ambition and your own proactive attitude. There's so much to be done here."

Ernst & Young Consulting

750 Seventh Avenue, Room 1800
New York, NY 10019
(212) 773-3000
Fax: (212) 773-6504
www.ey.com

LOCATIONS

New York, NY (HQ)
Cleveland • Houston • San Francisco • Washington, DC • Over 100 offices nationwide, and 650 around the world

THE STATS

Annual Revenue: $9.1 billion (1997)
No. of Employees: 82,000 (worldwide)
No. of Offices: 678 (worldwide)
A privately-held company
Chairman: Philip A. Laskaway

KEY COMPETITORS

Arthur Andersen
Andersen Consulting
Computer Sciences Corporation
Deloitte Consulting
KPMG Consulting
PricewaterhouseCoopers

UPPERS

- Training's a blast
- 16 weeks of family leave available to parents
- Daycare facilities
- Tuition reimbursement
- Generous vacation

DOWNERS

- Structured assignment system can be stifling
- Below average pay
- No private work space

EMPLOYMENT CONTACT

Human Resources
Ernst & Young Consulting
750 Seventh Avenue, Room 1800
New York, NY 10019

© Copyright 1998 Vault Reports, Inc. Photocopying is illegal and expressly forbidden.

HOURS BEST = SHORTEST HOURS	PAY BEST = HIGHEST PAY	PRESTIGE BEST = MOST PRESTIGIOUS	DRESS BEST = MOST CASUAL	SATISFACTION BEST = MOST SATISFIED
2	7	8	2	7

THE SCOOP

Here's EY!

If you like big firms, you should feel warmly about Ernst & Young – the product of a succession of mergers that started in the 1950s, the firm is more than a century old. The current incarnation of Ernst & Young was created from a 1989 merger of two members of what used to be called the Big Eight professional services firms – Arthur Young and Ernst & Whinney. In 1998, Ernst & Young had 82,000 employees in 132 countries around the world.

The rising star of consulting

Ernst & Young currently ranks as the second-largest integrated professional services firm in the U.S. (Total U.S. employment is 29,000.) Ernst & Young Consulting is a big part of this prominence, with 10,500 professionals. In the past two years, growth at Ernst & Young Consulting has far outstripped that of the consulting industry as a whole – the consultancy has enjoyed a 35 percent increase in revenue per year for the last few years.

No Bert

No doubt this strong growth is influenced by innovations like "Ernie," a popular online consulting service for small businesses. Ernie members pay a membership fee, and then can submit their queries to official Ernst & Young consultants via e-mail. Ernst & Young draws on its consulting expertise, and Ernie-users soon get a reasoned and usable answer. Ernst & Young Consulting also uses Ernie to feature "Trend Watch," a survey of most common concerns and questions. Another of E&Y's consulting innovations is the Ernst & Young Entrepreneurial Consulting group. While most of Ernst and Young's clients are big bruisers that earn over $100 million yearly, Entrepreneurial Consulting takes on smaller businesses hungry to grow.

Darn

Ernst & Young tried to grow bigger in 1998 by merging with its competitor KPMG Peat Marwick (as it was then called), another Big Six firm. The planned merger, however, foundered on the shoals of European regulatory concerns. (It didn't help matters that the mergers of competitors Price Waterhouse and Coopers & Lybrand was also pending at the time.)

GETTING HIRED

Ernst & Young Consulting has identified about eight "mega competencies," which include leadership, communication, technology, flexibility and teamwork. Each interviewer, insiders tell us, focuses on one of two of these competencies. The typical format to identify these skills goes as follows – "Tell me about a situation where you used your (competency) skill. What was your role? What did you do? What happened? What did you learn from this experience?" The candidate is also taken to lunch and evaluated during the meal on cultural fit and interest in Ernst & Young.

Case interviews are used only for candidates for Ernst & Young Consulting's Strategic Advisory Services Group. Neither brainteasers nor guesstimates are employed, insiders tell us.

Following the interviews, interviewers meet to discuss the candidate and whether or not to extend an offer. Apparently, the group must reach a consensus, or else no offer is made. In rare circumstances, a candidate will be telephoned if an interviewer has further questions, but the likelihood of this is reportedly slim. Better make a good first impression!

OUR SURVEY SAYS

CONSERVATISM STILL RAMPANT

Ernst & Young's size brings both advantages and disadvantages. On the less positive side, some consultants opine that Ernst is a conservative place. "I think it's a very conservative firm in terms of the way management acts, in the way projects are handled," says one consultant disapprovingly. Another contact notes: "It's a large firm, and if you're ambitious, it can be tough sometimes." The same contact continues: "[Ernst is] great if you want to settle down, but if you want to be making the most money of anyone your age, or if you want to do everything that interests you, you might get frustrated. It's more structured. You get assigned to something and that's your project – hopefully you'll like it, because that's what you'll be doing for a while." Note, however, that the rigid structure reported by those working in U.S. offices doesn't seem to exist in overseas E&Y offices. "In Canada, people do a mix of everything," says one insider, who adds: "In general, U.S. people are much more segmented."

GOING ABROAD?

E&Y insiders tend also to comment on the firm's increasing international outlook and encouraging attitudes towards going abroad. One contact notes that 30 to 40 percent of his office actively chose international assignments, and explains: "It's really encouraged, I guess because of globalization, and they know that a lot of these people would just leave if they couldn't go abroad. It's very easy to transfer between countries." One contact marvels: "On my first business trip ever, I went to Rio!" Another contact on the consulting side recalls an extraordinary assignment: "I went all over the world – you name it, I was there."

LESSER PAY

Pay doesn't seem to be one of E&Y's strong suits. "As for compensation," one contact tells us, "the general pattern is that you make a fair salary, but nothing spectacular." The same individual notes however, that the pay is "good lifestyle money," and that "you'll never have to beg on the floor of a car dealership for a loan." One former E&Y consultant, however, notes that "[for me] to get a big jump in pay, it just would have taken too long." Another ex-consultant says: "The pay was not going to do it for me." Note that, in consulting, there is no overtime and working all night "comes straight out of your salary."

E&Y seems to be taking steps to increase its compensation package. The firm, it is rumored, plans to institute a better bonus system to lure candidates away from bonus-happy jobs in investment banking and elsewhere. One contact reminds us: "[E&Y is] recruiting at the top business schools, so they must be willing to pay more."

CONSULTING FESTIVITIES

Insiders report frequent lunches, and regular soirees with colleagues. When asked about firm-organized activities, one consultant responds with a rather unsettling comparison: "There aren't as many as Andersen. I've talked to people there, and it almost seems like they want to make their employees a bunch of alcoholics." While perhaps more subdued than its competitors, Ernst & Young has its debauched spots. "There's the training and that's a blast," reports one consultant, who elaborates: "Every division has their own form of training. Basically you try and stay awake all day during some kind of class, and then you go out and drink all night."

BILLABLES ARE A DRAG

One source of complaints from consultants is the firm's "utilization" goals, targets that require consultants to bill 80 percent of all hours to clients. The goals are particularly pertinent for individuals at the lower levels, who focus more on project work and less on business development. While not as rigid or demanding as billable hours targets at law firms, consultants still feel the pressure. "They want you to bill those hours!" gripes one consultant. Another consultant levels particular criticism at the utilization goals: "If you're in consulting, when you're working on projects, there's a lot of down time, and then there's the recruiting and other non-chargeable time. Basically, the expectation is that you'll bill out eight hours a day and then do all the other stuff later, and the fact is that the people with the highest utilizations get noticed."

Vault Reports Guide to the Top Consulting Firms

Ernst & Young Consulting

To order a 50- to 70-page Vault Reports Employer Profile on Ernst & Young call 1-888-JOB-VAULT or visit www.VaultReports.com

The full Employer Profile includes detailed information on Ernst & Young's departments, recent developments and transactions, hiring and interview process, plus what employees really think about culture, pay, work hours and more.

First Manhattan Consulting Group

90 Park Avenue, 19th Floor
New York, NY 10016
(212) 557-0500
Fax: (212) 338-9296
www.fmcg.com

LOCATIONS

New York, NY (HQ)
Santa Monica, CA

THE STATS

No. of Employees: 100+ (consulting staff)
No. of Offices: 2 (U.S.)
A privately held company

KEY COMPETITORS

Booz•Allen & Hamilton
Greenwich Associates
Mitchell Madison Group
Oliver, Wyman & Company

UPPERS

- Excellent pay, bonuses
- Frequent promotions based on merit
- High profile clients
- "More frequent flyer miles than you can dream of"

DOWNERS

- Intense hours
- "No hand-holding" environment

EMPLOYMENT CONTACT

Human Resources
Consulting Staff Recruiting
First Manhattan Consulting Group
90 Park Avenue, 19th Floor
New York, NY 10016

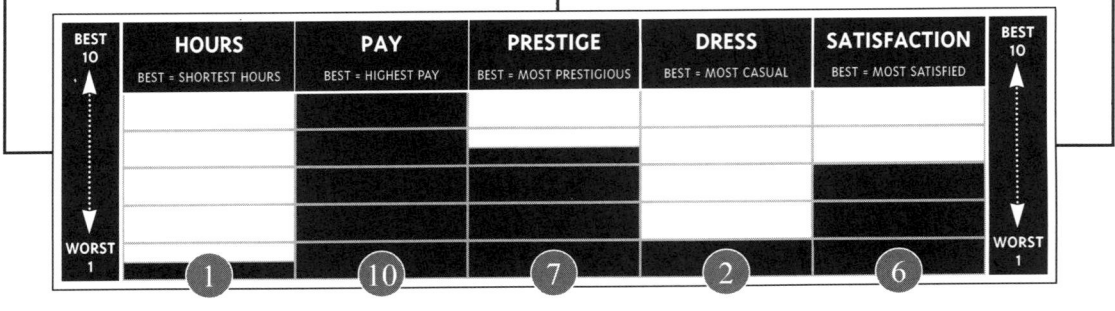

HOURS (BEST = SHORTEST HOURS)	PAY (BEST = HIGHEST PAY)	PRESTIGE (BEST = MOST PRESTIGIOUS)	DRESS (BEST = MOST CASUAL)	SATISFACTION (BEST = MOST SATISFIED)
1	10	7	2	6

Vault Reports Guide to the Top Consulting Firms
First Manhattan Consulting Group

THE SCOOP

GET THE NAME RIGHT

First things first – don't confuse this company with First Manhattan Co., an investment banking firm established in 1964. To prevent such missteps, First Manhattan Consulting Group is generally called FMCG within the consulting industry. And within its consulting niche, the firm doesn't take a back seat to anybody. Founded in 1980 by James McCormick, a McKinsey veteran, this boutique management consulting firm has grown steadily since its inception. Revenues per consulting staff member are among the highest in the industry. FMCG has served 80 percent of the 70 largest bank holding companies, half of the leading investment banks, a number of major foreign banks, and more than 25 technology and other vendors to the industry.

RESTRUCTURING THE FINANCIAL WORLD

First Manhattan specializes in the restructuring of financial companies. Its consultants have developed a comprehensive system that enables banks to analyze customer profitability. Termed Customer-Knowledge-Based-Management™, the technique studies the financial behavior of the small business customer, and allows banks to maximize profitability. The company also publishes benchmark studies for the financial industry, sometimes in conjunction with other firms or groups like the Bank Administration Institute. It is one of the more trusted providers of such information, and is regularly quoted by industry publications – from *The Wall Street Journal* and *Fortune* magazine to the *Journal of Retail Banking*.

DESIRED BY THE COMPETITION

Because it is such a well-respected industry monitor, FMCG experience is an extremely marketable asset. Recently, major utilities, telecom and new media companies have been looking specifically for individuals who have been trained at FMCG, because it is generally thought that FMCG consultants have strong skills and learn fast.

Vault Reports Guide to the Top Consulting Firms
First Manhattan Consulting Group

GETTING HIRED

Most new hires come in through campus recruiting, but FMCG accepts resumes and cover letters throughout the year. Consultants stress that "resumes should be perfect, and your cover letter should clearly state why you are qualified to work in such a demanding environment and why you want to work at FMCG." The company prefers that candidates send resumes via regular mail. Expect a response either by phone or mail within a month.

Interviews are usually done in two rounds – the first with a single consultant, the second with up to five or six. Veterans of the process say to expect "some sort of case, ranging from high-level business questions to brainteaser or estimate questions." Analysts are expected to make at least a two-year commitment to the firm. All new hires start in the firm's New York office. The company runs a formal orientation and training program for new analysts, and supplements that with further training sessions and luncheons.

OUR SURVEY SAYS

DOING WHAT IT TAKES

"If your primary criteria for where you want to work are such things as work hours and perks, this is not the place for you," warns a young analyst. What they do focus on at FMCG is "whatever it takes to get the job done for our clients." Insiders say that the corporate culture is "not unlike all the other management consulting companies, except we work a bit harder." They have a great deal of pride in the company, and say it's "the top consulting firm to the financial services industry," with the "the smartest collection of people I've ever seen." Employees "get along with each other, but are frequently too busy to mingle with colleagues."

INTENSE SCHEDULES

FMCG is not for the faint-hearted. "You have to be tough to make it here," warns one insider. "It's a pretty intense place to work." "You have to be really into the financial services industry to get the most out of it," comments another. Across the board, analysts say it's "a challenge just to keep up" with "high energy people" who "keep moving all day long and sometimes into the night." "You will come here not knowing what you're doing and will be expected to learn quickly." Analysts reportedly average about 65 hours a week, "with a number of major peaks where that figure can climb to 80 or 90 and beyond." In addition, "weekend work occurs with some frequency." Expect to travel a great deal. Although insiders say that firm consultants "always travel coach class," they note that "we generally stay in the best hotel in town." Plus, "you get to keep all your frequent flyer miles" – and there will be a lot.

AGGRESSIVE PAY

The company does compensate its employees handsomely, and "raises and bonuses are very aggressive when compared with the rest of the consulting industry." Starting analysts earn a $46,000 base, with an $8,000 signing bonus and an expected 15 percent bonus after the first year. After that, bonuses can climb to between 40 and 55 percent, "though the top end can stretch for the best performers." Insiders say First Manhattan is "pretty close to being a true meritocracy," though "there's no curve – if everyone does well enough to get a 60 percent bonus, everyone gets a 60 percent bonus." In addition, employees stress the fact that "opportunity for advancement is unparalleled throughout the industry." One of the more stressful aspects of working at FMCG is the fact that "you learn a lot in a really short period of time and it feels overwhelming at first."

NO GLASS CEILING

Women and minorities hold positions at all levels – insiders say "there does not appear to be any sort of glass ceiling." "The only discrimination I have seen is based on performance, enthusiasm, and attitude – all of which are not only legal, but logical," says one insider. "This isn't the place for people lacking self esteem," advises one neophyte, "you can get battered along the way." While those at the top are mostly "white males, aged 35 to 50," "younger personnel are very diverse in background." One insider admits that "it isn't the friendliest place towards women, though I've never seen any indication of harassment or favoritism." The dress code requires business attire from Monday through Thursday, with business casual on Fridays unless there is a client meeting.

"This isn't the place for people lacking self-esteem."

– *FMCG insider*

Gartner Group

56 Top Gallant Road
Stamford, CT 06904
(203) 964-0096
Fax: (203) 316-1100
www.gartner.com

LOCATIONS

Stamford, CT (HQ)
Offices in more than 40 countries in North America • South America • Africa • Asia • Australia and Europe

THE STATS

Annual Revenues: $642 million (1998)
No. of Employees: 3,300 (worldwide)
No. of Offices: 80 (worldwide)
Stock Symbol: IT (NYSE)
CEO: William T. Clifford

KEY COMPETITORS

American Management Systems
Computer Sciences Corporation
Deloitte Consulting
Diamond Technology Partners
Forrester Research
Renaissance Worldwide

UPPERS

- Ample opportunities for advancement
- Talented and smart staff
- Company on an "acquisition binge"

DOWNERS

- Company doesn't emphasize training
- Difficulties in integrating recent with seasoned employees
- Not enough information trading

EMPLOYMENT CONTACT

Heather Nelson
Director of Recruiting
Gartner Group, Inc.
56 Top Gallant Road
Stamford, CT 06904-2212

Fax: (203) 316-3445
heather.nelson@gartner.com

HOURS BEST = SHORTEST HOURS	PAY BEST = HIGHEST PAY	PRESTIGE BEST = MOST PRESTIGIOUS	DRESS BEST = MOST CASUAL	SATISFACTION BEST = MOST SATISFIED
4	6	6	8	6

© Copyright 1998 Vault Reports, Inc. Photocopying is illegal and expressly forbidden.

THE SCOOP

THE ROCKY HISTORY OF AN IT CONSULTING PIONEER

Gideon Gartner, computer analyst extraordinaire, founded The Gartner Group, an information technology consulting firm, in 1979. The Stamford-based information technology company was later acquired by the ad agency Saatchi & Saatchi in the company's failed effort to become a business services giant. A 1990 buyout led by the firm's management and assisted by Dun & Bradstreet eventually sent the firm's founder packing. The company went public again in 1993; three years later Dun and Bradstreet's stake in the company was transferred to Cognizant (a spin-off of Dun and Bradstreet).

ON THE ACQUISITION TRAIL

Presently, Gartner boasts more than 35,000 indiviual clients, representing more than 11,000 organizations. The firm has more than 3300 employees, including 750 analysts and 700 sales executives. Gartner's growth has exploded in recent years. The firm's revenue jumped from just under $400 million in 1996 to $511 million in 1997 and $642 million in 1998 – increases of greater than 25 percent each year. The firm's profits increased 20 percent in 1998 to $87 million.

Much of the firm's growth has come through acquisitions. In 1996 alone, Gartner purchased Dataquest, Internet vendor Fox Industries, the Productivity Management Group, CJ Singer, and Nomos Ricerca, an Italian IT consultant. In 1997 Gartner agreed to buy computer market researchers Datapro and Northern Business Information from McGraw-Hill. And in 1998, the firm bought a large stake in new media consulting firm Jupiter Communications. Also in 1998, the firm announced that William T. Clifford, formerly Gartner's president and COO, would become Gartner's CEO in 1999.

A PERSONAL TECH ADVISOR

The company thinks of itself as a comprehensive resource for information on the trends of the turbulent IT industry. Gartner's clients receive research and analysis through state-of-the-art delivery mechanisms like CD-ROM, Lotus Notes, Gartner Web, and a World Wide Web-based user forum named @vantage. All told, Gartner offers more than 80 personal advisory services. Its products and services include conferences, symposia, briefings, audioconferences, videoconferences, and vendor exhibits. Aside from providing information to clients, the firm, through its many published reports and engagements, also serves as something of an expert voice for the IT industry. In 1998, for example, Gartner research director Lou Marcoccio spoke before the U.S. Senate's Special Committee on Year 2000 Technology Problems. Also in 1998, in partnership with *Forbes*, the firm launched *Executive Edge* magazine, a bimonthly publication about IT targeting senior executives.

GETTING HIRED

Gartner applicants should expect fierce competition. One employee describes Gartner's selectivity, noting "the proportion of people chosen is very small given the number of resumes we receive." Garner conducts initial and final interviews on-campus. Due to Gartner's penchant for acquiring – and the fluctuation in company needs that this growth inevitably inspires – employment opportunities are often in flux.

OUR SURVEY SAYS

GROWTH AND HOT STOCK

"Gartner is a rapidly growing company with very talented people and the hottest set of products in a very hot area," declares one insider. "Salaries are pretty good and stock options are possible for top performers." Word on the dress code at Gartner varies. "Casual dress is OK except for two circumstances. First if you're meeting with a client, they make the decision (if they want business attire, we wear suits). Second, when you are on a sales call or at a conference, business attire is required." Yet, another insider says he wears his tie only a few times each year. "It's jeans or Dockers here, plus a knit shirt or sweatshirt."

ALWAYS IN SEARCH OF MORE CONSULTANTS

Diversity is something of a non-issue when you're growing as fast as Gartner. "Geez, we need more qualified women, men, minorities, non-minorities – it really doesn't matter," exclaims one consultant. "The issue, especially for the analyst area, is finding the few qualified and motivated people with the right intellect and attitude." An insider from a different department agrees that Gartner has a perennial need for qualified people, and believes that the company is sufficiently egalitarian in its hiring practices. "The majority of the analysts in my team (information security) happen to be female," says that contact. "I do not believe that prejudice is an issue here."

ALL-AMERICAN

One insider who makes frequent trip to Gartner's offices in Europe and Asia identifies a problem with Gartner's rapid growth and international dealings: "We have a very Americanized version of doing business. Not long ago, every decision in the international market had to run through the managers in the American office – even when they had no idea what we were dealing with. Gartner needs to grow up and learn how to be a global player."

THE CONSULTING-TECH WEDDING

In general, employees find Gartner "a happy marriage between the consulting and computer industries." Though most employees turn in the "long hours" expected of the consulting industry, many can work from their home by computer. "Despite the long workdays, Gartner makes a special effort to accommodate employee schedules," reports one Gartner insider. "I work out of an office I built at my house 50 percent of the time and spend another 15 percent of my time in our corporate headquarters. The rest of the time I spend on the road."

WHO'S THAT?

Perhaps the biggest gripe about Gartner has to do with its problems integrating new employees in a proper and healthy way. "It's crazy," declares one insider. "Because of the acquisitions, new colleagues suddenly appear all the time. Not only do they not know what to do, but the training process here is quite scant. By default, it's a learn-by-doing situation." Continues that consultant: "The people who do well here are the people who take initiative. They will ask for help, send e-mails, are bold, and attempt to trade information." What about the people who lack such nerve? "The people who don't take initiative feel isolated; they often produce work which goes unacknowledged." The bottom line: "You cannot be shy at Gartner."

"It's crazy. Because of the acquisitions, new colleagues suddenly appear all the time."

– *Gartner insider*

Gemini Consulting

25 Airport Road
Morristown, NJ 07960
(617) 491-5200
www.gemcon.com

LOCATIONS

Morristown, NJ (HQ)
Cambridge, MA • New York, NY • Barcelona • Frankfurt • Johannesburg • Lisbon, Portugal • London • Madrid • Milan • Munich • Oslo, Norway • Paris • Sao Paulo, Brazil • Stockholm, Sweden • Tokyo • Zurich, Switzerland

THE STATS

Subsidiary of Cap Gemini
CEO: Pat Elder
No. of Employees: 2,000 (worldwide)
Annual Revenues: $900 million (1997)
No. of Offices: 33 (worldwide)

KEY COMPETITORS

Andersen Consulting
Arthur D. Little
Electronic Data Systems
PricewaterhouseCoopers

UPPERS

- Profit-sharing
- Family leave
- Sabbatical option
- "Flexforce" program to reduce work for high-performing consultants
- "Life Balance" confidential counseling program

DOWNERS

- Up-or-out policy
- Frequent travel
- Specter of downsizing

EMPLOYMENT CONTACT

For Undergraduates:
124 Mt. Auburn Street, Suite 600
Cambridge, MA 02138

For Graduates:
25 Airport Road
Morristown, NJ 07960

HOURS (BEST = SHORTEST HOURS)	PAY (BEST = HIGHEST PAY)	PRESTIGE (BEST = MOST PRESTIGIOUS)	DRESS (BEST = MOST CASUAL)	SATISFACTION (BEST = MOST SATISFIED)
2	8	8	5	7

THE SCOOP

THE FIRST COMING OF GEMINI

Gemini Consulting was pieced together from five different consulting firms in 1991 by its parent Cap Gemini, a huge France-based technology firm. At first, Gemini's proffered holistic "transformation" was the hottest thing going – growing by 88 percent between 1991 and 1993. Prospective clients were attracted to Gemini's promise of reengineering. Clients also liked the firm's painstakingly thorough approach, which examined everyone at a company from the CEO to part-time salesmen. Gemini's philosophy cast organizations as living organisms that required total nurturing and care, not "organ by organ treatment." Historically, industry observers remarked that Gemini had "very strong theories and methodologies." Gemini would not tolerate friction among its employees on its engagements, and had squadrons of experienced troubleshooters ready to right potential wrongs.

HARD TIMES

In 1994, however, the firm fell on hard times. The re-engineering market had effectively collapsed a year earlier, and by 1994 the firm's revenues were flat. Gemini retrenched painfully, upsetting its own holistic positivity by laying off 300 of its then-1700 consultants. The consulting firm actually lost money at a time when virtually all other consultancies were showing gains. The firm closed its San Francisco office in early 1997. Currently, Gemini says it is "earning" the right to return to larger engagements in the U.S. by first taking on small and medium-sized jobs, often in IT consulting (a strength due to the connection with Cap Gemini) or operations. The firm is doing less strategy work in North America than before the retrenchment.

ON THE UPSWING

The new Gemini approach seems to be working. The firm is gaining confidence, taking on a large consulting job for Bridgestone in 1997. In January 1998, Gemini Consulting officially merged with Bossard Consulting, a European-based consultancy also owned by Cap Gemini. The merger has boosted the number of Gemini consultants to 2000 in more than 30 offices on five continents. The growth is expected to continue, particularly in Europe, where the firm is already the largest consultancy in France.

GETTING HIRED

The Gemini web site, located at www.gemcon.com, describes the firm's recruiting schedule at top undergraduate and graduate campuses. Candidates completing an MBA or advanced degree with some professional experience are typically considered for senior consultant positions. The senior consultant's responsibilities include analyzing data, problem solving, and assisting client teams. Additionally, the senior consultant must perform customer and client interviews and develop, present, and implement client recommendations. In North America, Gemini recruits from the Kellogg Graduate School of Management at Northwestern University and The Wharton School at the University of Pennsylvania. At Gemini, first-round interviews are conducted by consultants only one to two years ahead of the interviewee.

Internship opportunities exist at the senior consultant level. Candidates who are between their first and second years of an MBA program can work with Gemini for three months on a client site. Gemini's MBA Summer Internship Program is "global" and the firm claims to offer ample networking opportunities, training, and performance evaluations. The consulting firm holds events on campuses that focus on "showing how Gemini works," and is presented as an interactive event.

The consultant position is the entry-level role for undergraduate candidates. In some cases, for candidates with advanced degrees that may not be business-related. When they first join the firm, most new consultants will work in Gemini's Strategic Research Group in Cambridge, Massachusetts. Consultants who join Gemini directly from undergrad typically work with Gemini for two to three years before returning to business school. A handful stay with the firm and work their way up the ranks. The consulting hierarchy at Gemini goes: consultant, senior consultant, managing consultant, principal, vice president.

Gemini has smaller requirements for new consultants than some other firms – Gemini may hire 50 consultants in a year. "Sometimes it's difficult to compete with those churn and burn consulting firms," says one insider. "We need a dedicated consultant team, not just HR people, to reach out to the best students."

Recent graduates should send applications to the Cambridge office for consideration. Application dates vary by school, but all must include a resume, cover letter, and copies of both a candidate's SAT scores and his/her most recent transcript.

OUR SURVEY SAYS

A FIRM WITH POTENTIAL

The retrenchments of several years ago haven't helped the Gemini atmosphere much. Insiders say that "there are lingering repercussions about the layoffs. Things still haven't gone back to normal, and people still look over their shoulders." Despite these lingering concers, however, Gemini still has many intrinsic strengths. The "social," "team-based" approach gives recent hires "constant" exposure to their "down-to-earth," more senior colleagues. Gemini allows its consultants to live where they choose but requires them to be at the client site Monday through Friday. Explains one insider: "Gemini practices something called the virtual office, which means you fly to your client site Monday through Thursday and then you telecommute on Friday."

KIND AND RESPECTFUL CO-WORKERS

In its American offices, dress at Gemini is business casual, although it is still formal in the firm's European offices, insiders report. Gemini also provides "excellent" support staff, and consultants praise their "intelligent, proactive, interesting" co-workers. One consultant says "I have never seen anything other than mutual respect and trust for everyone in the organization." While the consulting industry is "full of individuals who are typically arrogant, the great thing about Gemini is that, while the arrogance does exist, it is held in check and does not impede working and social interactions."

LOTS OF TRAVEL, BUT FREE WEEKENDS

There isn't much formal training at the firm, but new employees learn "most of the ropes" from "project experience." Once Gemini consultants are familiar with their trade, "the amount of work can vary significantly from high to outrageous." Travel is intense and many consultants report wallowing in it: "If it were not for the significant travel, I could not imagine wanting to join another firm." Reveals another insider: "There is way too much travel and not enough vacation time." Fortunately, Gemini consultants "don't have to brown nose on the road or on weekends. They are expected to achieve a balanced life so that the workweek is something they look forward to." Apparently, this balance pertains to the body as well as to the mind. "I am able to work out daily," divulges another insider, "and have a weekend. I am one happy camper during the week."

TURNING THE CORNER

While "many people have left for other firms," other employees say "we've turned the corner in America." The merger with Bossard Consultants is "a great fit" and should "energize" Gemini, consultants say. One insider confidently summarizes the Gemini experience: "We care about the people we work with, including clients and co-workers, and it shows. I came to Gemini because of the interesting work. I'm staying not only for the work, but also for the culture."

Gemini Consulting

To order a 50- to 70-page Vault Reports Employer Profile on Gemini Consulting call 1-888-JOB-VAULT or visit www.VaultReports.com

The full Employer Profile includes detailed information on Gemini's departments, recent developments and transactions, hiring and interview process, plus what employees really think about culture, pay, work hours and more.

Greenwich Associates

8 Greenwich Office Park
Greenwich, CT 06831
(203) 629-1200
Fax: (203) 629-1229
www.greenwich.com

LOCATIONS

Greenwich, CT (HQ)

THE STATS

No. of Offices: 1 (U.S.)
A privately-held company
Managing Partner: Charles D. Ellis

KEY COMPETITORS

First Manhattan Consulting Group
Mitchell Madison Group
Oliver, Wyman & Company

UPPERS

- Contact with upper management
- Travel opportunities
- Cozy, stable client relationships

DOWNERS

- Sometimes administrative tasks
- Company claustrophobia

EMPLOYMENT CONTACT

Linda Triplett
Greenwich Associates
P.O. Box 2515
Greenwich, CT 06830

Fax: (203) 625-5126
lht@greenwich.com

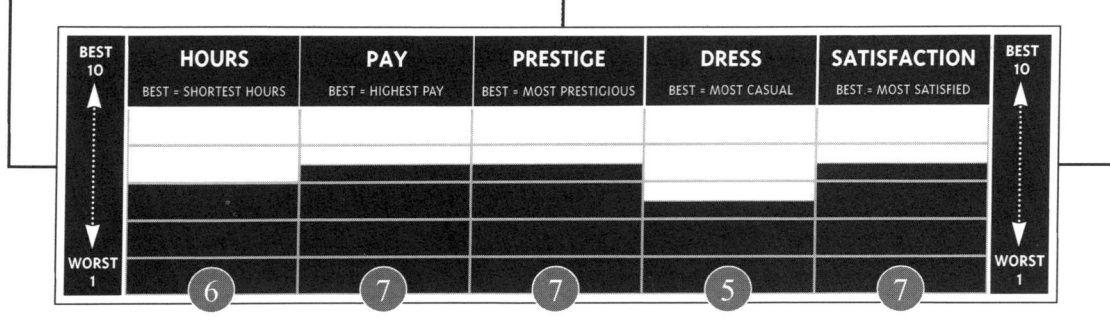

HOURS BEST = SHORTEST HOURS	PAY BEST = HIGHEST PAY	PRESTIGE BEST = MOST PRESTIGIOUS	DRESS BEST = MOST CASUAL	SATISFACTION BEST = MOST SATISFIED
6	7	7	5	7

© Copyright 1998 Vault Reports, Inc. Photocopying is illegal and expressly forbidden.

THE SCOOP

MANAGING KNOWLEDGE EVERY DAY

Greenwich Associates provides research-based consulting to leading commercial banks, investment banks, brokerage firms, bond dealers, investment managers, and other major institutions. At last count, Greenwich Associates worked in 100 major markets for professional financial services. Greenwich now stands abreast of one of the latest fads in management consulting – knowledge management, or as Greenwich calls it, "the art of informing, advising and advocating action."

SERVING THE FINANCIAL COMMUNITY, THOROUGHLY

There is a reason Greenwich Associates attacks its financial consulting jobs with unusual gusto – its clients are the leading firms in the financial services industry. Since its 1972 founding, the Greenwich, Connecticut-based consulting firm has built a reputation for strong client relationships, experienced consultants, and in-depth and complete research. Annual research efforts consist of more than 40,000 interviews in 16 languages conducted in 61 different countries. Greenwich shuns the world "survey" considering its research "more of a census, since we try to talk to 100 percent of the market."

(VERY) LONG-TERM CLIENTS

Over 95 percent of Greenwich's work is with continuing clients, often with relationships lasting over 20 years – perhaps why the consultancy likes to say that "the clients are the firm." The firm emphasizes that the clients come before the firm, and the firm comes before the individual. The firm is proud that many of its directors have stuck with Greenwich for 10, 15 or even 20 years each. Greenwich counts among its clients big names like ABN AMRO, Credit Suisse First Boston, Deutsche Bank, Donaldson, Lufkin & Jenrette, Fidelity, Fleet Bank, Goldman Sachs, J.P. Morgan, Nomura, PaineWebber, Salomon Smith Barney and Vanguard.

GETTING HIRED

Greenwich Associates looks for hard working and dedicated individuals for a variety of positions. Research associates must have a bachelor's degree or equivalent experience, strong organizational skills and analytical abilities, and top-notch communication skills. Visit the "Employment Opportunities" section of Greenwich Associates' web site (www.greenwich.com) for details on job opportunities. Send or fax resumes to Human Resources – the fax is (203) 629-1229.

Greenwich hires about three MBA associates per year; all associates are hired with the expectation that they will become partners in the pint-sized firm. Greenwich prefers that its hires have two to four years of experience in financial services or consulting to financial service organizations. Research associates are hired out of college; foreign languages are major assets for this position.

OUR SURVEY SAYS

GOING ABROAD – BUT STUCK IN CONNECTICUT AT HOME

Because they work at a global firm, Greenwich research associates can expect to take four to six overseas trips each year, with most lasting about a week. The firm is described as "a little on the conservative side," though consultants note many firms are even more stringent. In fact, the firm recently went from business dress to business casual. One contact reports being happy with the company and the people, although he notes that he would prefer New York to the firm's yuppie and bucolic Connecticut locale.

Hard hours for great rewards

Research associates at Greenwich are said to "put in long hard demanding hours at jobs that are somewhat administrative in nature." Associates "shouldn't expect to do a lot of consulting right away – that takes a long time, and a lot of associates never get there." However, hard workers are usually rewarded by "getting into a plum business school or starting a great financial services career." While consultants also work hard, "they have the opportunity to go on client visits to big financial firms and meet with the big cheeses there."

A very small firm

The firm is "really small. Only about 120 people work here." And don't expect much company, because "[Greenwich] is privately held and fairly unique in what it does, so there is little likelihood of a merger anytime soon." Consultants say that Greenwich has "decent perks, like health insurance, vision, profit sharing and tuition reimbursement for job-specific courses, but nothing incredible." Another perk for technophiles – "We've got full Internet access and aren't monitored too much." In this small and dedicated firm, "a lot of people find it's not what they thought or wanted," but "a lot of people find they like it and go with it."

Hewitt Associates

100 Half Day Road
Lincolnshire, IL 60069
(847) 295-5000
www.hewitt.com

LOCATIONS

Lincolnshire, IL (HQ)
Atlanta, GA • Bedminster, NJ • Newport Beach, CA • Rowayton, CT • The Woodlands, TX • Other offices in U.S. • Europe • Asia and South America

THE STATS

Annual Revenues: $858 million (1998)
No. of Employees: 9,600
No. of Offices: 70 (WorldWide)
A privately-held company
CEO: Dale Gifford

KEY COMPETITORS

Andersen Consulting
Buck Consultants
PricewaterhouseCoopers
Towers Perrin
Watson Wyatt Worldwide

UPPERS

- Two-year maternity leave
- Discounts on cars and cell phones
- Tuition reimbursement
- Profit sharing
- Free lunch and breakfast

DOWNERS

- Training and hiring unable to keep up with growth

EMPLOYMENT CONTACT

Human Resources
Hewitt Associates
100 Half Day Road
Lincolnshire, IL 60069

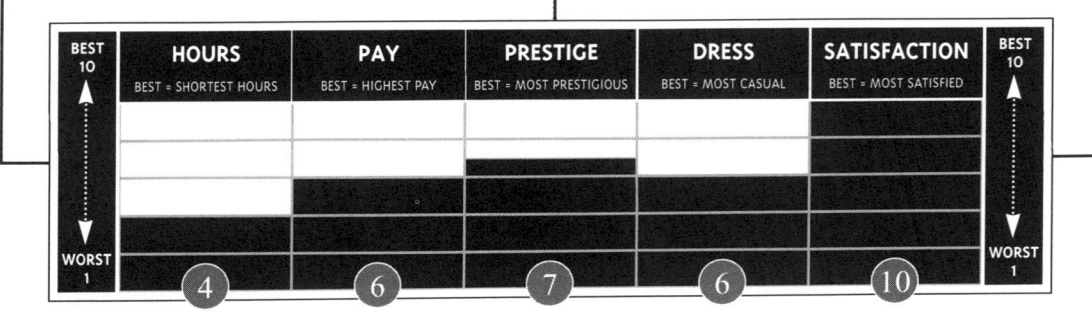

HOURS (BEST = SHORTEST HOURS)	PAY (BEST = HIGHEST PAY)	PRESTIGE (BEST = MOST PRESTIGIOUS)	DRESS (BEST = MOST CASUAL)	SATISFACTION (BEST = MOST SATISFIED)
4	6	7	6	10

© Copyright 1998 Vault Reports, Inc. Photocopying is illegal and expressly forbidden.

THE SCOOP

A TURN TOWARD CONSULTING

Ted Hewitt and Charles L. Kluss intended to open an insurance brokerage in 1940 in Lake Forest, Illinois. However, after working with their first client, Parker Pen, they realized what Parker Pen really needed was a well-designed benefits package for employees. Soon after, Hewitt Associates began to shift its focus from insurance to benefits consulting, which is now the firm's leading area of expertise. Currently, the firm boasts 70 offices in 31 countries, housing 10,000 employees.

A LEADER THAT CONTINUES TO GROW

The largest employee benefit consulting firm in the U.S., and the largest independent 401(k) record keeper, Hewitt is growing rapidly. In 1998, Hewitt posted revenues of $858 million – over a 20 percent increase from the previous year. Hewitt ranks as one of the world's 300 largest private companies. In the past couple of years, the firm has established major locations in Florida and Texas. Hewitt has become one of the largest providers of benefit outsourcing services. More than half of Hewitt's revenues – about $300 million – comes from benefits outsourcing. Client companies wishing to concentrate on "Core Competencies" contract eith Hewitt to run their employee benefit plans.

HEY, WAIT A MINUTE, WE'RE ONE OF THE TOP PLACES TO WORK

For the first time in 1998, Hewit Associates didn't rank as one of *Fortune* magazine's top 100 employers in the country. Not because quality of life at the firm has gotten worse, mind you – as a human resources consulting firm, Hewitt has always been mindful of its employees. Hewitt wasn't ranked because it partnered with *Fortune* in the project and removed itself from consideration. The authors of the article used Hewitt's People Practices Inventory (which includes categories like development and learning and work/life programs) to help choose and rank the 100 top employers. Previous to collaborating with the project, Hewitt had made *Fortune's* list every year since the inagural list in 1984.

GETTING HIRED

At the beginning of the hiring process, Hewitt usually meets with candidates on campus, over the phone, or on-site for an approximately half-hour first round interview. After that screening interview, Hewitt makes a decision about the person's chances for opportunities within the firm. Promising candidates are invited to a Hewitt office, at which time they have two to three interviews with associates and learn more about Hewitt's various departments.

Once part of the Hewitt team, most employees out of undergrad join the Total Benefits Administration (TBA) division. Hewitt hires a variety of majors, but often gives preference to those in the fields of computer science, MIS, accounting, economics, and math. Most new hires are placed in the firm's Lincolnshire headquarters, while a few are sent other offices. Entry-level compensation ranges, but the baseline is generally considered competitive with industry standards. For the past several years, Hewitt has been hiring extensively. College students who have completed their junior years and hold GPAs above 3.0 are encouraged to apply for internships – a good way to be hired at Hewitt permanently.

OUR SURVEY SAYS

THE PERSONAL TOUCH

For Hewitt has a surprising number of employees who wouldn't dream of being at a smaller, and presumably more intimate, workplace. Applauds one insider: "Hewitt's culture is open and honest." Says another: "Hewitt prides itself in being an open environment. Basically, teamwork is the key to our business." Part of this environment means taking junior employees seriously. Reports one insider: "Employees are important and are listened to." Another announces "any associate, using good judgment, can do just about whatever they want or need to do to meet business needs. The firm really trusts its associates." As an example of the team-oriented atmosphere, one consultant in the firm's headquarters points out that "there are few offices in our buildings, which means even the CEO/management sits in an open area." And it's not as if Hewitt employees are forced into teamwork, either. Says one contact: "The people at Hewitt are genuinely nice."

Insiders also consider their company's to be very prestigious (albeit in limited area). One insider gushes, "We are the premier firm in our business. Enough said!" An inspired, but less worshipful colleague states, "I think it means something to work at Hewitt Associates. We are the premier company in our industry and have been admired for years as one of the best companies in the United States."

THERE IS SUCH A THING AS A FREE LUNCH... AND FREE BREAKFAST

Insiders unabashedly laud the company's many perks and incentives. How many? How about "free birthday lunch at the restaurant of your choice, group outings on a quarterly basis; discounts on new cars and cell phones, movie tickets, theater performances, and daycare, on-site dry cleaning and an ATM machine." Then there are the "free breakfast, lunch, and re-heat dinners – if you work late hours." Hewitt headquarters also houses a credit union and "coffe stations fully stocked with soda, coffee, hot chocolate and tea." Says one associate about the perks at Hewitt: "Sometimes it's the little things that count. I remember each associate receiving a box of candies shaped in the form of a $100 bill on income tax day. And then there was multi-colored popcorn on 'all associate's day.'" Insiders also report disounts on amusement park tickets and "ice cream in the afternoon."

But it's not just quirky perks like discounts on computers and cell phones that Hewitt insiders count among their benefits. The firm offers profit-sharing bonuses and pays almost 100 percent of its employees' health insurance plans, insiders report. Says one insider: "There are so many benefits that we have a database setup solely for this, called Associate Benefits."

GREAT FOR WOMEN AND MINORITIES

Hewitt is known as an excellent employer for minorities and women, and our contacts couldn't agree with that reputation more. "Diversity is a very important part of the firm. There are many associate networks for people to become involved in," reports one insider, citing company organizations for expecting parents, gays and lesbians, and various ethnic minorities. Says one openly gay employee: "I can tell you the firm offers domestic partner benefits and sponsors the Chicago AidsWalk every year. I've always felt that Hewitt has supported me with open arms." Says another insider: "As a woman, I have not experienced any kind of discrimination, and find the organization very supportive of co-workers with families in terms of work flexibility." Another employee believes "there might be more females than males at Hewitt." Hewitt associates are also encouraged "to work on a volunteer basis at an organization of their choice two days a year."

NOT QUITE PARADISE, BUT ABOUT AS CLOSE AS IT GETS

Is there any dark side to this lovefest? There are occasional long workweeks at Hewitt. While most contacts report working between 40 to 50 hours a week, one reports that for some positions, Hewitt associates work "a minimum of 60 hours a week." Another says: "For me, the worst thing about working here is that it's not a 9 to 5 job. Depending on what type of position you're hired into, most administrative consultants and systems consultants work upwards of 50 hours a week."

GROWING PAINS A SMALL PRICE TO PAY

Hewitt is also experiencing some growing pains. "Lack of communication between upper management and associates and lack of information sharing is a problem," discloses an insider. "And training capacity has not grown with the company. There is not enough space for all the people who want – and need – to attend classes." Says another: "Growing at such a fast rate places a training burden on experienced associates. It's often difficult for recruiting to keep pace with needs."

But overall, Hewitt associates are about as satisfied as one could expect. "I'm very satisfied with my job," reveals one Hewitt-happy individual. "Every day is different here and the environment's always great." Says another: "I'm extremely satisfied with Hewitt Associates. The benefits are great and the people are even better." Says another fan: "I would recommend this company to anyone."

ICF Kaiser

9300 Lee Hwy.
Fairfax, VA 22031-1207
(703) 934-3600
Fax: (703) 934-9740
www.icfkaiser.com

LOCATIONS

Fairfax, VA (HQ)
Numerous locations throughout the U.S. and worldwide

THE STATS

Annual Revenues: $1.1 billion (1997)
No. of Employees: 4,772 (worldwide)
No. of Offices: 80 (worldwide)
Stock Symbol: ICF (NYSE)
CEO: James O. Edwards

KEY COMPETITORS

American Management Systems
Booz•Allen & Hamilton
Ernst & Young Consulting
Towers Perrin

UPPERS

- Excellent treatment of ethnic minorities
- 401(k) plan with company match
- Company gym at headquarters

DOWNERS

- Relatively low prestige

EMPLOYMENT CONTACT

Human Resources
ICF Kaiser
9300 Lee Hwy.
Fairfax, VA 22031-1207

Fax (703) 218-2680
resumes@icfkaiser.com

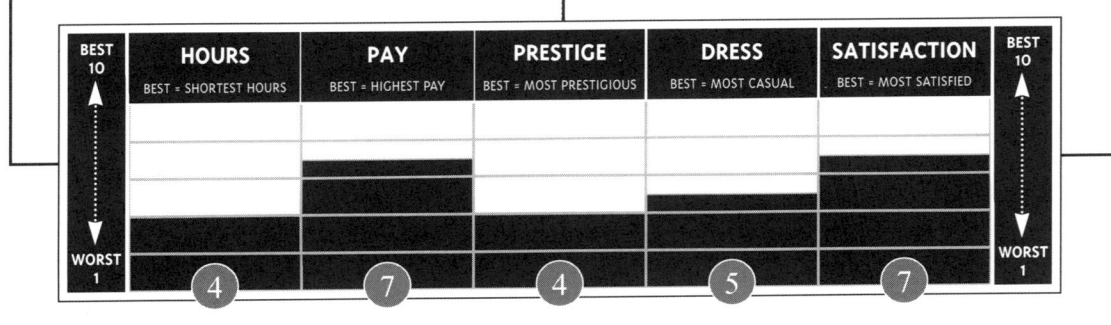

HOURS	PAY	PRESTIGE	DRESS	SATISFACTION
BEST = SHORTEST HOURS	BEST = HIGHEST PAY	BEST = MOST PRESTIGIOUS	BEST = MOST CASUAL	BEST = MOST SATISFIED
4	7	4	5	7

THE SCOOP

DEEP IMPACT

When the government issues policies that affect business, ICF Kaiser tells big name corporations what to do. Providing engineering, construction, program management, and consulting services, ICF Kaiser helps clients understand the impact of public policies and develop alternative corporate strategies in response.

A FAST-GROWING, GOVERNMENT-LOVING HYBRID

The firm is a hybrid of Kaiser Engineers, an engineering and construction company founded in 1914 by Henry Kaiser, and ICF, a firm that consulted to the U.S. government. Based in Fairfax, Virginia, ICF Kaiser was born in 1988, when ICF purchased Kaiser. The company continues its public sector work, and serves nearly every major agency and department of the federal government with a range of consulting services. With more than 5000 employees and 12 international offices, the company is also now a major player in the worldwide engineering, procurement, construction, and construction management fields. The firm is currently growing at a rate of 14 percent per year.

GETTING HIRED

ICF Kaiser looks for creative individuals with analytical skills, and the ability to translate them into sound, practical assistance. Applicants should have career interests in public policy, economic analysis, and strategic planning issues for both private and public clients. Hiring is based on academic records, relevant work experience, and expressed interest in the firm.

The company conducts on-campus interviews at several top business and public policy schools and provides correspondence opportunities at many others. On average, ICF Kaiser hires 40 to 50 professionals from a range of different graduate and undergraduate programs each year. Most MBAs will work at ICF Kaiser's Fairfax headquarters. Insiders report that the company has no strict up-or-out policy.

OUR SURVEY SAYS

DUAL CULTURES

Composed of a large engineering firm and a smaller consulting firm, ICF Kaiser's dual make-up prompts one employee to say that "the corporation really has two cultures, though both are professional services firms in the business of selling people's time." Moreover, employees also say the firm has many "minicultures, depending on who you work with and the primary client organizations with which you will be working." But employees willing to take a stab at an overall company culture say that "in general, the culture is less formal than many Fortune 500 firms." The dress code "isn't written in stone." Instead, most employees dress to mirror the clients they work with. Work hours vary by job function and level, but are "usually 40 to 45 hours a week, generally 9 to 5."

PERKS BOTH HAPPY AND HEALTHY

The company offers a competitive benefits package, small tuition reimbursement for work-related college courses, 401(k) retirement plan with a company match. One employee at company headquarters notes "a modest on-site health club facility." Employees say women and minorities are treated well. In addition to many females "rising through the ranks," one employee stresses that "the ICF president is Indian, and one of the co-founders was African American, so there is a strong tradition of respect and appreciation of diversity."

"The president is Indian, and one of the co-founders was African American, so there is a strong tradition of respect and appreciation of diversity."

– *ICF Kaiser insider*

Integral

One Brattle Square, 5th Floor
Cambridge, MA 02138
(617) 349-0600
Fax: (617) 864-3862
www.integral-inc.com

LOCATIONS

Cambridge, MA (HQ)
San Francisco, CA
Los Angelos, CA
Menlo Park, CA
Cambridge, U.K.

THE STATS

A privately-held company

KEY COMPETITORS

Mars & Company
Parthenon Group
Monitor Company
Charles River Associates
Strategic Decisions Group

UPPERS

- Plenty of opportunities to display leadership
- Chance to work abroad
- Plenty of upward mobility
- Intellectually rigorous atmosphere

DOWNERS

- Lack of support staff
- Can be political and cliquish
- Occasional dry spells in terms of workload

EMPLOYMENT CONTACT

Melissa DellaRusso
One Brattle Square, 5th Floor
Cambridge, MA 02138

(617) 349-0600
recruiting@integral-inc.com

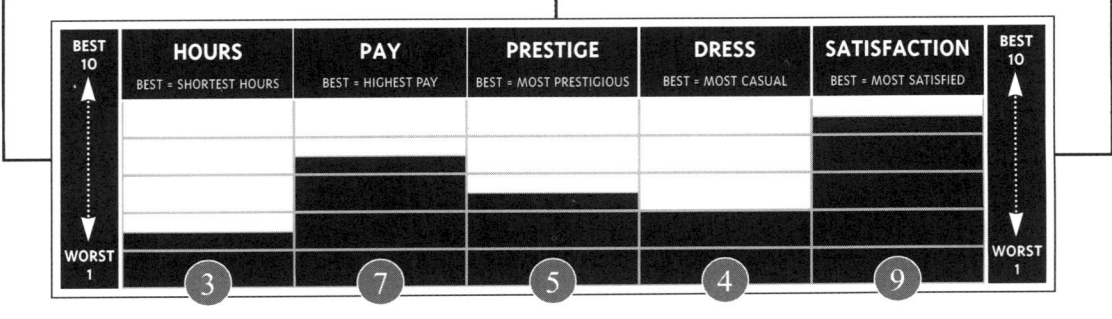

HOURS BEST = SHORTEST HOURS	PAY BEST = HIGHEST PAY	PRESTIGE BEST = MOST PRESTIGIOUS	DRESS BEST = MOST CASUAL	SATISFACTION BEST = MOST SATISFIED
3	7	5	4	9

© Copyright 1998 Vault Reports, Inc. Photocopying is illegal and expressly forbidden.

THE SCOOP

INTEGRALLY INTERESTING

Where can a consultant travel to exotic locations, work in the midst of intellectual giants, and go on the occasional canoe trip with fellow employees? Look no further than Integral. "Integral is a very stimulating place," exclaims one enthusiastic associate. The company was founded in 1988 by a distinguished intellectual triumvirate: Harvard Business School professors Kim Clark and Steven Wheelwright and economist Bruce Stangle. Since its inception, Integral has maintained close ties to numerous well-respected academic affiliates at leading business schools. Indeed, the company prides itself on its academic approach to problem solving and has no plans of changing its methods.

WORKING WITH MANY INDUSTRIES

Integral works with Fortune 100 companies worldwide in a variety of industries from pharmaceuticals to telecommunications to utilities. Integral consultants tend to be highly qualified in specific areas, yet also possessed of a general knowledgeable of business and technical fields. Services include finely tuned economic and financial analysis, among other niceties. Currently employing over 80 professionals, Integral is commanded by six so-called principals. The company's three corporate offices are located in Cambridge, MA; Menlo Park, CA; and Cambridge, U.K. Since its birth, Integral has sustained an average growth rate of 30 percent per year.

STRONG TRAINING

Integral considers itself devoted to professional development. The firm holds year-round company meetings and work sessions devoted to training. New associates are invited to attend an intensive program covering basic consulting skills, firm values, and various approaches to problem-solving. First-year employees also learn about Integral's more original projects such as Vusion, an innovative Intranet-based project monitoring tool which – irritating name aside

– has earned a fair share of acclaim. Other unique Integral projects include the Resource Mountain Chart, a tool for resource allocation decisions, and the Consumer/Technology Matrix, a tool for managing portfolios of development projects.

GETTING HIRED

Integral accepts candidates from all academic disciplines, including the liberal arts. Those applying to Integral should underscore any mathematical or economic accomplishments, since the firm emphasizes quantitative ability. Not surprisingly, the company also keeps an eye out for graduates of big name schools and prestigious MBA programs. Those who have served out a summer internship at Integral also have a leg up on the rest of the applicant pool.

Prospective employees can expect three tough rounds of interviews, insiders tell us. Each round is meant to test critical reasoning skills, quantitative understanding, and conceptual and strategic interpretation. Be ready for tricks which seem to serve only one purpose: to measure one's prowess at forming absurd answers to even more absurd questions. Here's an example: You're rowing your boat in a pond. When you throw in your anchor, will the water level rise, fall, or stay the same? A word of advice: on questions such as this one, interviewees are looking less for the appropriate answer and more for creativity and ingenuity in a person's problem solving method.

Those good enough to make it past the first two interview rounds can expect a rigorous final round which lasts half a day and is jam-packed with more Q&A rounds. Fortunately, there is a little light at the end of the tunnel, insiders say. Many of the interviewers are said to approach their task in a friendly and even light-hearted manner.

(By the way – the water level falls.)

OUR SURVEY SAYS

SMALL IS BEAUTIFUL

Integral is the quintessential small company, equipped with both the perks and the pitfalls of micro-size. It suffers from a "perpetual lack of support and resources," but has a "bounty of amazingly smart people." One insider remarks, "Integral is a small company that still acts like a small company." Part of what this means is notable internal politics. "There is a lot of internal hiring. And there are social cliques. People here tend to be recognized as experts in their fields. They tend to work with the same people – the people they are most familiar and comfortable with."

A WELL-GREASED MACHINE

Nevertheless, for the most part, our contacts say that the people of Integral make the machine work well. "Across the board, the people at Integral are a talented, ambitious, and steady-handed bunch. There could be more diversity – especially racial diversity – but the company's getting better about that issue." There's also an undeniable academic slant to the company. "It doesn't hurt to work around a professor of the Harvard Business School," reveals one consultant. "I'm constantly learning. Working around PhDs all the time, well, to be honest, it's kind of humbling."

TRAVEL CAN BE FUN

And there are other perks. Says one insider "I know some people view consultant travel as a bad thing, but I've enjoyed all of my stints abroad." Reports another consultant: "One of the reasons I chose Integral was the travel. I had the privilege of living abroad in my first year."

KPMG Consulting

Three Chestnut Ridge Road
Montvale, NJ 07645
(201) 307-7000
www.kpmgcareers.com

LOCATIONS

Montvale, NJ (HQ)
Offices in 1,100 offices in over 150 countries

THE STATS

Annual Revenues: $2.0 billion (1997)
No. of Consultants: 5000 (worldwide)
No. of Offices: 1100 (worldwide)
A privately-held company
CEO: Stephen Butler

KEY COMPETITORS

Andersen Consulting
Arthur Andersen
Deloitte Consulting
Ernst & Young Consulting
PricewaterhouseCoopers

UPPERS

- Aggressive in promoting diversity
- Sporting event and theater tickets
- Daycare assistance
- Flexible hours
- Community involvement assistance

DOWNERS

- High turnover
- Starting pay below competing Big Five firms

EMPLOYMENT CONTACT

Human Resources
KPMG Consulting
Three Chestnut Ridge Road
Montvale, NJ 07645

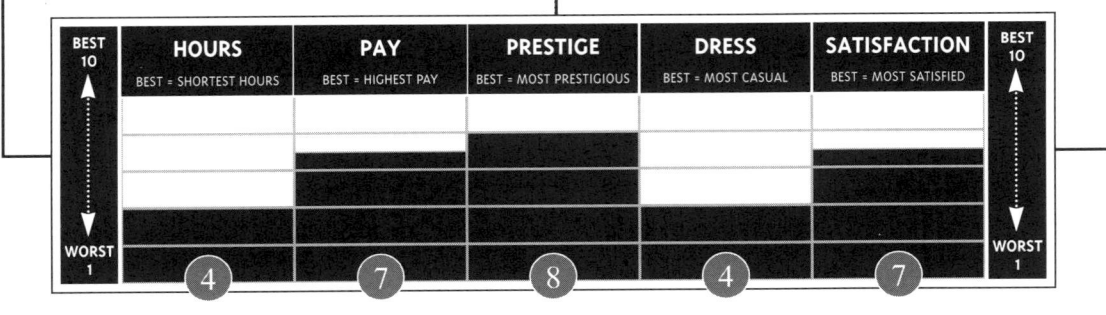

HOURS	PAY	PRESTIGE	DRESS	SATISFACTION
BEST = SHORTEST HOURS	BEST = HIGHEST PAY	BEST = MOST PRESTIGIOUS	BEST = MOST CASUAL	BEST = MOST SATISFIED
4	7	8	4	7

© Copyright 1998 Vault Reports, Inc. Photocopying is illegal and expressly forbidden.

THE SCOOP

THE CHEESE – OR THE KPMG – STANDS ALONE

After scratching plans to join forces with fellow Big Five professional services firm Ernst & Young, KPMG stands alone. But KPMG (formerly called KPMG Peat Marwick in the United States) is hardly in need of any sympathy. The professional services firm has been adding business steadily, figure that the firm aggressively plans to increase to $6 billion by the year 2000. The consulting arm has risen dramatically in recent years, earning $1.5 billion in the U.S in 1998.

SELF-PROMOTION ABOUNDS

KPMG refuses to stand pat, however, and is launching an ambitious $60 million promotional campaign aimed at bolstering its already considerable name recognition. And a proposed plan to go public with part of the consulting business could spell even more big bucks for the firm and its employees. Truly, in more ways than one, KPMG is a firm on the move. KPMG has a lot of dizzying numbers attached to its name. The humongous firm has 85,291 employees (of which 59,663 are professionals) in 155 countries worldwide.

ONE POWER

Despite all these big numbers, KPMG's new philosophy, proclaimed from the mount (i.e., by CEO Stephen Butler) rests on a very small number – the campaign is called "The Power of One." This transcendent "guiding vision" has three major components: becoming No. 1 in the marketplace, functioning as a unified firm, and involving all KPMG employees in the firm's success. "The only acceptable position for this firm," proclaims KPMG, "is to be No. 1 in all of the businesses in which we choose to compete."

IMPRESSIVE AMBITION

That's a rather ambitious aim, for KPMG Consulting is a relatively young branch of the firm. Yet it already totals more than 5000 consulting professionals. But the first time, in 1998 the consulting division surpassed assurance (auditing services) in terms of U.S. revenue, grossing $1.5 billion of the firm's $3.8 billion total. The practice's revenues have more than tripled since 1994, and KPMG now seeks to retain 5 percent of the worldwide consulting market (which would be 400 percent more that the consultancy's current market share).

GETTING HIRED

Be confident, job seekers! The consulting industry is champing at the bit to hire qualified new candidates. In fact, KPMG intends to boost its North American employee base from 20,000 to 30,000 in the coming years. To accomplish this, the firm has 70 full-time hiring professionals on staff, and many of the highest ranking members of the organization dedicate a large portion of their time to recruiting.

The firm is also expanding its recruitment of consultants. "A few years ago, the firm only hired MBAs. But now a lot of that has changed. We have a lot of work and are widening the net," reports one savvy consultant. First-year MBA students looking for summer positions are another new group now being treated to the lavish parties and dinners that are an integral part of the wooing process. Of course that does not mean that jobs are just handed out like Halloween candy. But for the adequately ambitious and analytical, the opportunities are plentiful.

KPMG puts a premium on interactive, non-stressful interviews, so prepare to answer several questions with a somewhat lighter tone than you might expect. But this doesn't mean that KPMG isn't serious. Because KPMG tends to hire consultants with significant industry or technical experience, the firm hardly ever uses case interviews to evaluate its consulting applicants, instead directing questions about work experience and computer expertise. Recalls one veteran of the interview process, "[they asked] what I had done in my internships and what I was interested in."

OUR SURVEY SAYS

A MULTIFACETED CULTURE

It's unsurprising that at a firm as large as KPMG, employees have many different takes on the corporate culture. One employee praises the "open door" atmosphere, where "managers are able to answer questions and provide guidance." Another employee has a slightly different take. "It's nurturing for newbies," says that contact. "This means you find a manager you are compatible with and become a sponge." We're told that KPMGers should "prepare your psyche for high turnover. Since I came to the firm six months ago, four people I worked with closely have left. Two defected to another Big Five firm, one went over to industry, and one transferred to another KPMG office."

SPECIFIC BY OFFICE?

Insiders report that "Culture varies somewhat between offices. In DC, for example, there's a Gay/Lesbian support group, but Raleigh is very stuffy and 'old-boy.' In general, the smaller offices tend to be more rigid and controlling." Now's the time to sign up for your frequent flyer card. "Consultants travel, on average, about 70 percent of the time. We try to stay regional in our business, but when the client has offices all over the country, sometimes it is necessary to work at all those offices." As for the employees themselves, they are "fairly young, with most large projects staffed by people in the 20- to 30-year-old range."

FLEXING TIME

At KPMG, "community involvement is encouraged and you are paid for four workday hours per month to perform volunteer work, provided that you match these hours with volunteer hours on your own time." One consultant reports that "some offices have flex time. For example, I work 10 to 7 to avoid rush hour traffic." Additionally, "continuing education opportunities abound and usually involve travel, with KPMG picking up the tab." Employees say that "when you start with the firm, KPMG gives you a new laptop, supplies and briefcase with the firm logo," and that the firm offers "five weeks of vacation." Well, not exactly. One insider comments that "KPMG is a bit unusual in that it combines vacation time with sick leave, so it's great if you're young and healthy, maybe not so great if you're sickly." Be forewarned that "some perks vary from office to office, or partner to partner, or even manager to manager."

DOES ANYONE ACTUALLY WORK THOSE HOURS?

In consulting, "the hours are officially 8:30 to 5:30, expecting that you'll take an hour for lunch. Sometimes I do leave at 5:30, other days [I stay] until 7:30." Another consultant concurs that "10 or 11 hours a day is typical." At times, "hours can be very long [for consultants], with late nights spent compiling and analyzing data, or preparing a presentation for a project meeting or board meeting."

To order a 50- to 70-page Vault Reports Employer Profile on KPMG call 1-888-JOB-VAULT or visit www.VaultReports.com

The full Employer Profile includes detailed information on KPMG's departments, recent developments and transactions, hiring and interview process, plus what employees really think about culture, pay, work hours and more.

"It's nurturing for newbies"

– *KPMG insider*

Kurt Salmon Associates

1355 Peachtree Street, NE
Suite 900
Atlanta, GA 30309
(404) 892-0321
www.kurtsalmon.com

LOCATIONS

Atlanta, GA (HQ)
Greensboro, NC • Los Angeles, CA • Miami, FL • Minneapolis, MN • New York, NY • Princeton, NJ • San Francisco, CA • Chicago, IL • International offices in 9 countries

THE STATS

Annual Revenues: $92 million (1997)
No. of Employees: 697 (worldwide)
No. of Offices: 16 (worldwide)
A privately-held company
CEO: Peter Brown

KEY COMPETITORS

Andersen Consulting
Booz•Allen & Hamilton
Deloitte Consulting
McKinsey & Company
Swander Pace

UPPERS

- Rapid career advancement
- Thorough job training
- Innovative specialties

DOWNERS

- Frequent travel
- Stressful examination
- Poor vacation policy

EMPLOYMENT CONTACT

Marian Crandal
Human Resources
Kurt Salmon Associates
1355 Peachtree Street, NE, Suite 900
Atlanta, GA 30309

Fax (404) 898-9590
recruiting@kurtsalmon.com

HOURS (BEST = SHORTEST HOURS)	PAY (BEST = HIGHEST PAY)	PRESTIGE (BEST = MOST PRESTIGIOUS)	DRESS (BEST = MOST CASUAL)	SATISFACTION (BEST = MOST SATISFIED)
4	7	7	6	7

© Copyright 1998 Vault Reports, Inc. Photocopying is illegal and expressly forbidden.

THE SCOOP

FROM HOSE TO CONSULTING

Before he founded his consulting firm, Kurt Salmon worked in a stocking factory. He studied engineering in Germany, and came to the U.S. in 1930. He became a consultant because it paid more than working in a hosiery mill (one would hope!). He later switched his focus to the apparel industry and opened his own firm in 1935. Since then, Kurt Salmon Associates has expanded across the globe, offering premier managerial advice to the retail, consumer products and healthcare industries. Today the Atlanta-based firm employs 697 professionals, and is the world's largest consulting firm focused on the retail and consumer products industries. Training is extremely important to this small and specialized firm: In addition to an intense two-week orientation when they start with the firm, all consultants take part in a minimum of 60 hours a year in professional development training.

HEALTHY BUSINESS

Hamilton HMC, the firm's healthcare consulting division, was formed in 1986 with the acquisition of Hamilton Associates. The division has recently emerged as a leader in its field, advising on such issues as strategy improvements, technology implementation, managed care, and facility planning. One in five hospitals in the United States has engaged the services of Hamilton KSA, which also finds clients in academic medical centers, research organizations, government health agencies, long-term care facilities, clinics, and physician groups.

RETAILERS PAR EXCELLENCE

The company's Retail and Consumer Products Division's major groups include strategy, supply chain management, operations, IT, logistics and corporate finance. Although Kurt Salmon Associates is smaller than most of its management consulting competitors (which the firm identifies as A.T. Kearney, McKinsey, Andersen Consulting/Arthur Andersen, Deloitte Consulting and Booz·Allen Hamilton), it is the largest firm specializing in the consumer product and retail industries. Kurt Salmon has averaged approximately 22 percent annual growth over the last five years, with at least 75 percent of the firm's business coming from previous clients. Its engagements usually last anywhere from six weeks to over a year. The firm serves a wide range of firms, from small manufacturers to large department stores. However, the firm's focus has moved up the supply chain over the years, from operations to retail. Recent clients include Tiffany, Nike, Liz Claiborne and Home Depot.

THE NEW WAVE

In June 1998, Kurt Salmon launched an investment bank subsidiary, which specializes in M&A, capital formation and financial consulting services. Soon after, the firm formed an alliance with QRS Corporation, an e-commerce software firm. Together, the firms offer e-commerce consulting services for retailers – Kurt Salmon provides business and process engineering consulting, and QRS brings its e-commerce expertise.

GETTING HIRED

Kurt Salmon's employment web page, located at www.kurtsalmon.com/recruit.htm, describes the firm's current openings. The firm hires about five to ten new MBA-level consultants each year. Summer internships are rarely offered, and sources say "KSA will not reimburse summers for their second year if they come back." U.S. and foreign nationals (with permanent work status in the U.S.) may apply for positions in the U.S., but overseas positions are only open to foreign nationals. Resumes may be posted, faxed or e-mailed to the firm. New consultant hires often start out in the Performance Enhancement, Corporate Finance, or Logistics practices and the firm occasionally encourages its consultants to go on short- or long-term assignments overseas. During their first year, consultants attend an intense two-week orientation program. New MBA hires usually have three years of work experience, come from the top 10 percent of their class, and typically have prior experience in consulting, retail or consumer products. Fluency in a second language and additional degrees are considered pluses as well. New undergraduate hires come from the top 10 percent of their class, have strong quantitative and analytical skills, and have a good understanding of business issues, the firm repots.

Insiders report that "the firm is very concerned with fit, and big egos don't really fit in here." Interviews are done in three rounds: the first and second rounds "is to gauge fit," and is followed by a series of analytical/quantitative tests. If you are called back, you will meet with a manager. The second round "is also behavioral," says one source. "We want to get a sense for fit, and to see whether the candidate has taken the time to really think about KSA." At this stage, interviewers will generally pose case questions. The third round is "the office interview," where candidates meet with "more senior people." A recent interviewee at Kurt Salmon reports: "It was the most intensive interview I have ever had. I went through eight people in three days before I was made an offer. This included two tests after the initial interview. One test is a twelve-minute multiple choice test with 50 questions – the goal was to answer as many of the questions correctly in that period of time. The second test is a killer – 12 pages of word problems. These are supposed to test logic and thinking speed. You also get a personality test in human resources. They never tell you how you did on the test, only if you passed or failed."

OUR SURVEY SAYS

CUDDLY CO-WORKERS

Kurt Salmon consultants cite their "friendly, helpful" co-workers and "rapid" career advancement paths as two of the best things about the firm. They also comment that they receive "far superior training" and "more serious responsibilities" than their peers at other consulting firms. However, salaries "are somewhat below market level," insiders report. "The firm has always been conservative when it comes to keeping up with the market," says one.

However, one insider remarks that KSA "has moved up over the past year or two." Benefits are "on par with the rest of the [consulting] industry," and employees like the fact that "the retirement plan vests in only seven years." Perks include "standard expense account stuff when you're traveling." Consultants in the New York office "can call a car service if they work late, but in Atlanta, pretty much everyone drives to work, so it's not necessary."

CULTURE OF RELAXATION — OR IS IT?

Dress codes vary widely by office. At the Atlanta headquarters, "it's business casual every day, and on Friday, you can wear anything – within reason – no jeans with holes in them or anything." In the New York office, on the other hand, "it's suits Monday through Thursday, and casual Friday means khakis and collared shirts." Whatever they wear, Kurt Salmon consultants work in "what could be described as a casual work environment." "To give you an example, the president of the company came to one Christmas party wearing a tux and white sneakers," says one insider. As at most consulting firms, the age range at KSA "is pretty young," which makes for "a bit more of a relaxed culture." "Some of our principals are 33, 34 years old," one source points out. The firm sponsors "periodic happy hours" to encourage mingling, but consultants in the firm's headquarters say "there's not too much socializing out of the office. There are a lot of married people here."

FRIENDLY AND FLEXIBLE

KSA is "a family-friendly firm," with "diverse senior management in terms of background and ethnicity." Overall, the firm has "a fair amount of Hispanics and foreign nationals – but few black Americans."

A source gives us the breakdown for the U.S. offices: 11 percent principals are female, and 11 percent of the firm's officers/partners are minorities; six percent of the firm's professionals are African American, 4 percent are Hispanic, and 7 percent are Asian. Kurt Salmon is "pretty flexible about hours as long as you get your work done." "If you want to work from home sometimes, that's fine." In addition, when it comes to choosing your projects, "if there's a reason why you don't want a real travel-intensive period – if your wife is pregnant, for example – you can let that be known, and the firm will try to accommodate that."

Undergraduates usually stay with the firm "for about four years, after which many go to business school." Insiders confirm the company's claim that "we hire believing each new consultant has the potential to one day become a principal." "The firm makes a sincere effort to assess whether hires will make it," reports a consultant, "if you get in, your chances of becoming a principal are significantly higher than at other firms – KSA doesn't have that churn and burn attitude." In addition, "you can make principal if you don't have an MBA."

ON THE ROAD AGAIN

Kurt Salmon insiders say "travel is no worse than other consulting firms," and note that it "tries to focus more on lifestyle." "We generally work less hours than they do in the Big 5 firms," says a contact, though "there are spikes because the work is project-driven." Travel is also "unpredictable, since it depends on the project." Several contacts report working "on average between 50 and 60 hours a week," and say "weekends are rare." "There's no face-time issue here, or at the client," adds one insider. Strategy-oriented projects can be handled largely out of the home office. In those cases, travel is only about two to three days a week." As for travel abroad, "if you would very much like to be transferred to a foreign office," reveals a consultant, "you can do it, but a move like that would never be forced on you."

LEK/Alcar Consulting

101 Federal Street
Boston, MA 02110
(617) 951-9500
Fax: (617) 951-9392
www.lekalcar.com

LOCATIONS

Boston, MA (HQ)
Chicago, IL • Los Angeles, CA • Aukland • Bangkok • London • Manila • Melbourne • Milan • Munich • Paris • Sydney

THE STATS

No. of Offices: 12 (worldwide)
No. of Employees: 350 (worldwide)
A privately-held company
CEO: Iain Evans

KEY COMPETITORS

First Manhattan Consulting Group
Marakon Associates
McKinsey & Company
Mitchell Madison Group
Parthenon Group

UPPERS

- Profit sharing
- Free meals and taxis
- International opportunities
- Not as much travel as other consulting firms

DOWNERS

- Insensitive upper management
- Limited vacation entitlement
- Long hours for consulting

EMPLOYMENT CONTACT

Human Resources
LEK/Alcar Consulting
101 Federal Street
Boston, MA 02110

HOURS (BEST = SHORTEST HOURS)	PAY (BEST = HIGHEST PAY)	PRESTIGE (BEST = MOST PRESTIGIOUS)	DRESS (BEST = MOST CASUAL)	SATISFACTION (BEST = MOST SATISFIED)
1	8	7	3	7

© Copyright 1998 Vault Reports, Inc. Photocopying is illegal and expressly forbidden.

THE SCOOP

THE BANK/CONSULTING HYBRID

Three ex-partners of Bain & Company founded the LEK Partnership in London in 1983. Since then, the firm has expanded through Europe, North America, Australia and the Pacific Rim. It has offices in 12 cities and employs 250 consultants. In 1993, the firm's U.S. operation was merged with The Alcar Group. The resulting operation is called LEK/Alcar, and it's a mix between an investment bank and a consulting firm. Half of the firm's work is in strategy and half is in M&A consulting. In its strategic consulting capacity, LEK/Alcar conducts extensive research and advises management from a variety of industries on improving performance and increasing shareholder returns. The firm also offers educational services and shareholder value consulting. Areas of expertise include financial services, health care, startups and emerging-growth companies, telecommunications, consumer goods, media and entertainment, utilities and agribusiness. Since 1992, LEK/Alcar has been involved in over 300 transactions valued at more than $200 billion.

LITTLE AND FLEXIBLE

LEK/Alcar offices are small, with an average of 25 consultants per office. In addition, the firm is unusually flexible in its international assignments – employees switch easily between offices. The firm does not require its consultants to specialize in a particular practice area, though generally they gravitate to two or three preferred industries. While LEK consultants do travel frequently, these trips are generally short in duration, perhaps two to three days in a given workweek. Associates (BAs) typically return to graduate school, while consultants (MBAs) can expect to be promoted to the managerial level within two to three years.

GETTING HIRED

LEK/Alcar seeks entrepreneurial applicants with a record of academic and professional excellence. Recent college graduates are recruited for associate positions, and MBAs are eligible to apply for consultant openings. According to employees, the firm looks for well-rounded candidates with a strong work ethic who are "smart, smart, and um, smart." The firm performs on-campus interviews at several leading undergraduate and business schools, though it encourages applicants from schools where it does not actively recruit. The firm offers five to eight summer (MBA) positions in the U.S., and the London office also has a formalized summer associate program. LEK reimburses its summer MBA interns for their second year if they choose to return to the firm. For detailed information on job descriptions and opportunities, visit the "Career Opportunities" section of LEK/Alcar's web site, where applicants can e-mail questions and comments. Send or fax resumes to the recruiting coordinator at any U.S. office location.

Interviews are conducted in three phases, insiders say. The first round consists of two half-hour interviews with post-MBA consultants. Questions are "tailored to judge case and fit." In the second round, there are two 45-minute interviews with managers, and "there are more case questions, though they're still looking for fit." In the final round, candidates meet with five partners for one hour each. "These meetings are somewhat [to gauge] fit, though they will give you some highly technical cases." Sources say not to worry, "you'll start off just kind of chatting, and then you get to the case questions." Veterans say "the whole thing is kind of unstructured – your interviewer will pick up something they're working on at the time and walk you through it. They are trying to gauge whether you can pick things up and see what kind of approach you take." One source describes the case interviews (for MBAs) as "similar to a pop quiz for a B-school class."

OUR SURVEY SAYS

YOUNG AND DRIVEN

Employees describe LEK's company culture as "young, intellectually driven and intense." Though "it is in competition against firms like McKinsey and Bain," LEK still gets "the best and the brightest" from "the best schools." They're a "highly sociable" group with "eccentric interests and an entrepreneurial spirit rarely found in consulting." "Our cases are much shorter than those at other firms," explains one source, "you're not going to get stuck on one case for nine months." Another bonus: "we work with businesses ranging from veritable start ups all the way to Fortune 500 companies." Thus, "when you come off a case, they need to staff what comes in the door, so you end up dealing with lots of different industries and projects." Our contacts say turnover at the firm "is lower than at a lot of other firms," though "most people eventually move on to something else."

AN ENTREPRENEURIAL FEEL

Because "LEK doesn't have the structure you find at huge consultancies, things are slightly different," say insiders. "There's a more entrepreneurial feel to it than at more established companies." MBA grads like that fact that "you have immediate management responsibility. You structure the work, delegate tasks and analyze results." Undergrads value the opportunity for on-the-job learning, though one source complains that "because we're a small firm, they immediately throw you out to the sharks."

Sources say LEK is full of young people – "most of the professional staff, with the exception of the partners, is under age 30." "At all offices," say employees, "the young lively crowd bodes well for after hours entertainment." At the same time, the firm is also "pretty family friendly – most of the partners are married with families." One source reveals that "they have even let a female manager work part-time so she could spend more time with her child." Despite this reported flexibility, "women and minorities are underrepresented," at LEK, which is typical for the consulting industry. However, insiders assert that "women do get promoted to top positions."

EXTENSIVE TRAVEL – IN SANDALS?

As far as travel opportunities, consultants can choose between "international swap programs" and regular case travel. The former is "entirely voluntary and somewhat like a student exchange program," while for typical case travel, "consultants average one night per workweek." Some LEK/Alcar consultants escape the travel hell usually associated with the industry because "the M&A advisory services are rarely performed on-site."

Dress is typically formal, with dress-down Fridays in some offices. In the London office, there's no casual day – "there are credibility issues when the consultants are so young," explains one source. On the other side of the spectrum, the Los Angeles office reportedly has casual days on Monday and "fantastically casual" Fridays when "Teva sandals are a recurring fashion theme."

LONG, HARD HOURS

Some insiders complain about insensitive upper management at LEK. "Management used to not give a damn about how hard people worked," reports one former employee. "We had consultants working 80 hours a week, which is very high for the consulting industry." However, now "the firm gives you comp time if you work over 70 hours a week, so managers have to come up with a really good reason to have consultants work that hard." In some senses, LEK is "like a typical investment bank, very professional, heads-down and intense." In fact, says one associate: "On occasion, I have to remind myself that I'm not an investment banker."

NOT GREAT PERKS, BUT GREAT BONUSES

Compounding the long hours, insiders say, the firm offers limited vacation time. Salaries are "above average," though "perks are minimal." The firm is not going to subsidize your gym membership or your lunch, but insiders say "the lack of extras is more than compensated for by our annual bonuses," and they will pay for your dinner and a ride home if you work after 8 p.m. Benefits include a comprehensive health plan, profit sharing, and a 401(k) plan.

AN ADAPTABLE REVIEW PROCESS

To address some complaints, the company has implemented "a formal 'upward review' process to complement the traditional performance review process." The results of these reviews "are incorporated into managerial performance appraisals." Associates typically stay with the firm for three years: "They spend two years as associates, then they're promoted to associate consultant, where they're directing other people's work." Insiders say "not having an MBA won't stop you from succeeding at LEK," in fact, "some go straight through and become consultants." Says one contact: "We have partners who don't have MBAs."

Mars & Company

Mars Plaza
124 Mason Street
Greenwich, CT 06830
(203) 629-9292
Fax: (203) 629-3916
www.marsandco.com

LOCATIONS

Greenwich, CT (HQ)
San Francisco, CA
London, UK
Paris, France

THE STATS

No. of Employees: 200 (worldwide)
No. of Offices: 4 (worldwide)
A privately-held company
CEO: Dominique G. Mars

KEY COMPETITORS

Boston Consulting Group
Integral
McKinsey & Company
Parthenon Group
William Kent International

UPPERS

- BAs can make MBA-level salaries
- Exposure to higher-ups within the firm and on the client side
- Serves top players in industries

DOWNERS

- Lack of formal training
- No one makes partner
- Overbearing chairman

EMPLOYMENT CONTACT

Francine Even
Human Resources
Mars & Co.
Mars Plaza
124 Mason Street
Greenwich, CT 06830

HOURS	PAY	PRESTIGE	DRESS	SATISFACTION
BEST = SHORTEST HOURS	BEST = HIGHEST PAY	BEST = MOST PRESTIGIOUS	BEST = MOST CASUAL	BEST = MOST SATISFIED
3	10	8	3	7

THE SCOOP

THE FAITHFUL CONSULTANCY

Former BCG director Dominique Mars founded his eponymous international consulting firm in Paris in 1979. Unlike his reputedly Casanovan countrymen, Dominique Mars claims to have created "the only consulting firm of any consequence to guarantee 'fidelity'" to its clients. Mars believes that consulting firms are afforded an extremely intimate view of client businesses, and thus cannot justifiably work for competing corporations. Mars & Co. therefore only serves a limited (and highly exclusive) group of companies. They are all Fortune 100 or similarly powerful international companies and normally the top one or two corporations in their industries. For the sake of discretion, Mars does not publish the names of its clients. In fact, it does not even reveal them to prospective hires until very late in the interview process.

Mars focuses on business strategy – helping clients allocate their resources in order to maximize returns. It also assists clients with international acquisitions, joint ventures, and other methods of penetrating foreign markets. Like many strategy consulting firms, Mars defines "critical paths" (strategies) for its clients, but it does not facilitate implementation.

ENTERING THE UNITED STATES

In the mid-1980s, Mars & Co. opened its first U.S. office in Greenwich, Connecticut. Harvard Business School professor Malcolm Solter was then hired to be the company's president. Solter is a major force behind the development of the firm's business concepts, and insiders also say "has a pretty extensive list of contacts on his Rolodex," which he often uses to bring in new clients. There are no partners at Mars – the firm is owned and controlled 100 percent by its founder. Dominique Mars travels frequently between all of the offices, maintaining relationships with clients and courting new business.

A CLOSE-KNIT OPERATION

Though the firm's 200 consultants work in four separate offices, the firm is extremely integrated – in many cases, client teams are composed of consultants from two or more offices. Because their clients come from so many different industries, Mars associates gain familiarity with a wide variety of industries and tasks. The firm plans to expand further throughout North America and Europe, and eventually employ 400 to 450 consultants who will serve between 30 and 40 clients, insiders say. The firm operates as "a pure meritocracy," and is serious about promoting from within. In fact, it refers to new hires (both BAs and MBAs) as 'apprentices,' and will promote undergrads to the consultant level (read: six-figure salary) without MBAs.

GETTING HIRED

Mars & Co. hires 10 to 15 consultants per year. Undergraduates are hired as associate consultants; MBAs are hired as consultants. The firm recruits exclusively at top colleges and business schools, and posts recruitment information on its web site. It also "makes limited use of headhunters," say consultants. All interviews are conducted at the firm's offices. Mars looks for undergraduates with degrees in engineering, math, economics or any hard science, and MBAs with undergraduate degrees in one of those areas. Resumes should be forwarded to the office you hope to work for – company contacts for each outpost are listed on the company web page. The firm prefers to hire multilingual individuals with diverse backgrounds. One source describes the ideal candidate as "young, single, willing to relocate, bilingual, analytical and hard working."

The firm has a strict policy of promoting from within; it claims that successful candidates have the opportunity to move up rather quickly. Candidates interview with senior staff members, and the company encourages applicants to contact junior staff to "get their direct unfettered opinion of life at Mars & Co." Interviews are "not case intensive" – the first round "is mainly with senior consultants on the project manager level," and generally includes some "brainteaser-type" case questions. The second round is "with two VPs and a senior project manager." The final round consists of "a half-hour interview with Dominique Mars." One contact warns applicants that "Dominique is reputedly fluent in a number of languages." So if you claim to speak a second language fluently, "he'll conduct the whole interview in that language just to throw you off." Either way, "he'll usually start off with a question like 'Why are you here?' – to see how you react to being put on the spot." One source tells Vault Reports he "thought the interview with [Dominique] Mars was only a formality, but after I was hired I found out that only 50 percent of candidates that meet with him actually get hired."

OUR SURVEY SAYS

THE STEALTH FIRM

Mars & Co. is "a private firm" with a "stealthy reputation, and sources say "it makes no effort to attract attention to itself." "A quantitative background is a total prerequisite," one source notes. "In fact they've been hiring a lot of people with masters degrees and PhDs in engineering." "The quality of work and the projects at Mars are very high," adds another. "From the start you get to work with high-level consultants, and you deal with CEOs and presidents from the companies you are working for." One insider attempts to reassure prospective hires, asserting that "if you went to the right school, MIT or Ivy, and know something about business, you'll be OK."

UNDER HIS THUMB

If you manage to get in, expect to be thrown into a "work hard, play hard" environment where you will be "under the thumb of the chairman, who maintains 100 percent of equity in the firm." Some say Dominique's attitude "tends to breed self-loathing" among the ranks." Consultants also complain that there is "limited space for innovation" in this "old school" company – one source says this is partially a due to fact that the company is "French, with an HBS Chairman." Overall, though, our sources agree that the firm is "a great opportunity for undergrads."

APPRENTICE AT MARS

Some new consultants complain that "there is no official employee training program." (Mars & Co. says it "works under the apprenticeship format.") Most of the firm's consultants say they thrive as they learn on the job, though new hires "could benefit from an official introduction to strategy consulting." The good thing about the 'apprentice format' is that "if you show that you can take on significant responsibility, you're going to get it." "You move beyond number crunching," explains an insider. "Early on, you're working with CEOs of some really important companies." In addition, an insider reveals that the firm will promote non-MBAs to the consultant level – which means "MBA-level salaries." Reportedly, "after three years, you can make a six-figure salary." One contact explains that "with that kind of money, you work a few more years and you won't have to take out loans for grad school."

NEVER A PARTNER

Though most undergraduates leave the firm for graduate school after about three years, "the firm will not kick them out." One insider estimates that "about 20 percent of the firm's professionals above the consultant level are homegrown through the Mars system." What employees do gripe about is the fact that "no one will ever make partner – Dominique owns the company, and that's that." However, "in terms of compensation, VPs make as much as partners at Bain or BCG. Some might even make more."

RECENT GRAD HEAVEN

Mars & Co. "is a very young firm, in the sense that a lot of the people working here are recent grads from both undergraduate and business school." This makes working at Mars "fun – all week we bust our butts, so on Fridays, especially in the summer, we go out to a bar in Stamford and have some drinks." There are also company softball and basketball teams – "Dominique used to play, now he'll come to a game once in a while." "Women seem to be more the exception" at Mars & Co. Several of our contacts explain that "we're interviewing lots of women and making offers, but it's hard to convince them to join the company when there are so few here." Employees say there are no problems with ethnic minorities, "there are just not many of them – it's a small company." They do point out that "we do have a lot of international people."

THE PURITY OF STRATEGY

Hours "are determined by the client, the nature of the project, and the VP you're working with." "There's no real face time – people show up at 9:30 or 10 a.m. and that's okay." On the flip side, "if there's work to be done and you're not in the office, there's a problem." Insiders admit that "people do sometimes take two- or three-hour lunches, or run errands if they have to. They just make sure to get their work done." Travel "can be pretty extensive, in that you may be staffed on site somewhere for a while." But one source points out that "the good thing about pure strategy consulting is that the travel is not always so intense. A lot of the work you do is analyzing a client's competitors or markets." Not only does this minimize travel time, "you benefit from the resources in the office," most importantly by "being around everyone else in the firm."

Oliver, Wyman & Company

666 Fifth Avenue, 16th Floor
New York, NY 10103
(212) 541-8100
Fax: (212) 541-8957
www.oliverwyman.com

LOCATIONS

New York, NY (HQ)
Frankfurt, Germany
Madrid, Spain
Paris, France
Singapore
Toronto, Canada

THE STATS

No. of Offices: 6 (worldwide)
A privately-held company

KEY COMPETITORS

First Manhattan Consulting Group
Greenwich Associates
Mitchell Madison Group

UPPERS

- Profit-sharing
- Challenging work environment
- Lots of relevant on-the-job training

DOWNERS

- Upward mobility not standardized
- Unimpressive employee diversity
- Extremely young employee pool

EMPLOYMENT CONTACT

Human Resources
Oliver Wyman & Co.
666 Fifth Avenue, 16th Floor
New York, NY 10103

recruiting@owc.com

HOURS (BEST = SHORTEST HOURS)	PAY (BEST = HIGHEST PAY)	PRESTIGE (BEST = MOST PRESTIGIOUS)	DRESS (BEST = MOST CASUAL)	SATISFACTION (BEST = MOST SATISFIED)
4	8	6	2	6

© Copyright 1998 Vault Reports, Inc. Photocopying is illegal and expressly forbidden.

THE SCOOP

SPLITTING FROM BOOZ

In July 1984, five consultants from Booz•Allen & Hamilton and The Boston Consulting Group pooled their consulting expertise to form Oliver, Wyman & Company, one of the few management consulting firms dedicated to the financial services industry. The firm splits its business into several major practice areas: Capital Markets, Retail Finance Services, Wholesale Leading, Risk Management, Emerging Markets, and Insurance and Investment Management. Now in seven offices worldwide, the company has close to 200 consulting professionals.

SELECTIVE AND TARGETED

Oliver Wyman seeks to distinguish itself from other consulting firms in three main ways: first, by concentrating almost exclusively on the financial services industry; second, by assigning consultants to projects that effectively utilize their academic and work experience (in most consulting firms associate consultants are assigned to a "generalist pool" from which they are designated to projects by demand and availability); and finally, by implementing extremely selective hiring practices.

PROMISING FIRM

According to one piece of the firm's literature: "We hire people who have what it takes to become a director in our firm, and we realistically have the expectation that a significant number of our directors will do so (of our 20 directors, eight were hired from undergraduate or graduate schools)." The company's strategy appears to be paying dividends: its clients include major investment banks and commercial banks.

GETTING HIRED

Oliver Wyman recruits on campus at several prestigious undergraduate colleges and business schools around the U.S. Candidates are encouraged to either meet the company's campus representative, or send a resume, cover letter, transcript, and standardized test scores to the director of recruiting at the company's headquarters in New York (candidates in Europe should send their information to the London office). Oliver Wyman seeks individuals with outstanding intellectual capabilities and an interest in finance from an array of academic disciplines. Individuals without prior experience in consulting are hired as associate consultants.

Interviewing at Oliver Wyman is an exhausting affair. Most insiders report going through three rounds. The first two are full of case and "fit" interviews. Oliver, Wyman's case interviews range from the challenging to the ridiculous – insiders say there is absolutely no uniformity to the case interviews, and that interview styles are partner-specific. Alex Oliver, the firm's chairman, has a reputation for asking the weirdest cases, insiders report. Historically, the company has also stumped candidates with guesstimate questions.

The interviewers are, of course, examining the way a candidate analyzes each scenario. The key is to ascertain the specifics; as such, candidates should ask questions until they uncover complications and details of each case. Because each case tends to be quantitative, you should bring along a pencil and pad to work out difficult sums. However, insiders warn that candidates should be able to do the easy math in their heads. Because Oliver Wyman hires a number of mathematical wizards, hesitation on a simple addition or subtraction problem will not make a good impression. Once past the first two rounds, candidates are asked to a third and final round that can last a full day and is filled with more rigorous interviewing. "Oliver Wyman is basically looking for really, really smart people," reports one insider. "But we also want people who are pleasant to be around. We do the airport terminal test. In other words, if we can't stand the idea of being stuck in an airport with someone for a few hours, that person probably won't get hired."

OUR SURVEY SAYS

ONLY THE BRIGHT

Oliver Wyman's corporate culture tends to be on the young side, says one insider. "Oliver Wyman takes people straight from undergrad and then trains them on-the-job. The result is that people move up the ranks pretty fast around here. It's not unusual to find a 24-year-old manager." Not everyone is a fan of this on-the-job training, although most agree it is crucial in an industry as narrow as financial services. "People tend to have little or no 'real world' experience here. They are plucked right out of college and have no experience in either other firms or in the financial services industry itself."

WMS

"White male syndrome" is also a gripe of insiders at Oliver Wyman. "In the New York office," declares one contact, "we used to have more men named 'John' than we had women." That contact continues: "Oliver Wyman talks a lot about improving gender diversity, but it hasn't come through yet. Even though the partner-to-consultant ratio is good, in the history of the firm there has only been one female partner. And she left." Racial diversity tends to be a little bit better, but it still leaves "plenty of room for improvement."

A MIXED BAG?

In general, Oliver Wyman employees seem a mixed bag. Insiders call them "intelligent," "insecure," "smug," "talented," "good at what they do," and "immature." Regardless of reputation, however, the Oliver Wyman employees have plenty of opportunity for advancement. "If you're staffed on good projects and earn a name for yourself, you climb the ladder quickly," reports one contact "There are a lot of politics here, so it's important to prove yourself early in the game. If not, you'll get bogged down in all the competition."

Parthenon Group

200 State Street
Boston, MA 02109
(617) 478-2550
Fax: 617-478-2555
www.parthenon.com

LOCATIONS

Boston, MA (HQ)
London, England

THE STATS

Annual Revenues: $22 million (1997)
No. of Employees: 100 (U.S.)
A privately-held company

KEY COMPETITORS

Bain & Company
Boston Consulting Group
Mars & Company
McKinsey & Company

UPPERS

- Innovative equity compensation program
- Diverse array of case projects
- Paid benefits for maternity leave

DOWNERS

- Narrow recruitment from only a few select schools
- High performance pressure

EMPLOYMENT CONTACT

Eileen McBride
Recruiting Coordinator
Parthenon Group
200 State Street, 14th Floor
Boston, MA 02109

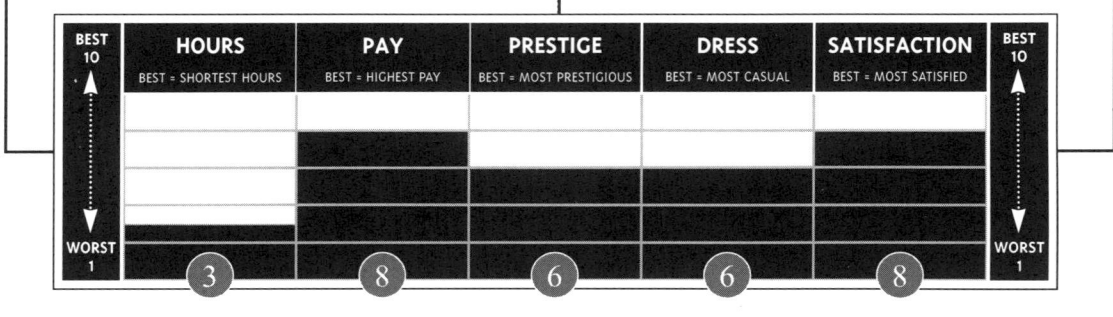

HOURS BEST = SHORTEST HOURS	PAY BEST = HIGHEST PAY	PRESTIGE BEST = MOST PRESTIGIOUS	DRESS BEST = MOST CASUAL	SATISFACTION BEST = MOST SATISFIED
3	8	6	6	8

THE SCOOP

The Parthenon Group took its name from the Acropolis temple honoring Athena Parthenos, the Greek goddess of wisdom and war. In a similar spirit of smarts and aggression, Parthenon has emerged a promising competitor in the eternal battle of strategy consulting firms. Founded in 1991 by William Achtmeyer and John Rutherford, two former directors of Bain and Company, Parthenon has expanded at warp speed despite its tender age. The company's revenues have jumped 20 percent annually.

Originally focused on financial services, Parthenon has expanded into a variety of other sectors, including media, publishing and communications, and retail. It has plans to expand to the West Coast and has already earned international recognition by planting an office in London. Despite fierce competition, Parthenon has managed to amass an impressive client list, which includes Microcom, Laura Ashley, Pepsi, Ocean Spray, and the AT&T Online Division. Like other small consulting firms, Parthenon also advises high-potential startups. Partheon claims that 80 percent of its assignments are CEO-level and is looking to further strengthen such boardroom relationships.

Parthenon is fond of separating itself from the pack on the basis of specific company codes. The firm prides itself on offering equity incentives to its employees because such compensation seems "a powerful tool for achieving peak performance." Since there is no requirement to specialize by level, MBA graduates who join Parthenon as "principals" are said to work on a broader-than-average range of client issues. Moreover, Parthenon likes to consider itself community-friendly and has actively supported public service projects like Bridge Over Troubled Waters and the Inner City Scharship Funds.

GETTING HIRED

Like all consulting firms, Parthenon seeks individuals with superior intellectual and interpersonal skills. It focuses its recruiting at a select number of top undergraduate and business schools. The number of full-time employees Parthenon hires per year varies, as that figure depends on the company's mercurial business needs. Parthenon also hires a limited number of business school students as summer associate. The program is designed to provide an opportunity for individuals interested in a consulting career to get their feet wet. During their stints, summer associates will receive extensive training and receive in-house mentors. Currently, summer associates are hired exclusively for Parthenon's Boston office.

Determined Parthenon interviewees would do well to acquaint themselves with the recruitment rhetoric of the industry. Since Parthenon's company literature is chock full of standard corporate phrases like "team player," "entrepreneurial spirit," and "risk taking," a careful and thoughtful response to these ideas is likely to earn points. Once on board, Parthenon employees begin as principals (MBAs) or associate consultants (undergrads). The organizational pyramid narrows to managing director, and at the pinnacle, the two founding partners. Parthenon states that there is no standard promotional track; rather, the pace of a new principal's progression is set by his or her experience and project team success. Consultants are hired as generalists, rather than being assigned to practice groups.

OUR SURVEY SAYS

Clients of Parthenon tend to be satisfied with the job performed. "They do the best analytical work around," reveals one enthusiastic client, while another states, "They make fairly aggressive and dramatic moves."

Parthenon is reported to have a better-than-average working environment as well. "Parthenon is a very exciting place to work – fast-paced, challenging, and very client-driven," says one insider. An associate reveals, "I often work side-by-side with senior clients and senior people at Parthenon. The level and rate of learning is high and requires associates to be creative, driven, and very analytical." Says another: "Working here is fun – we try to work hard, play hard, and enjoy some of the benefits of being in this field." As for the work culture: "Our environment is casual, both in dress and relationships. The hours are typical for the profession, as is the travel and pay."

Pittiglio Rabin Todd & McGrath

9 Riverside Drive
Weston, MA 02193
(617) 647-2800
www.prtm.com

LOCATIONS

Weston, MA (HQ)
Costa Mesa, CA • Dallas, TX • Mountain View, CA • Rosemont, IL • Stamford, CT • Washington, DC • Oxford, United Kingdom • Paris, France • Frankfurt, Germany • Glasgow, United Kingdom

THE STATS

No. of Consultants: 250 (worldwide)
No. of Offices: 12 (worldwide)
A privately-held company
Managing Directors: Michael McGrath and Robert Rabin

KEY COMPETITORS

Andersen Consulting
Booz•Allen & Hamilton
Diamond Technology Partners
Gartner Group

UPPERS

- Good lifestyle firm
- Genuinely helpful co-workers

DOWNERS

- No consulting positions for undergrads
- Business dress

EMPLOYMENT CONTACT

Karen O'Sullivan
Human Resources
Pittiglio Rabin Todd & McGrath
9 Riverside Drive
Weston, MA 02193

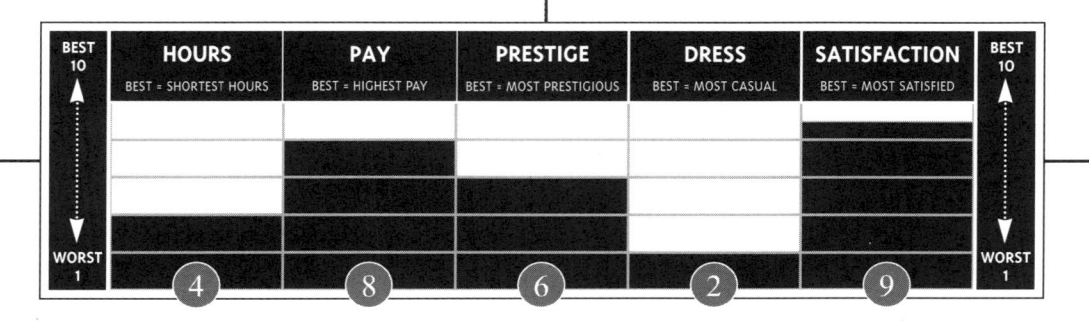

HOURS (BEST = SHORTEST HOURS)	PAY (BEST = HIGHEST PAY)	PRESTIGE (BEST = MOST PRESTIGIOUS)	DRESS (BEST = MOST CASUAL)	SATISFACTION (BEST = MOST SATISFIED)
4	8	6	2	9

THE SCOOP

ALL TECH, ALL THE TIME

With headquarters in both California's Silicon Valley and Boston's Route 128, Pittiglio Rabin Todd & McGrath is positioned to serve as the management consulting firm of choice to the technology industry. But this company, founded in the bicentennial year of 1976, does not reserve its technical know-how just for the high-tech elite. Pittiglio also dispenses its knowledge to small and mid-sized companies, and even a few startups. Thanks to annual revenues that have risen by an average of 30 percent over the last two years, the firm is expanding its reach into the biotech, pharmaceutical, and telecommunications industries and has plans to double its consulting force by the year 2000.

THE CURRENT STATE OF AFFAIRS

Doubling in size by 2000? An ambitious goal – especially – since the millenium is so close. Right now, Pittiglio Rabin Todd & McGrath (PRTM) is a smallish consulting firm, with about 300 consultants worldwide. The firm has three geographic regions: the Eastern, with offices in Weston, MA; Stamford, CT; Chicago, and Washington DC; the Western division, which has offices in Dallas, Costa Mesa and Mountain View, CA; and the European region, with offices in Frankfurt, Paris, Oxford and Glasgow. Consultants must be pleased with all the changes at PRTM – the turnover rate has been running less than 10 percent for some years, well below the industry average.

GETTING HIRED

PRTM's hiring qualifications are very stringent. All of the firm's consultants have MBAs (most from from top schools) and have technical and management backgrounds (including technical undergraduate degrees). Volunteers one insider: "We have many consultants with multiple masters degrees or doctorates." The firm posts contact information and its on-campus MBA recruiting schedule at its web site, located at www.prtm.com. PRTM hires first-year business school students as summer associates. The firm also hires undergrads for a two- to three-year research analyst position.

Applicants can mail resumes to the firm's Eastern headquarters in Weston, MA, or to the Western regional headquarters at 650 Town Center Drive, Suite 820, Costa Mesa, CA 92626. Recruiting contact e-mail addresses are available at the firm's web site.

MBA candidates can expect one or more on-site visits with "three or four 45-minute interviews." Insiders suggest that candidates highlight their experience with actual company operations: "Since we implement improvements in companies, we want to hire people who have actually done something in a company, rather than those who have just performed studies or analysis."

OUR SURVEY SAYS

ENJOYING THE LACK OF STRUCTURE

Pittiglio consultants enjoy their "unstructured environment" and "autonomy" so much that they leave their firm far more infrequently than their peers at other consulting firms; the turnover rate at Pittiglio is 10 percent, "well below" the industry average. Part of the reason for the high morale is the "pretty laid-back" culture, "especially for a management consulting firm." Says one insider: "We have a very supportive environment in which we all do our best to help each other out."

THE LIFESTYLE FIRM

Moreover, Pittiglio consultants neither travel as frequently nor work as rigorous a schedule as those at rival firms; 70-hour workweeks, insiders say, are a "rarity." One consultant reports working from "40-hour weeks to 70 – normally, [workweeks are] closer to 45 or 50." Says one consultant: "While other firms talk about a focus on lifestyle, PRTM puts its money where its mouth is. Traveling consultants get every other Friday off, and nobody works weekends." The firm's travel policy in the past has also allowed spouses to "travel for visits on weekends." Still, PRTM consultants cannot escape the grueling travel that characterizes the consulting industry. One insider reports that PRTM "can spend up to a year working at a client site, but we always go home on weekends and usually go home on Thursday nights." And the consultants at PRTM don't get to kick back with business casual dress, it's "business dress unless the client requests differently."

IMPLEMENTATION ORIENTED

One insider also distinguishes the firms from its competitors when it comes to its business model. "We are very implementation oriented," he says. "We do not just write a report for a client and leave. We will do an initial diagnosis and requirements study." Recent hires say that they are "constantly impressed" by the expertise of their colleagues, including senior consultants who are "eager to help new consultants grasp the subtleties of the business."

PricewaterhouseCoopers

1251 Avenue of the Americas
New York, NY 10036
(212) 596-7000
Fax: (212) 790 6620
www.pwcglobal.com

LOCATIONS

New York, NY (HQ)
PricewaterhouseCoopers has offices in 116 cities around the U.S. and 867 offices worldwide.

THE STATS

No. of Employees: 140,000 (U.S.)
No. of Offices: 116 (U.S.)
A privately-held company
CEO: James Schiro
Chairman: Nicholas Moore
Year Founded: 1998

KEY COMPETITORS

American Management Systems
Andersen Consulting
Deloitte Consulting
Ernst & Young
KPMG Consulting

UPPERS

- Hiring like mad
- Huge company = wide choice of locations and opportunities
- Solid benefits
- Solid benefits, nifty laptops

DOWNERS

- Gigantic and confusing
- Hideous logo
- Nifty laptops needed due to extensive travel

EMPLOYMENT CONTACT

Human Resources
PricewaterhouseCoopers
1251 Avenue of the Americas
New York, NY 10036

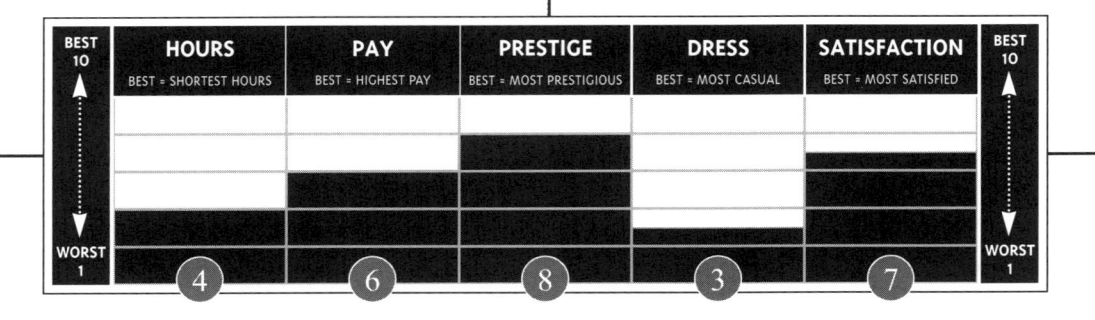

HOURS	PAY	PRESTIGE	DRESS	SATISFACTION
BEST = SHORTEST HOURS	BEST = HIGHEST PAY	BEST = MOST PRESTIGIOUS	BEST = MOST CASUAL	BEST = MOST SATISFIED
4	6	8	3	7

THE SCOOP

THE BIGGEST OF THE BIG FIVE

Those of you who thought the Big Six financial services firms were due to become the Giant Four are half right. While the planned merger of KPMG and Ernst & Young fell by the wayside, Price Waterhouse – the smallest and perhaps most prestigious of the former Big Six – and Coopers & Lybrand managed to put one and one together. On July 1, 1998, the awkwardly named PricewaterhouseCoopers was born. To celebrate, employees in Los Angeles supped "Merger Beer," brewed especially for the occasion.

The joke around PwC is that the companies paid a design firm $10 million to create its new logo and look – upon which Andersen Consulting paid that designer $20 million to screw it up. But no one's going to mess with PricewaterhouseCoopers right away – this is a daunting firm. PwC has 140,000 employees and 9000 partners around the globe, with projected annual revenues of $15 billion yearly. Consulting revenues, if the firm had been combined in 1997, would have been $3.23 billion (that's just a jot behind leader Andersen Consulting). More than 30,000 PricewaterhouseCoopers employees currently work as consultants.

THE FRIENDLY MONOLITH

Despite its jaw-dropping size, PricewaterhouseCoopers would like to convey the message that it is no faceless monolith. The firm began a huge advertising drive in September 1998, featuring mostly black and white photos of staff members, in order to promote the "human face" of gigantic PricewaterhouseCoopers. PwC plans to use its new size to truly bring about a globally integrated firm. Roughly 90 percent of its revenues will be generated within the integrated organization, though some practices, such as those in Japan and Korea, will not be integrated for some time (owing to regulatory and cultural concerns). The leaders of PwC believe that the bigger a firm is, the faster it grows, and that the new bulk of PwC will create an inexorable "breakaway firm" that will far exceed the reach of any competitor.

A FEW MINOR ISSUES

Competitors point out that skills also matter. Already, competitors have been taking advantage of the changes at PwC to steal away its "network" firms. Five percent of PwC member firms are still talking terms, and branches from Chile to Zambia have defected to competitors like Grant Thorton and Arthur Andersen. PricewaterhouseCoopers clearly sees these defections as short-term considerations. The firm has stated that it plans to become a $30 billion firm by the year 2005. Post-merger, PricewaterhouseCoopers has become a true giant; in a time when every company that has ever made an overseas call touts itself as having an international presence, PwC is truly a globalized firm with a presence in 152 countries and 867 offices worldwide.

SCHIRO'S WORDS

New CEO James Schiro has been traveling the world to rally PricewaterhouseCoopers' 9000 partners. "I was born excited," Schiro was quoted as saying. "I tell our partners that if they were born excited, they have to stay that way. If not, they should get excited." And, if nothing else, the massive new firm on the scene, PricewaterhouseCoopers, is something to get excited about.

GETTING HIRED

PricewaterhouseCoopers Consulting has adopted an approach that Coopers & Lybrand used to good effect in 1997.

"First, we will do presentations on campus," confides one insider. "We will tell people who are interested to apply online. Then, we use the online applications to screen through the on-campus applicants and make up our recruitment schedules. So it's really not possible to sneak into the interviewing schedule." Candidates will be notified by phone (and also online, if they're enterprising enough to check). Interviews are given on campus by a partner or senior manager. Those brought back to the office are interviewed by three or four partners and managers. Two associates or analysts will take the consulting candidate out to lunch in the middle as a de-stresser. Despite this break, "it's a long day."

OUR SURVEY SAYS

A RELAXED ATMOSPHERE

PwC insiders enjoy their culture. "The people here are young – between 24 and 35," reports one insider. "It is a relaxed atmosphere, and people feel very comfortable about going out for a drink together after work. It is a very social place if that is what you choose, but you are never made to feel guilty for not participating in any activities or parties." Speaking of parties, "there are usually lots of them going on – mostly going away parties. Big Five firms are notorious for high turnover. That's not a reflection on the company, just the nature of the beast." "The people here are friendly and fun," says one consultant. "There is always lots of work to do, and you also have lots of freedom to do whatever you have to in your personal life outside of work, even during work hours."

DRESSING LIKE CONSULTANTS OR ACCOUNTANTS?

On-site dress for consultants varies according to the client's specifications, "though we always try to dress a bit better than the client employees." While at the office, "it's professional Monday through Thursday, and business casual Friday and all summer."

ON THE MERGER

What do insiders say about the massive merger? Most are cautiously optimistic. "With the merger, we are expected to gain more experience from the increased clientele base that we already have as the merged firm," suggests one consultant. Another points out that "since the merger our benefits have increased. We now get three weeks vacation, healthcare and a 401(k) (the firm matches 20 percent). PwC employees have 10 paid holidays, plus 15 vacation days to start (and 22 vacation days after two years)."

Another consultant speculates about the PwC kulturkampf. "Coopers was known to be the most laid back of the Big Six firms in terms of things like dress code and workplace environment. The merger with the more conservative Price Waterhouse presents interesting questions regarding clashing cultures." That insider continues: "There is no way to know what type of personality the combined firm will take on, particularly at this early stage, when most offices haven't even been combined yet. Both firms were huge and the combination results in a sort of a colossus."

LONG HOURS ON OFFER

Like most consulting firms, PwC offers its employees long hours. For most, "work hours are what you make them. If you become a workaholic, like many do, then you can work all the time. If you're disciplined enough, you can work 8 to 5, Monday to Friday." However, says that contact: "No one gets overtime – you just work until the job gets done." Another business consultant complains: "The hours suck. I won't lie. You will have to work an average of 50 to 60 hours a week." Much of this long workweek involves travel – though consultants say that the "traveling policies are nice." When traveling, you "have a very nice laptop," and "stay at nice hotels and have enough money to eat well. Most people are on the road during the week, leaving on Monday and returning Thursday evening." Though Big Five firms aren't known for their generous pay, "I feel that the pay is competitive," says one consultant. "The truth is that three years ago the pay was very low, but the firm has taken strides in improving that."

BIG BUT FLEXIBLE

"An organization as big as PwC will need everyone it can get," says one insider, and befittingly, PricewaterhouseCoopers has shown marked signs of flexibility. "The firm would rather see you stay part-time than leave because of their inflexibility," reports one contact. "While the truth is that there are few female partners, that seems to be changing." "I know a woman," says one consultant, "who was recently promoted to partner while working part-time." Ethnicity and race seems to be "no consideration whatever, though a firm with 140,000 employees is bound to have one or two bad apples. But only one or two!"

To order a 50- to 70-page Vault Reports Employer Profile on PricewaterhouseCoopers call 1-888-JOB-VAULT or visit www.VaultReports.com

The full Employer Profile includes detailed information on PwC's departments, recent developments and transactions, hiring and interview process, plus what employees really think about culture, pay, work hours and more.

Renaissance Worldwide

189 Wells Ave.
Newton, MA 02159
(617) 527-6886
Fax: (617) 965-4807
www.rens.com

LOCATIONS

Newton, MA (HQ)
More 100 offices in the U.S. and worldwide

THE STATS

Annual Revenues: $286 million (1997)
No. of Employees: 6,500 (worldwide)
No. of Offices: More than 100 (worldwide)
Stock Symbol: REGI (NASDAQ)
CEO: G. Drew Conway

KEY COMPETITORS

Arthur Andersen
Booz·Allen & Hamilton
Cambridge Technology Partners
Gemini Consulting
Computer Sciences Corporation

UPPERS

- Company gym
- Off-site meetings
- Employee stock option plan
- Friday company lunches
- Profit sharing
- Three weeks vacation for new full-time employees
- Tuition reimbursement

DOWNERS

- Long hours
- Skimpy 401(k) program

EMPLOYMENT CONTACT

Worldwide Recruiting
Renaissance Worldwide Inc.
70 Wells Ave.
Newton, MA 02159

(617) 527-4812
mforbes@rens.com

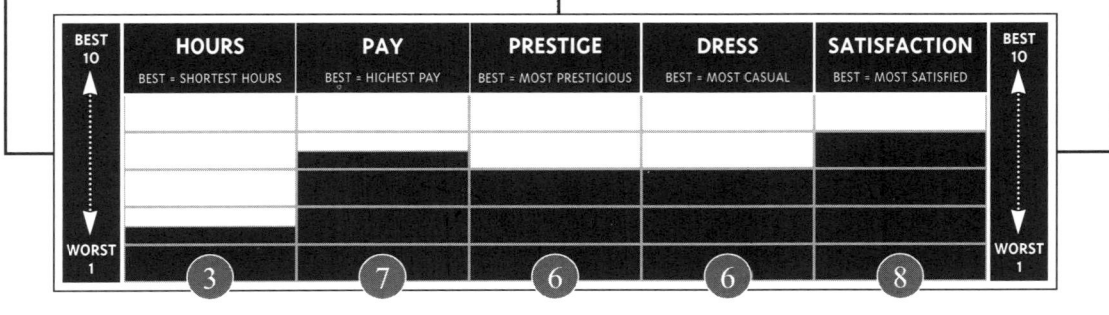

HOURS BEST = SHORTEST HOURS	PAY BEST = HIGHEST PAY	PRESTIGE BEST = MOST PRESTIGIOUS	DRESS BEST = MOST CASUAL	SATISFACTION BEST = MOST SATISFIED
3	7	6	6	8

THE SCOOP

CHILD OF MERGERS

Renaissance Worldwide is the product of a 1997 merger between Massachusetts-based management consulting firm Renaissance Solutions and IT consulting firm the Registry Inc. The firm offers strategy consulting – and can help you install your software too. (That's what's called implementation.)

SCORE!

Previous to the merger, Renaissance Solutions won accolades in both *Fortune* and the *Harvard Business Review* for its Balanced Scorecard concept. The Balanced Scorecard is the creation of Renaissance Solutions CEO David P. Norton, who is president of Renaissance Worldwide's strategy group, and who helped found Renaissance Solutions in 1992. The fundamental premise of the Scorecard is that "measurement motivates behavior;" the Scorecard modifies that behavior to provide a forward-looking management system. *Fortune* once estimated that "less than 10 percent of strategies effectively formulated are effectively executed." However, Renaissance claims that the Balanced Scorecard supplies a framework that ensures that its business strategies are part of the small percentage that are successfully implemented.

GOING SHOPPING

In December 1996, Renaissance Solutions bought ISS Corporation in the first of its major acquisitions. In February 1997 Renaissance acquired two other firms, COBA Boston and COBA Consulting in the U.K., giving the firm a considerable boost in its computer, telecommunications, energy, and utility industry services. And in July 1997, Renaissance merged with The Registry, Inc., then a 350-member firm offering information technology consulting services. Companies contract techies such as software engineers from the firm rather than hire on a full-time basis.

AN IT BENT

Since the merger, the firm has continued to gobble up competitors, buying IT consulting and systems integration firms. Most notably, the firm acquired The Hunter Group, a leading international consulting firm providing management consulting and systems implementation. (The Hunter group has been an implementation partner for PeopleSoft since 1989.) In 1998, the firm's name was changed to Renaissance Worldwide. Including the tech consultants, Renaissance Worldwide now includes more than 6,500 consultants.

GETTING HIRED

Renaissance seeks associate candidates with liberal arts degrees and GPAs of 3.6 or higher. Candidates should be poised under pressure, possess strong analytical and problem-solving skills, writing, editing, and research skills, a familiarity with basic business concepts, the ability to master database software, and they must be proficient with major software packages. The firm especially likes candidates with degrees in computer science, electrical engineering or management information systems, and with computer programming language proficiencies such as C/C++, Visual Basic or other higher-level languages.

The firm also hires MBAs for higher-level positions. For its MBA/MS recruiting, Renaissance targets the top MBA programs as a key source for consultants. Renaissance lists its openings on its web site at www.rens.com/employmt.htm. Inquiries and resumes should be addressed to: Cynthia Tsakonas, director of Recruiting & Employment, at the firm's Massachusetts headquarters or via the Internet at cynthia tsakonas@rens.com.

OUR SURVEY SAYS

AN INNOVATIVE ENVIRONMENT

Employees describe the corporate culture at Renaissance as "innovative," "creative," and "a place where risk-taking is rewarded." The dress code is "casual all summer, and on Fridays the rest of the year." The hours are "long, but typical for consulting," and the perks include travel – one associate reports spending 10 months on a project in Amsterdam and four on a U.K. engagement. The people are "friendly, fun, and helpful, especially compared to other consulting firms."

THE HISTORIC RECORD ON DIVERSITY

With regard to the treatment of minorities, one contact cites the philosophy of David Lubin, co-founder of Renaissance Solutions, who "expressly brings up the example of Pompeii on this subject; archaeologists found evidence of many different cultures in the ruins of Pompeii, and this was the strength of the city." Similarly, Renaissance is "very aggressive on promoting diversity," not as "an end in itself but because it brings strength to the organization."

THE ART OF RENAISSANCE

Insiders say the work at Renaissance is "definitely more art than science." And while that art transpires during "long" and "demanding" hours, one consultant claims to have "only worked seriously on three weekends in the four years I've been here." Employees, even those in the graphics department and other support staffs, "always feel like part of a team." One respondent reports that the "traits" for which he was hired are "given full reign."

Vault Reports Guide to the Top Consulting Firms

Renaissance Worldwide

To order a 10- to 20-page Vault Reports Employer Profile on Renaissance Worldwide call 1-888-JOB-VAULT or visit www.VaultReports.com

The full Employer Profile includes detailed information on Renaissance's departments, recent developments and transactions, hiring and interview process, plus what employees really think about culture, pay, work hours and more.

Consulting Job Seekers: Receive free e-mailed job postings matching your interests & qualifications! Register at www.vaultreports.com

"I've only worked seriously on three weekends in the four years I've been here."

– *Renaissance insider*

San Francisco Consulting Group

49 Stevenson Street
7th Floor
San Francisco, CA 94105
(415) 777-0721
www.sfcg.com

LOCATIONS

San Francisco, CA (HQ)

THE STATS

No. of Employees: 20 (worldwide)
No. of Offices: 1 (U.S.)
A privately-held company
CEO: Craig L. Doré

KEY COMPETITORS

Diamond Technology Partners
Monitor Company
Mitchell Madison Group
Marakon Associates

UPPERS

- Reasonable hours
- Full array of medical and dental insurance with no cost to the employee
- 5-10% salary bonuses

DOWNERS

- Pay below industry norms
- Very small firm

EMPLOYMENT CONTACT

Human Resources
San Francisco Consulting Group
Three Embarcadero Center
Suite 1700
San Francisco, CA 94111

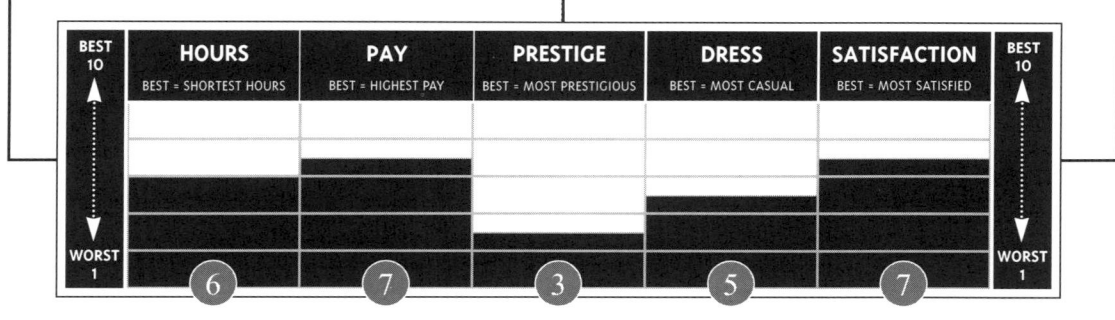

HOURS	PAY	PRESTIGE	DRESS	SATISFACTION
BEST = SHORTEST HOURS	BEST = HIGHEST PAY	BEST = MOST PRESTIGIOUS	BEST = MOST CASUAL	BEST = MOST SATISFIED
6	7	3	5	7

© Copyright 1998 Vault Reports, Inc. Photocopying is illegal and expressly forbidden.

Vault Reports Guide to the Top Consulting Firms
San Francisco Consulting Group

THE SCOOP

A HOME IN TELECOM

Founded in 1976, the San Francisco Consulting Group (SFCG) has found its niche in the highly competitive telecommunications industry. Acquired by KPMG Peat Marwick in 1995, the firm made its name providing consulting services to phone giants like AT&T, MCI, Sprint, and the baby Bells. The firm focuses on the regulatory, competitive, and technical changes in telecom. SFCG also serves smaller carriers and government and corporate telecommunications operations, and offers advice on the telecommunications industry to manufacturers, systems developers, and the investment community. SFCG doles out advice in four main areas: Business Strategy, Network, Systems, and Performance Improvement. A small but growing company, SFCG's sales have grown about 40 percent annually for the past five years, as the deregulation of the telecom industry drives companies to seek out new markets.

GETTING HIRED

SFCG looks for applicants who can work well with clients and attack problems from a general management perspective, with a strong record of academic achievement and work experience. Hiring two to three consultants each year, the firm actively recruits at top business schools in the U.S. The recruiting process usually includes a few rounds of on-campus interviews followed by an invitation to a daylong visit and interviews at SFCG's offices. There is no formal summer internship program at SFCG. Visit the "Career Opportunities" section of SFCG's web site for details on positions including research analyst, consultant, manager, director and others.

OUR SURVEY SAYS

THE PAY/LIFE TRADEOFF

SFCG gives employees time to enjoy their West Coast surroundings, with most consultants working less hours (for less pay) than industry norms. "We tend to work 40 to 55 hours per week," says one employee, "as opposed to 55 to 75 for most other firms." Employees describe a friendly atmosphere and speak highly of co-workers. Says one insider, "The culture is very friendly. Everyone is very bright and driven, while at the same time relaxed, nice, and interesting."

EVERYONE LIKES KPMG

With a relatively diverse work force, one employee notes that "we are definitely an equal opportunity employer," especially when it comes to research analyst positions. Employees say the recent acquisition of SFCG by KPMG Peat Marwick (now called KPMG) yielded positive changes, including a jump in vacation time from two to four weeks each year. The dress code is "formal with casual Fridays."

"Everyone is very bright and driven, while at the same time relaxed, nice, and interesting."

– *SFCG Insider*

Stern Stewart & Company

1345 Avenue of the Americas
New York, NY 10105
(212) 261-0600
Fax: (212) 581-6420
www.sternstewart.com

LOCATIONS

New York, NY (HQ)
Chicago, IL • London, England • Sydney, Australia • Johannesburg, South Africa • Buenos Aires, Argentina • Bogota, Colombia • Sceaux, France • Munich, Germany • Wellington, New Zealand • Lidingo, Sweden • Danderyd, Sweden • Istanbul, Turkey

THE STATS

No. of Offices: 2 (U.S.) 13 (worldwide)
A privately-held company
CEO: G. Bennett Stewart

KEY COMPETITORS

Boston Consulting Group
KPMG Consulting
Marakon Associates
McKinsey & Company

UPPERS

- Opportunities to work in international branches
- Self-managed pension plans

DOWNERS

- Strict dress code – women are not allowed to wear pants
- Few women in the company

EMPLOYMENT CONTACT

Mr. Ashley Joffe
1345 Avenue of the Americas
New York, NY 10105
Fax (212) 581-6420

ajoffe@sternstewart.com
careers@sternstewart.com

HOURS	PAY	PRESTIGE	DRESS	SATISFACTION
BEST = SHORTEST HOURS	BEST = HIGHEST PAY	BEST = MOST PRESTIGIOUS	BEST = MOST CASUAL	BEST = MOST SATISFIED
2	8	5	1	6

© Copyright 1998 Vault Reports, Inc. Photocopying is illegal and expressly forbidden.

THE SCOOP

THE VALUE-ADDED FIRM

Stern Stewart was founded in 1982 by Joel M. Stern and G. Bennett Stewart III. They were the developers of the Economic Value Added (EVA®) system, a value-based performance-measurement tool at the center of Stern Stewart's consulting business. Since the company was founded, more than 300 corporations have hired the firm to install the EVA system. Among these are AT&T, Coca-Cola, and Eli Lilly. Stern Stewart's program rates a company's profitability by determining the difference between returns and the cost of capital. The companies that employ EVA adjust executive bonuses and stock options according to the system.

MAINTAINING THE LEAD

Other companies have introduced similar products, including The Boston Consulting Group's Total Business Return (TBR); but for the moment, New York-based Stern Stewart is the leader of the fiscal measurement pack, mainly because it was the originator of that type of tool. It has also maintained its status with strong marketing efforts. The company publishes articles in financial journals and trade magazines, and offers seminars around the world. In addition, G. Bennett Stewart, the original "EVAngelist," (an officially trademarked term) wrote a book on the subject called *The Quest for Value*. Because EVA only rates a company's past performance, Stern Stewart recently introduced a companion performance measurement, Market Value Added (MVA®), which allows companies to gauge how current fiscal strategies will pan out.

SCANDAL

In 1995, while auditing Stern Stewart's books, accounting firm KPMG Peat Marwick created its own consulting service, based on unusually familiar tool called "EVM," or Economic Value Management. The company then hired away three Stern Stewart employees: Senior Vice President Thomas Jones, and two consultants to set up the practice. Stern Stewart filed a lawsuit against the firm charging that Jones stole client lists, a laptop, and computer disks containing an EVA manual. However, the firm had difficulty proving that EVA was a proprietary concept, as the company had promoted its publication

THE FEUD

In August 1997, a judge ruled that KPMG had abused its relationship with Stern Stewart, but did not find it accountable for unfair competition theft of trade secrets. In November 1997, the feud was revived when KPMG sponsored a conference on EVM, and invited several Stern Stewart clients to address the participants. An incensed G. Bennett Stewart wrote to several of those clients, reminding them of EVM's tainted origins. Three of the candidates reneged, prompting KPMG to retaliate with a federal lawsuit, charging Stewart with libel and slander.

GETTING HIRED

Click on the "Career Opportunities" link on the Stern Stewart web page, located at www.sternstewart.com, for information on the analyst and associate positions. Undergraduates with a background in finance, accounting or economics may apply for the analyst position. Associates should hold an MBA or equivalent higher degree, and have several years of professional experience. Overall, the firm looks for candidates with strong analytical and computer skills. In addition, the company prides itself on being an entrepreneurial organization, and particularly favors self-starters.

Resumes and cover letters should be posted, faxed or e-mailed to Mr. Ashley Joffe at the firm's New York headquarters.

LONG HOURS IN INTERESTING SURROUNDINGS

Analysts and associates at Stern Stewart "typically work from 9 a.m. to 9 p.m. or later," and "at least one day per weekend, especially in the beginning." But you'll be surrounded by "fun, interesting" co-workers who "actively share information," and "are very helpful when you have questions." Plus, late-night dinners and car service can be charged to the client. Insiders describe a "strong team spirit" in the firm's "academic environment." One says there's "very little attitude or office politics" to deal with. However, contacts do warn that the corporate culture "demands that you really apply yourself," and that "it takes a while to perform some of the analysis." This "can be really frustrating," sources say, "but once a problem is resolved, you feel very gratified."

LOVE THAT PENSION PLAN

Salaries "are competitive with other top consulting firms," and employees enjoy "lots of vacation time." Stern Stewart also offers a unique pension plan in which employees manage their own accounts. Newcomers to the company like the fact that "many first-year analysts travel internationally within six months of arrival." There is also the option to work in one of Stern Stewart's international offices. Insiders stress the fact that working at Stern Stewart "opens up your options for the future." They point to the company's "good reputation," and the schmoozing opportunities "in a diverse range of industries and companies."

NO CREATIVITY IN DRESS

For a company founded in the 1980s, Stern Stewart has an extremely restrictive dress code. The company goes way beyond 'professional dress,' requiring women to wear skirts every day. They are only 'officially' allowed to wear pants suits when they are traveling. "On occasion one deviates," says a female analyst, "but risks a scolding from our office manager (a woman)." She goes on to say that employees "are all hoping that this will change as more women join the firm." Aside from the dress code, women in the company report being "treated as total equals" by male co-workers, "though there are no female VPs to date."

"There are no female VP's to date."

– *Stern Stewart insider*

Strategic Decisions Group

2440 Sand Hill Road
Menlo Park, CA 94025-6900
(650) 854-9000
www.sdg.com

LOCATIONS

Menlo Park, CA (HQ)
Boston • New York • Houston • London, England • Caracas, Venezuela • New Delhi, India • Singapore

THE STATS

No. of Employees: 250 (worldwide)
No. of Offices: 8 (worldwide)
Year Founded: 1981

KEY COMPETITORS

Booz•Allen & Hamilton
Boston Consulting Group
Integral
Monitor Company
Parthenon Group
ZS Associates

UPPERS

- Associates can choose their projects
- Real possibility for partnership
- Well-stocked kitchens
- Good representation of women

DOWNERS

- Not a party firm
- Few ethnic minorities
- Erratic schedules

EMPLOYMENT CONTACT

Human Resources
Strategic Decisions Group
2440 Sand Hill Road
Menlo Park, CA 94025-6900

recruiter@sdg.com

HOURS (BEST = SHORTEST HOURS)	PAY (BEST = HIGHEST PAY)	PRESTIGE (BEST = MOST PRESTIGIOUS)	DRESS (BEST = MOST CASUAL)	SATISFACTION (BEST = MOST SATISFIED)
3	8	6	3	8

© Copyright 1998 Vault Reports, Inc. Photocopying is illegal and expressly forbidden.

THE SCOOP

THE SMART CONSULTING FIRM

SDG was founded in 1981 in Menlo Park, California, with an eye toward mixing academia and business. It has since grown to 260 employees in six worldwide offices, but its consultants have maintained their bookish bent. Jim Matheson, a co-founder of the firm and managing director of the firm's Boston office, and his son David Matheson, a principal in the London office who heads the European arm of the firm, recently published a book called *The Smart Organization*, in which the father-son team argues that today's corporations need to overhaul their decision-making strategies.

A PANOPLY OF INDUSTRIES

SDG's international management consulting group serves senior management from some of the world's largest corporations in a variety of industries, including oil and gas, high tech, automobiles, information services, and pharmaceuticals. SDG also helps smaller companies looking to expand. One third of the firm's engagements involve research and development strategy, mostly in technology and portfolio strategy at business unit and R&D management levels. The firm's counts among its clients 27 Fortune 500 companies, including Bayer, Shell, Hewlett-Packard, General Motors, and GE Capital. In addition, SDG does pro bono work for non-profit organizations.

HELLO TO INDIA

In February 1998, SDG entered the Indian market through the formation of a joint venture with Eicher Consultancy Services Ltd., India's top private consulting firm. The new company, based in New Delhi, will be comprised of two divisions: ECS-Operations Consulting, and SDG-Strategy Consulting. Each side controls a 50 percent stake in the company, and ECSL acts as the holding company for the new firm. ECS will focus on the operations consulting market, and SDG will deal with strategy issues. ECSL's managing director is CEO of the new firm; SDG's Dr. Carl Spetzler is its chairman.

GETTING HIRED

SDG hires BAs as business analysts; MBAs and PhDs are hired as associates. Candidates are hired through a three-round process. First-round interviews are conducted on the phone, on campus, or in one of the firm's offices. The second round consists of several 'case questions' so that "we can measure the candidate's business, analytical and interpersonal skills." Sources say questions "are not stressful by design, and do not include any 'trick' questions." The third round is "primarily used to verify 'cultural fit'" with the company. Several employees point out that senior partners make the time to take part in the process – in fact candidates "usually meet with one of the founders of the firm."

"No mind games" reports one source about SDG's hiring process, who says few other firms were as honest as SDG in the recruitment process. One of our contacts reveals that interviewees "are allowed to talk as much as you want with real people about their work at the firm." Another consultant observes that SDG's interviews "are more interesting and in-depth than those of others I've experienced," but says one negative aspect of the process is that "it's decentralized across offices." Another reported negative is that the firm sticks to "somewhat low-budget" recruiting presentations – some insiders complain that there is "not enough 'glossy material.'"

Although the firm may not expend a lot of energy on written recruiting materials, insiders note that for candidates, it's important to put a lot of effort into your resume and cover letter – one insider remarks that during the initial screening of resumes, there is a "real likelihood of passing over hidden gems." The fact is, "we look at 200 resumes to hire five people." The process doesn't get any easier once a candidate gets through the resume screen. SDG consultants describe the interview process as "very intense," but "personal and friendly." "Talk to us about values," advises one recent hire. "SDG knows exactly what skills it is seeking, and is very up front about that." One source tells Vault Reports that "we actively seek individuals with strong analytical skills," which translates into "a major or minor in a quantitative discipline, such as economics, mathematics or the physical sciences."

OUR SURVEY SAYS

HAPPY AND CHAOTIC

SDG certainly has its fans – and a lot of them work for the firm. "If you want to do real strategy consulting," SDG is "the best place to work," claims one happy insider. "The firm has a strong methodological bent, which makes our work analytically challenging and interesting." Just make sure you're "comfortable working every day with technical modeling tools and explaining your results to senior management teams." Employees describe SDG as a "team oriented," "entrepreneurial firm" where "anyone can achieve anything." One contact warns that "the unstructured environment can be a bit chaotic at times," so SDG "may not be a good fit for someone who likes the road well-traveled." "The firm is very receptive to proactivity," says one source, "and there are plenty of opportunities to take initiative." In addition, associates are actively involved in shaping their careers at the firm: "I completely choose which projects to work on," one consultant insists, "based on my professional development goals." That consultant adds: "Besides the travel requirement, the firm basically allows [associates] to create the job we want in life."

THERE IS NO BOSS HERE

SDG consultants are "very intellectual and collegial," "honest," and "passionate about shared values." Our contacts also point out that they are "supportive, not competitive." "There are very few incidents of empire building or other selfish behavior" one consultant says. "People work for the benefit of all." In addition to "really challenging and interesting work," recent hires appreciate being able to "speak directly and honestly with anyone at any level."

"SDG pushes the non-hierarchical envelope" reports a principal. Employees on every level at SDG agree. "We typically don't think supervisor/subordinate," says one associate. "People are encouraged to treat others with respect, regardless of position." "The barriers between levels of people at SDG are very low," says another associate. "I am treated as an equal by everyone – including the CEO – and I treat everyone with that same respect." "We have a very rectangular organizational structure at SDG," explains one associate (that's as opposed to the rigid hierarchical "pyramid" structure of most organizations). One senior associate, however, makes sure we know that there is still some sense of hierarchy at SDG: "We're quasi-democratic. Everyone's voice gets heard. Good ideas are implemented. But there is still a place where the buck stops."

DREAM ON

Although those who come into the firm with undergraduate degrees generally leave for business school after two or three years, others at SDG generally plan to grow old with the firm. SDG "has an extremely low turnover rate for the industry [the firm reports an 8 to 10 percent attrition rate], and most MBAs at this selective firm say they're in it for the long haul." Says one insider: "Much of our turnover is voluntary, and individuals who have the desire to stay with the firm are usually successful in making partner." Another contact agrees: "The attitude is that there is room at the partner's table for everyone."

Not surprisingly, many consultants at SDG call it their "dream company." "If you just want to work somewhere for two years, this is not the place for you" remarks an associate. "This company is more a place to build a career than a jump-off point." "I do not believe I would enjoy my job as much with another firm," one consultant says. "I turn down a lot of calls [from headhunters]." Another source concurs: "I would not work in consulting if it weren't for SDG."

ERRATIC HOURS

Hours "tend to be erratic," say consultants. "Some weeks are 80, some are 35, but it balances out." Most insiders report hours evening out at between 50 and 60 hours. One source claims that SDG "doesn't have the 'churn and burn' style of other companies," and says, "you do have a fair amount of control over the timing." Consultants say they're "on the road three weeks out of four, sometimes more," but most feel that the firm has "respect for lifestyle issues." Don't think that this means extra time to party with your colleagues, though. After hours, most of the firm's consultants are "more family-oriented than firm-oriented in their off hours"

ADEQUATE PAY, PERKS, DIVERSITY

Business analysts and associates describe their salaries as "adequate." Those at higher levels, on the other hand, are quite delighted. Including bonus, business analysts can expect to make upwards of $56,000. Associates make anywhere from $96,000 to $125,000. Senior associates earn anywhere from $100,000 to $175,000. Principals pull in around $400,000, while directors make approximately $600,000. "After the first year, everyone's salary is measured by the same standard, regardless of their prior education and experience."

Perks at SDG include Friday lunches and "generous provisions in staff kitchens." Luckily, the firm subsidizes gym memberships so consultants can work off all the extra calories. Employees also praise the firm for sponsoring "good, family-oriented social events," including annual picnics and holiday parties. Then, of course, there are "all the perks associated with frequent business travel" (mostly tons of frequent flyer miles). In addition, the firm provides each consultant with a professional development account – that's "$2000 each year to spend on anything that contributes to your professional development, such as books, magazines, computer software, association membership fees, etc." Benefits are "outstanding," and the firm offers (in-house) "graduate-level courses to employees in a number of different disciplines." Consultants throughout the firm office praise the "top-notch" support services. One of our contacts at the company's Menlo Park headquarters praises the "editorial and desktop publishing units" in particular, noting that they "are extremely competent and professional."

Contacts report that there are many female consultants and partners at SDG, "including the managing director of the Menlo Park office – the firm's largest office." In addition, the firm is very receptive to minorities – "particularly gays," notes one source. However, insiders admit that "the firm has not been successful in attracting as many [minority] candidates as we would like."

Towers Perrin

335 Madison Ave.
21st Floor
New York, NY 10017
(212) 309-3400
www.towers.com

LOCATIONS

New York, NY (HQ)
Other locations in the U.S. • Europe • South America • Asia

THE STATS

Annual Revenues: $1.1 billion (1997)
No. of Employees: 7,251 (U.S.)
No. of Offices: 89 (worldwide)
A privately-held company
CEO: John Lynch

KEY COMPETITORS

Andersen Consulting
Buck Consultants
Ernst & Young Consulting
Hewitt Associates
PricewaterhouseCoopers
Watson Wyatt Worldwide

UPPERS

- Flexible and relatively short hours
- Revamped training programs

DOWNERS

- Low pay relative to other management consulting firms
- Stigma of being HR shop

EMPLOYMENT CONTACT

Human Resources
Towers Perrin
335 Madison Ave.
21st Floor
New York, NY 10017

recruiting@towers.com

HOURS (BEST = SHORTEST HOURS)	PAY (BEST = HIGHEST PAY)	PRESTIGE (BEST = MOST PRESTIGIOUS)	DRESS (BEST = MOST CASUAL)	SATISFACTION (BEST = MOST SATISFIED)
4	6	7	7	6

© Copyright 1998 Vault Reports, Inc. Photocopying is illegal and expressly forbidden.

THE SCOOP

THE TOWER OF HR

Towers Perrin, a firm especially known for its human resources consulting services, has been in the business for more than 60 years. It offers services through three operating units: Towers Perrin, the management consulting unit; Tillinghast, which offers actuarial and risk management services, primarily to the insurance industry; and Towers Perrin Reinsurance, a major reinsurance intermediary. The firm serves clients throughout the world, including governments, the private sector, educational institutions, and nonprofit organizations. Among these clients are 333 of the world's 500 largest companies and nearly 700 of the Fortune 1000. Towers Perrin has repeatedly reaffirmed its commitment to remaining a privately-held company. Instead of offering stock to the public, the firm distributes stock to its employees through an incentive program.

THE LONG HISTORY

Towers Perrin traces its roots back to 1871 and a Philadelphia firm called Henry W. Brown and company. In 1934, four of that firm's partners formed Towers, Perrin, Forster & Crosby, specializing in reinsurance and employee benefits consulting. By the 1960s, the firm had branched out throughout North America, and by the 1970s, it had an international presence. At that point it began acquiring other consulting firms, thereby expanding its offerings. In 1987, the firm changed its name to Towers Perrin. Throughout this decade, the company has continued to grow through acquisition. Its prime targets have been international firms and health care consultancies. In 1998, the firm bought the North American Risk & Insurance Services arm of Watson Wyatt, a Bethesda, MD-based consulting firm. The unit was absorbed by Tillinghast-Towers Perrin, the firm's insurance and risk-management division. Soon after, the firm purchased Miller/Howard, an Atlanta-based change-management specialist.

THE EXPERTS ON WHAT YOU WANT

Towers Perrin has responded to the rising demand for expert assistance by narrowing the range of expertise of each individual consultant while broadening the range that these consultants cover together. Within Towers Perrin (the management consulting unit, as opposed to, say, Tillinghast), there are three major divisions: human resources and general management consulting; employee benefit services; and health industry consulting.

The human resources and general management consulting division, which is the division that offers services most like traditional management consulting in the mold of McKinsey or BCG, has four broad categories: business strategy, organization strategy, people strategy, and change management. Because of the rest of the firm's expertise with human resources policies, "people strategy" is perhaps Towers Perrin's best-known offering. The firm stresses "alignment," making sure that all HR activities – from staffing to pay and performance management – support their clients' business strategy.

STREAMLINING ITS BUSINESS

Recently, Towers Perrin has been streamlining and consolidating its business in an effort to become more profitable. The firm dumped several of its smaller defined contribution clients in early 1998, citing the prohibitive cost of making all of its customized software Y2K compliant. According to executives, the firm only dropped clients in cases where the cost of repairing the individually customized software outweighed the value of its relationship with the client. Also in 1998, Towers decided to grow its asset consulting practice (like asset management for retirement and pension funds, only on a consulting basis). At the same time however, it wants to limit clients of that business to those which bring other business, like actuarial or benefit design work.

GETTING HIRED

Students as well as applicants from the working world can submit resumes for consulting positions via conventional mail or e-mail (for students: crecruiting@towers.com; others: recruiting@towers.com). The firm's web site is chock full of recruiting information. One employee cautions that "you may want to ask about turnover in your interview. Some offices and units are more turbulent than others, and you should be cautious if there is quite a bit."

Insiders say that "generally, at the undergraduate analyst level, the company looks for people with degrees in communications, math, economics, or another business-related degree." As far as MBA grads, the firm prefers people with at least two or three years of work experience, though "whether the job experience or the MBA comes first is not important." The firm feels work experience gives candidates "a better understanding of what business is all about." Towers Perrin would reportedly rather hire someone "with common sense and a good attitude" than a "summa cum laude Harvard graduate," although "a hot GPA never hurts."

Insiders report a three-round hiring process. The first round usually consists of "two half-hour case interviews." In the second round, insiders say, you get two "45-minute case interviews." For the third round, candidates "are given a case and 45 minutes to develop a presentation, which you give in front of the interviewer." Our contacts say this type of case interview "is nerve wracking in the beginning, but it's easier than the traditional case questions because you have time to organize and prepare." What's important is that you understand the industry mix the firm deals with – "that way you can anticipate what the case questions will be about."

New MBAs join as "unaffiliated associates." Guided by officers and/or principals, consultants work with clients early on, and perform duties such as fact finding, analysis, survey planning, and report preparation and presentation. MBAs thus develop a specialty and preferred area of concentration on their own. MBAs also have the flexibility to determine their degree of specialization. As Towers Perrin says: "If you're one of the world's most knowledgeable people in a given area, no matter how narrow, demand for your skill is usually tremendous. On the other hand, if someone combines consulting skills with managerial skills, there are many opportunities for further growth and development."

OUR SURVEY SAYS

NOT JUST HR

Consultants give the firm high marks: "Towers Perrin is a great home away from home," where "business keeps booming and the company takes care of you," says one. Though most people know it as "the HR consulting firm," insiders are quick to point out that Towers has a "significant and growing general management consulting division." Several contacts say that "most people in general management consulting want nothing to do with the human resources side." "People are supersensitive about proving that they are not HR," says one put-off insider. The irony is, "a lot of the work has an HR bent – the management consulting side tends to take the 'people' aspect into account."

BELOW-AVERAGE PAY AND A BIT SKIMPY ON THE PERKS

However, consultants complain about the "rigid promotion schedule" and confide that "Towers does not pay particularly well." The pay "does not quite match up," says one. "Starting consultants get the going rate, but as you go up the scale, the increases are less," says one insider.

Consultants get some of the typical industry perks: "frequent flyer miles," and "good, comfortable travel." Back at the office, "if you are working on a client account, you can bill meals and a ride home after 8 p.m." If they're on a long business trip, Towers pays for consultants to fly home on weekends. However, insiders say, "we don't have the option of flying to another city if it's cheaper – like in most other firms." Contacts also report that vacation "isn't great" – "two weeks a year for the first five years, and then it goes up to three weeks."

BUT GOOD WORK/LIFE BALANCE

But employees say they are drawn to the firm because "it's good at balancing work and life. You can easily have a decent career and not be working every weekend." As one recent summer associate recounts, "there was one female partner had to leave early every day to relieve her nanny, and a male consultant who had a long commute. As long as you get your work done, they allow for things like that." Insiders say the firm is "seriously committed to allowing consultants to achieve a balance between work and life outside of it."

"Towers Perrin officially has a 7.5-hour workday," says one insider, "but everyone generally puts in eight hours or more." "There's no face time," says another source, "you don't have to be there until 9 at night if you're done with your work." Consultants "might have to work a weekend or two," but "hours are still less than at other consulting firms, and travel is not so bad."

WE HAVE AGENCY

Sources say one of the best things about working for Towers Perrin is "the level of responsibility they give you once you proved you can handle the work." Summer associates and recent hires also appreciate "the opportunity to deal with senior management both at Towers Perrin and the client organization." Another plus – "you can ask to be staffed on projects – you basically keep your ear to the ground and find out what projects are coming up, and you ask if you can work on them."

The firm recently "improved its training programs, so now undergrads are guaranteed two or three weeks of training every year in addition to the initial orientation program." New hires "start working right away for a few months, and after they begin to understand what the business is all about, they go to consultant training – where they learn things like supply chain analysis, how to run a focus group, how to do better presentations, and other skills." The firm also offers the Towers Perrin Institute, where consultants are trained in areas where their skills are weak. One insider from the general management consulting side, however complains that "the Towers Institute focuses more on the HR side."

THE TOWERS PERRIN CONSULTANT CADRE

Towers Perrin culture "really varies by office," but sources from different outposts say they enjoy a "small company culture within a more secure big corporate structure." The firm now "has a business casual dress code" which "saves a lot on dry cleaning bills," though some consultants are still "rarely seen out of sharp suits." Some insiders describe the office atmosphere at Towers as "loose" and "relaxed," even to the point that it is sometimes "disorganized."

Consultants enjoy working with "razor-sharp" colleagues in a "rigorously professional" environment where the level of competition is "healthy" but "definitely not negative." "The people are terrific to work with and are, for the most part, in their mid-20s to mid-30s," reports one insider.

When it comes to the diversity of the consultants, most insiders say Towers is doing well. "Women are well represented on every level in both HR and management consulting," reports one source. In many offices, report consultants, "there are more women than men." The numbers aren't so good for other minorities, however. Says one insider: "They treat minorities and gay people well, though there are very few here." Another Towers consultant offers an explanation. "We have difficulty recruiting women and minorities," reports that contact. "The qualified candidates tend to go to more prestigious firms."

"Most people in general management consulting want nothing to do with the Human Resources side."

– *Towers Perrin insider*

Vertex Partners

10 Post Office Square, Suite 700
Boston, MA 02109
(617) 292-0990
Fax: (617) 292-0994
www.vpartners.com

LOCATIONS

Boston, MA (HQ)

THE STATS

No. of Employees: 55 (U.S.)
No. of Offices: 1 (U.S)
A privately-held company
CEOs: Mike Evanisko, Jim Kalustian

KEY COMPETITORS

Integral
Parthenon Group
Pittiglio Rabin Todd McGrath
Strategic Decisions Group
ZS Associates

UPPERS

- Friendly company with excellent training program
- Personal-growth oriented corporate culture
- Lots of responsibility for new employees

DOWNERS

- Small size of company can lead to claustrophobia and stress
- Few locations

EMPLOYMENT CONTACT

Ms. Rachel Golder
Associate Director of Recruiting
Vertex Partners
10 Post Office Square, Suite 700
Boston, MA 02109

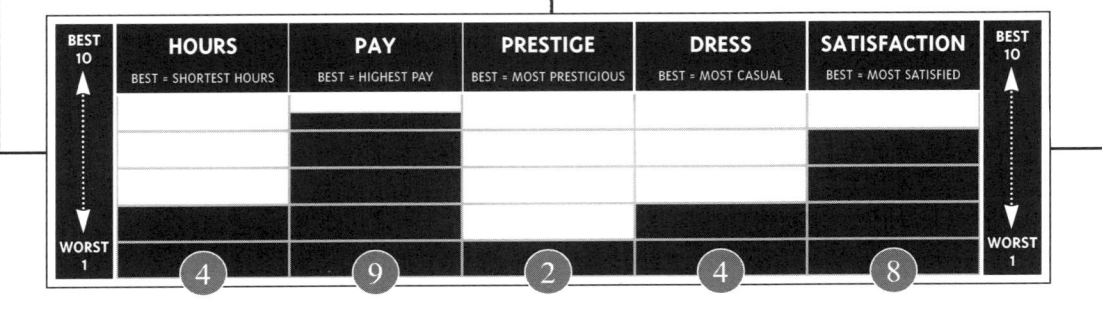

HOURS	PAY	PRESTIGE	DRESS	SATISFACTION
BEST = SHORTEST HOURS	BEST = HIGHEST PAY	BEST = MOST PRESTIGIOUS	BEST = MOST CASUAL	BEST = MOST SATISFIED
4	9	2	4	8

© Copyright 1998 Vault Reports, Inc. Photocopying is illegal and expressly forbidden.

THE SCOOP

THE NEW KID ON THE BLOCK

With squadrons of suit-wearing consultants already streaming through companies worldwide, could there be room for one more consulting firm? Vertex thinks so, and the rapid growth of their partnership may have proved them correct. Founded in 1994 by disenchanted consultants formerly employed by many leading management consulting firms (including Mike Evanisko, the founder of Boston consulting company Corporate Decisions Inc.), Vertex claims that the industry norm involves storming into client companies, behaving obtrusively, then producing impractical, "C+" solutions. Vertex, on the other hand, concentrates on clearing up strategy and implementation troubles in a pragmatic and workable manner. This "roll up the sleeves" attitude has thus far boosted the growth of the young company.

MAXIMIZING VALUE

Vertex, true to its name, strives to offer a sharp focus to its clients. The firm works mostly with Fortune 500 companies, especially those involved in healthcare, and their international equivalents. The company does not reengineer, downsize hapless workers, or implement information technology. Its goal is maximizing the profit margins of its clients without resorting to these large-scale changes.

CREATING A PLEASANT PLACE FOR CONSULTANTS

At the same time, Vertex aims to optimize the workplace experience for employees. The company professes to support creative thinking, a balance between personal and professional life, and teamwork rather than turbulent competition. Most notably, Vertex claims to offer hours which do not detract from – and may even be conducive to – a personal life. Since the founders of Vertex were themselves refugees from other consulting firms, the company actively battles employee attrition and likes to boast of a better-than-average retention rate. Still, to stay at Vertex one must first get in the door. Although Vertex is rapidly growing, only

20 percent of first-round interviewees are called back for the second round, making this fledgling company as competitive as its elders.

GETTING HIRED

The new and ambitious Vertex is in an expansion phase, with both associate and consultant positions available. The company recruits at prestigious liberal arts universities (Harvard, Yale and Brown) and business schools (Wharton, Yale, and Harvard Business School) in the East, but welcomes applicants outside its recruitment cycle. The firm also hires a small number of summer associates (four in 1998). That program includes a two-day orientation program and two days of off-site training, along with a slew of social events, like Red Sox games and barbecues.

Vertex hires consultants from a variety of majors and backgrounds, but warns candidates to do their homework on both the company and consulting in general before coming in for their interviews. Indeed, candidates must be thoroughly prepared if they are to have any chance of being hired. Vertex accepts only 20 percent and 30 percent of candidates for first- and second-round interviews, respectively. Candidates should expect to meet with "at least six" consultants before receiving an offer. After interviews, interviewers meet as a group to discuss candidates. Once accepted, employees can look forward to an intense, two-week training program, but should not expect a systematic program of advancement. At a small firm like Vertex, it's almost impossible to predict career paths.

Applications are accepted via letter and fax. Vertex has a flat organizational structure, with four positions on the professional consulting staff – associate consultant (the lowest rung), consultant, manager, and partner. Undergraduates and those with advanced degrees outside of business fields generally enter as associate consultants, while MBA-holders from top business schools start as consultants.

OUR SURVEY SAYS

THE BIG LITTLE COMPANY

For a "little company," employees say they work on "a wide variety of projects, from mergers and acquisition cases to salesforce restructuring." Major clients include, but are not limited to, the "pharmaceutical industry and communications and technology industries." The consensus seems to be that "Vertex is a great place to work" and a "worthwhile experience." Benefits and salary are "competitive with other leading consulting firms"; perks include tuition reimbursement for associates who return to Vertex after business school, a 401(k) plan and health club membership subsidies. The firm's year-end bonus for consultants has two components: a bonus based on corporate performance targets, and a bonus based on individual performance.

Consultants report that the company "fosters an environment that values creativity, teamwork and a balanced lifestyle." Furthermore, employees enjoy "a high degree of autonomy" if they display the proper initative. Says one consultant: "Because the firm is still very small, you have excellent access to the top people and a minimum of bureaucracy and office politics."

However, lilliputian size does have its drawbacks. Employees cite "nonexistent" opportunities to work at overseas branches since Vertex is still based only in Boston, although "we have golobal clients, so some consultants will experience international travel." Overall, however, Vertex consultants agree that the best aspect of the firm is the network of people. For the most part, the intimate size of Vertex fosters camaraderie and collaboration among all employees, from the associates to the seasoned partners. One insider sums up: "The people here make a tremendous difference."

Watson Wyatt Worldwide

6707 Democracy Boulevard
Suite 400
Bethesda, MD 20817
(301) 581-8056
www.watsonwyatt.com

LOCATIONS

Bethesda, MD (HQ)
Other offices in the U.S. and international locations

THE STATS

Annual Revenues: $513 million (1998)
No. of Employees: 5,100
No. of Offices: 89 (worldwide), 30 (U.S)
A privately-held company
CEO: A.W. Pete Smith Jr

KEY COMPETITORS

Andersen Consulting
Buck Consultants
Hewitt Associates
PricewaterhouseCoopers
Towers Perrin

UPPERS

- Flexible relocation policies
- HR experience means ultrasensitivity to consultant concerns
- Employee-owned firm
- Business casual dress

DOWNERS

- HR concentration less prestigious than strategy
- Stress on billable hours

EMPLOYMENT CONTACT

Steve Sharpe
Director of Business Services
Watson Wyatt Worldwide
6707 Democracy Boulevard
Suite 800
Bethesda, MD 20817

careers@watsonwyatt.com

HOURS (BEST = SHORTEST HOURS)	PAY (BEST = HIGHEST PAY)	PRESTIGE (BEST = MOST PRESTIGIOUS)	DRESS (BEST = MOST CASUAL)	SATISFACTION (BEST = MOST SATISFIED)
4	7	6	5	7

© Copyright 1998 Vault Reports, Inc. Photocopying is illegal and expressly forbidden.

Watson Wyatt Worldwide

THE SCOOP

CONSULTING FOR PEOPLE

With more than 5000 associates in 36 countries, Watson Wyatt is one of the world's leading consulting firms focusing on human resources consulting. Traditionally, the firm's core businesses have been actuarial work and designing benefit and pension plans for clients. More recently, Watson Wyatt has built a business around helping clients set up benefit "call centers"– a service used by a company's employees (especially those in foreign lands) who have human resources questions.

For more than 50 years, Watson Wyatt has worked with companies of every scope, from the largest multinationals to public employers to nonprofits. The Maryland-based firm traces its origins to an actuarial firm founded in 1946 called The Wyatt Company. In 1995, the firm merged with British benefits firm R Watson & Sons, becoming Watson Wyatt Worldwide. The firm counts corporate giants in a wide array of industries, such as high tech (America Online, IBM), aerospace and defense (Lockheed Martin) and pharmaceuticals (Glaxo Wellcome), among its clients. In the last decade, the firm has expanded aggressively internationally, which it feels is increasingly necessary to serve clients with their own worldwide businesses – and employees stationed around the world. "We first went global because we thought it might be practical," Vice President Kevin Meehan told the *Washington Post*. "But we didn't start becoming profitable globally until we started concentrating on clients and clients' needs globally."

MOTIVATED AT WATSON

Watson Wyatt has some very motivated employees: The firm is wholly owned by its active staff. Watson Wyatt likes to present itself as a learning firm, committed to the growth of its people. Individual career development at Watson Wyatt is focused on developing employees in technical and/or consulting expertise, industry knowledge, consulting process, and business management acumen. A highlight of employee training is the Watson Wyatt Harvard Leadership Program, a weeklong program held at the Harvard Business School and led by prominent HBS faculty. The program covers critical leadership concepts in management, strategy, and implementation.

RECENT PROBLEMS

With its rapid international expansion, Watson Wyatt has hopes to become the world's leading workplace consulting firm. In recent years, however, the firm has seen revenues stagnate and profits drop, as it struggled with a venture into total benefit oursourcing (completely taking over a client's management of benefits). Called Wellspring, and owned 50/50 by Watson Wyatt and State Street Global Advisers, that venture was launched in 1996. Although Wellspring counted major American companies like AT&T and Sears, Roebuck & Co. among its clients, Watson Wyatt backed out of the capital- and systems-intensive business in 1998, taking a $59 million write-off to cede ownership of the venture to State Street. Largely because of the problems with Wellspring, Watson Wyatt took a $126 million loss in 1998. In exiting the venture, the firm said it would be able to concentrate on its core HR consulting businesses.

GETTING HIRED

Watson Wyatt's hiring criteria are demanding. Associates must have top grades and be prepared to demonstrate their academic performance by providing test scores, papers, and honors from rigorous programs. Open positions, which can be searched for by geographical region, are listed on the Watson Wyatt web site at www.watsonwyatt.com. According to the company, "a degree or background in computer science, communications, mathematics, economics, health care, or business will provide a foundation for success with Watson Wyatt," though "many of our associates have degrees in the sciences, humanities, or the law." The firm will respond to all electronic inquiries, but not to telephone inquiries. To apply for a position, fax or send a resume by regular mail.

OUR SURVEY SAYS

A FLEXIBLE WORKPLACE

Watson Wyatt is recognized by its employees as "one of the leading benefits consulting firms in the world," with a "broad range" of careers within the company. There is a "definite growth track" for consultants with Watson Wyatt, as well. A "recent perk" to the job is that the firm has implemented "year-round business casual dress." There are many "financial incentives" within the company. In addition to "more than generous base salary," employees receive "periodic bonuses." Another bonus – a "two-day training seminar each fall, with ample time devoted to fun." While there are "few set holidays," the firm offers "adequate paid time off (PTO) which, if not used, can be moved forward, within limits." One employee says that the "co-workers and pay are what keep me here." Another insider, a late sleeper, is happy that "Watson Wyatt offers flex time – we can start any time between 7:30 and 10:00."

EVER ON THE ROAD

Consultants "travel constantly" and, for that reason, "it is not your typical 9 to 5 job." "Billable hours are important here," says one consultant, "the more, the merrier everyone is." However, "the company is willing to transfer employees, and has been known to create openings in offices where there aren't any, just to accommodate an employee who needs to relocate." Employees report no "overt, or covert" attempt to "keep women or minorities out of career growth goals," and several employees report having female supervisors. According to insiders, Watson Wyatt "is a company that cares as much about keeping its employees happy as it does about making a profit."

William Kent International

2101 Wilson Blvd., Suite 1100
Arlington, VA 22201
(703) 351-7654
Fax: (703) 351-7654
www.wkint.com

LOCATIONS

Washington, DC (HQ),
Los Angeles, CA
Beijing and Shanghai, China
Mumbai, India
Rio de Janeiro, Brazil

THE STATS

No. of Employees: 120 (worldwide)
No. of Offices: 6 (worldwide)
A privately-held company
President: William H. Kent

KEY COMPETITORS

Bain & Company
Boston Consulting Group
Mars & Company
McKinsey & Company

UPPERS

- Performance-based promotions
- Tuition subsidies (75%) for relevant external classes
- Short-term projects (3-5 months)
- Exciting international travel

DOWNERS

- Recent restructuring
- Less than lavish salaries (for consulting)
- Minimal administrative support

EMPLOYMENT CONTACT

Betsy Shimko, Recruiting Director
William Kent International
2101 Wilson Boulevard, Suite 1100
Arlington, VA 22201

(703) 516-7920
Fax: (703) 276-7749
bshimko@wkint.com

HOURS (BEST = SHORTEST HOURS)	PAY (BEST = HIGHEST PAY)	PRESTIGE (BEST = MOST PRESTIGIOUS)	DRESS (BEST = MOST CASUAL)	SATISFACTION (BEST = MOST SATISFIED)
3	7	6	3	8

THE SCOOP

A UNIQUE NICHE

William Kent International (WKI), the international strategy consulting specialist, occupies a unique niche within management consulting. Founded in 1966 by William H. Kent in response to globalization trends in industry, WKI focuses solely on helping its clients take advantage of international opportunities. Guided by the philosophy that the future, for most companies, lies in international markets, WKI developed a process known as the Global Resource Repositioning to find untapped markets for its multinational clients. In its more than 30 years, WKI has provided its services in 85 countries, including nearly every developing nation worldwide. WKI works primarily for large, multinational Fortune 500 companies or their international equivalents. WKI's industrial and consumer industry clients range from aerospace to food to companies, and include U.S.-based Rockwell International and DuPont International, and Japan's Toshiba.

INCREDIBLY DIVERSE GROUP OF CONSULTANTS

WKI consists of 120 employees worldwide, from Mongolia to the Ukraine, who offer considerable international expertise and experience, and together speak 37 languages. Every WKI consultant has a country of expertise, but also internationally diverse work experience. Based on thorough analysis, case teams come up with a strategy and help to implement an action plan for their clients. In some cases, the firm's consultants even start up and run the client's new business in the target market. This expertise doesn't come cheap. Fees for three- to five-month projects have price tags with five- to seven-digit figures. Recent projects include a product manufacturing strategy in Australia and a market entry project in Turkey.

GETTING HIRED

WKI recruits for two positions. Undergraduates are recruited primarily from top Ivy League schools to fill associate consultant positions. For consultant positions, WKI actively recruits MBAs from the top B-schools. WKI also advertises in *The Economist*, and accepts mailed applications and resumes from other "leading institutions." (Roughly 80 percent of MBAs come from seven top business schools, mainly Stanford, Wharton and Chicago.) WKI looks for candidates that have very strong quantitative, analytical and communication skills, and an international background. Previous experience overseas is prized and speaking a foreign language is said to be "highly regarded," although based on the WKI employee profile, it appears to be a requisite. Over half of the firm's consultants speak three or more languages. WKI uses a resume screen and multiple interviews to evaluate candidates. Applications should be addressed to Recruiting Director, Betsy Shimko.

Veterans of the recruiting process say WKI has a very simple approach: "They're not into bells and whistles during the presentation," explains one source. "They just make it clear that they are looking for a definite sort of candidate." They want people "who are interested in all the basic consulting shit, but really want an international focus." Our contacts reveal that "there are some people who only speak one language, but they definitely have that commitment to dealing internationally."

OUR SURVEY SAYS

WKI IS THE WORLD

WKI consultants say the diverse composition of the workforce makes the firm's corporate culture pretty unique. Insiders say the firm's CEO is pretty conservative, thus "the corporate culture exists despite him, not because of him." "Because we're all kind of well-traveled," one source explains, "we tend to be very liberal." On average, consultants "speak at least three languages, though there are some who speak only one." Though you will probably travel to countries where you'll put your language skills to use, consultants point out that because the company is so small, "everyone eventually gets sent to a country where they don't know the language. So sometimes it doesn't matter whether you know those extra languages."

My pals at WKI

One of our contacts reports that "the people that get hired here are from completely diverse backgrounds, but we fit a very specific profile – we're all international. Most of us are world culture kids, we've moved around all our lives, lived in lots of places. It's cool working with group of people who have had such similar types of experiences, though they may be completely different."

These similar backgrounds foster a unique level of camaraderie, which is strengthened by the fact that WKI consultants are basically forced (by circumstances) to socialize with each other outside the office. "If you're hanging out after work," one consultant explains, "it's probably with someone from WKI." The reason? Timing. Explains one contact: "You travel internationally all the time, and when you're home, you're usually in the office." When they're spending a third of their time overseas and an average 60 hours in the office the rest of the time, it's no wonder consultants complain that "it's hard to maintain a social life." "You end up hanging out with people from work." Another contact agrees: "You have to devote so much of time to the company that eventually all your friends are from WKI." Consultants at the company headquarters (right outside Washington, DC) say "we all go out in DC together – we tend to drink heavily and party a lot." Some insiders claim that "we do more dancing than boozing." One source describes the office as "a very collegiate atmosphere" where you start to view your co-workers "as your brothers and sisters." He goes on to add that "because we're all from different ethnic groups, there are a lot of slightly off-color jokes going around – I think that's really another indicator of how comfortable we are with one another."

THE POWER OF THE POSITION

Most WKI employees live in DC, and the average consultant is around 23 or 24 – "the only 'older' people there," reports one contact "are the CEO, who's probably in his 60s, and the VPs, who are between 30 and 35." Consultants are generally recruited straight out of college. "Most of us spend two years there and move on." You're not required to leave, but as one source puts it, "after a while, people sort of realize it's about that time." One former consultant who describes the job as "totally amazing," describes a typical consultant's experience: "For the first nine months you are working hard, and engrossed in making ends meet. You spend an inordinate amount of time trying to get your work done, and worrying that you just won't be able to. But then you reach the level where you realize you can get it all done. This is the most enjoyable period, because you have such a sense of power and control in your job." Continues that one contact: "But after a while, the job becomes predictable. The people that are attracted to this place are the kind who thrive on challenges, variety and excitement – they're used to moving around. So when things becomes predictable, they leave."

MOVING ON

After WKI, consultants do a wide variety of things, though "just about everyone does something international." Some travel or go to business school; some move to the client side, move to other firms, "one even went to Canada and opened a bakery." The relationships built at William Kent last far beyond the company's halls. One former consultant says: "Even though I'm not there anymore, I know what's going on in the office every day; and I have several friends [who have also left] that I speak to almost every day." Employees also like the fact that they get to meet people as they travel. As one sentimental WKI insider puts it, "William Kent will definitely change your world view – it makes you realize the world is a very small place."

LACKLUSTER SALARIES BUT, OH, THE TRAVEL!

Salaries are "not very competitive for the industry" sources say, "entry-level consultants make 40k to start." However, consultants say "we stay in five-star hotels, all of our expenses are covered, and we get to take an amazing number of cool vacations." When at home, consultants "bill late meals" and get to take a car home after 8 p.m." In addition, there are a lot of business dinners and company functions – including the yearly retreat to the CEO's farm in Pennsylvania, which one insider describes as "two or three days, of games, sports, and lots of boozing." Oh yeah, and everyone gets full benefits, three weeks vacation, a 401(k), and flextime for employees with children. On the downside, sources say the company "has always had minimal administrative support." For example, there is no production department, one source says. "Everyone does their own slide production."

WOMEN RARE BUT WELCOME

There are very few women at WKI – one insider estimates that they account for only 15 percent of consultants. But that source goes on to add that women are "absolutely treated as equals. There are absolutely zero respect issues." The company is quite racially diverse, however – as one source put it, "we don't have a lot of 'minorities' according to the American definition, (there are no African Americans, for example), but many people here are immigrants. There are people from India, China, South America and Europe." In response to changes in the international scene, WKI implemented a significant restructuring in October 1998, paring down some of its staff while hiring others.

ZS Associates

1800 Sherman Ave., Suite 700
Evanston, IL 60201
(847) 492-3600
www.zsassociates.com

LOCATIONS

Evanston, IL (HQ)
Menlo Park, CA • Princeton, NJ • London, England • Frankfurt, Germany • Paris, France

THE STATS

No. of Employees: 225 (worldwide)
No. of Offices: 6 (worldwide)
A privately-held company
CEO: Andris A. Zoltners
%Male/%Female: 70/30

KEY COMPETITORS

Andersen Consulting
Arthur Andersen
Arthur D. Little
Booz•Allen & Hamilton
Strategic Decisions Group
Vertex Partners

UPPERS

- Great client contact
- Casual dress
- Paid maternity leave
- Deep area knowledge

DOWNERS

- Limited exposure to diverse industries
- Little travel
- Small consulting firm means somewhat limited choice of engagements

EMPLOYMENT CONTACT

Sally Johnson
Human Resources
ZS Associates
1800 Sherman Ave., Suite 700
Evanston, IL 60201

Fax: (847) 492-3409
zshr@zsassociates.com

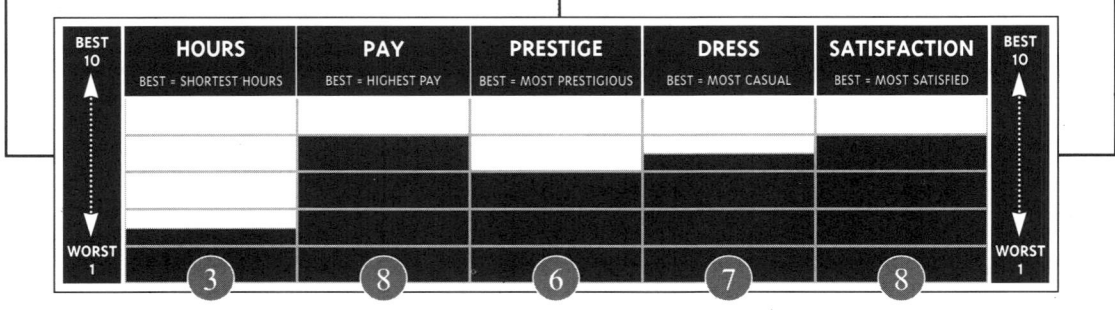

HOURS BEST = SHORTEST HOURS	PAY BEST = HIGHEST PAY	PRESTIGE BEST = MOST PRESTIGIOUS	DRESS BEST = MOST CASUAL	SATISFACTION BEST = MOST SATISFIED
3	8	6	7	8

THE SCOOP

AN ACADEMIC BIRTH

ZS Associates was the brainchild of two professors at Northwestern University's Kellogg Graduate School of Management. What began as moonlighting for Andris Zoltners and Prabha Sinha (the Z and the S in the name) quickly became a global management consulting firm. The two entrepreneurs realized that they could apply their academic research to "real life," and much more profitably. Since 1983, ZS Associates has expanded its expertise in the pharmaceutical industry to 18 industries in 60 countries. Today, the firm maintains Zoltners and Sinha's academic bent: half of all ZS consultants have graduate degrees. Forty percent of ZS consultants are MBAs or MS holders; 10 percent are PhDs. The consultancy has its headquarters in Evanston, Illinois, a stone's throw from Northwestern, where the two founders still teach at the Kellogg Graduate School of Management. Other offices are in Princeton, New Jersey (another college town), Menlo Park, California, and Reading, England. In an effort to strengthen its Latin America business, the firm will open a Miami office in 1999.

TEAM ZS

Associates at ZS form "teams" of two to four people, which include technical associates (who design and develop software for specific projects) and associates who analyze the data. ZS Associates emphasizes its status as a "global" consulting firm – it conducts 40 percent of its business outside of the U.S. Its clients are primarily Fortune 500 companies and their affiliates. ZS engagements are concentrated within the pharmaceutical, health care, and biomedical industries. Almost half of the firm's engagements involve marketing strategy and strategic marketing analysis. Other ZS specialties include forecasting sales and geographic sales territory alignment. Sales territory alignment is aided by ZS' specialized software, MAPS. From 1988 to 1995, ZS enjoyed a 21 percent annual growth in revenue, and more than 80 percent of ZS business each year comes from repeat customers. While ZS has worked in industries ranging from health care to media and communications to durable goods, keep in mind that since its founding, close to 90 percent of its hours have been spent on clients in the pharmaceutical industry. In addition, the firm tends to have long-standing relationships with its clients. As one consultant puts it: "ZS is very specialized. We almost exclusively work with pharmaceutical firms and their sales and marketing strategies – some people might want more variety."

GETTING HIRED

ZS Associates hires BAs as business associates, and MBAs as senior-level consultants. The company wants "smart, ambitious people" with strong math and quantitative skills. See the company web site for the latest recruiting calendar. Though it encourages students from other institutions to apply. Resumes and cover letters should be mailed, not faxed, to the Human Resources department. Potential applicants can also email resumes to careers@zsassociates.com.

Interviews for undergraduates usually consist of two "painless" rounds: "one on campus and one in the office." MBAs endure three "case interview-based rounds," the last of which "involves a group case and presentation." "The firm stresses quantitative ability," notes a consultant, who adds, "it's important not to get bogged down by the case questions." One source describes them as "easy quantitative questions to test your problem solving skills." A recent interviewee advisesthat "the case is likely to deal with a sales force issue, so it would be a big plus if you already know something about sales forces."

Prospective employees also field behavioral and background questions meant to assess your "fit" with the company and how you work with others. Interviewers will "also ask you about leadership skills." Sources say it's crucial that you "demonstrate interest in ZS and show you have learned a little about the firm beforehand."

OUR SURVEY SAYS

THE CASUAL, SEA LION-RIFE CULTURE

ZS Associates is similar to other consulting firms in its selective hiring, "demanding" hours and "competitive" salary. What sets it apart is its casual corporate culture. Insiders say "jeans are the uniform." Consultants only wear suits "when they're going to meet with a client." The firm encourages employee interaction by holding meetings "away from the office" and sponsoring various social events, including company outings and a holiday party. "Most of the people here are single and not more than three years out of undergrad or grad school," one recent hire reports. "We get together fairly frequently after work to have fun." Employees report that "there is a very strong feeling of camaraderie and everyone is willing to help out."

The typical employee at ZS is "very bright," "highly motivated," and "under 30 with a can-do" personality. According to employees, ZS has its own motivational mantra: "If it has to be, it is up to me" (said three times fast). ZS has "a fairly good mix of minorities in the company at all levels" and "women are well represented." While there is "certainly room for improvement," both women and ethnic minorities report being "treated equitably and with respect." One insider estimates that "half of the firm's employees are minorities," though "we are sadly underrepresented in the African American sector."

COMPENSATION

Employees say compensation is "competitive with consulting industry averages" and is supplemented by "good annual bonuses." Starting salaries in 1997 were in the low $40,000s for business associates, and around $70,000 for MBA-level applicants, plus a signing bonus and yearly performance bonuses. In addition to medical and life insurance, ZS offers tuition reimbursement if the courses you take are "relevant to work." Outside of that, "the company doesn't really provide many perks," one source complains. "ZS does pay for your dinner if you work past 8," but the consulting firm only "pay for cabs home past 10, if you commute."

JUST YOU AND A COMPUTER

ZS is not your run-of-the-mill consulting firm. There are no business trips to exotic locales or elbow-rubbing with media moguls – most of the project work is done in front of a computer and the only moguls you're going to meet are in the pharmaceutical or biotech industry (the creators of Viagra, perhaps?). The hours can range from 40 to 80 a week (if you do the math, you know this means occasional weekends). Like most other consultancies, ZS is "a high stress, heavy workload environment," but one source claims "some people are happier in [the 80-hour] weeks." Hard work notwithstanding, the company awards its employees with an "amazing degree of client contact" and "lots of responsibility," making the firm "a good place to learn the ins and outs of the consulting business."

LIKE DRUGS? LOOK AT ZS.

"There are three things you need to know about working at ZS," one source points out, "We work mainly in the pharmaceutical industry, our work is very data-driven, and we work with sales and marketing issues." If you are looking for variety on the job, keep looking. However, another consultant at the firm says "I had almost no exposure to the pharmaceutical industry or sales forces before I came here, but have enjoyed the issues very much." That source goes on to add that "I use my brain a lot, I work in teams with interesting people, and I deal with new issues on a regular basis." Recent grads commend "the level of responsibility and client contact you receive within your first year." After only a year, one source looks forward to "managing a small project with a prominent Fortune 500 company. I doubt that there are many 21-year-old women who can say that."

PICKY, PICKY (HAPPY)

There are a few other drawbacks. One insider complains about "finicky" clients that "keep changing the data and make us redo everything six or eight times." That contact also dislikes "being staffed on a project that goes over 100 hours a week, and then having nothing to do the next week." However, he admits "it's probably just the nature of consulting." As one contact explains, "consulting is a lifestyle choice – you need to be able to make your clients happy" and find satisfaction "working on a team as opposed to seeking individual 'glory.'"

ABOUT THE AUTHORS

Marcy Lerner: Marcy is executive editor of Vault Reports. She graduated from the University of Virginia with a BA in history and holds an MA in history from Yale University. Marcy authored articles on management consulting and other career topics for *The Wall Street Journal Interactive Edition* and the *National Business Employment Weekly*.

Chandra Prasad: Chandra is an associate at Vault Reports. She graduated from Yale University in 1997 with a degree in English, with a concentration in Women's Literature. She joined Vault Reports after confusing it with a club in New York with a similar name.

Nikki Scott: Nikki is news editor of Vault Reports. She graduated from Amherst College in 1997 with a degree in English Literature, with a concentration in Caribbean Literature. After a brief stint in the advertising world, Nikki joined Vault Reports.

Samer Hamadeh: Samer is co-founder and managing director of Vault Reports. Previously, he served as an associate consultant with LEK/Alcar Consulting working on strategy cases from the firm's Los Angeles office. He graduated with a BS in chemistry and an MS in chemical engineering from Stanford University.

CONSULTING JOB SEEKERS:
Have job openings that match your criteria e-mailed to you!

VAULTMATCH™
FROM VAULT REPORTS

A free service for Consulting job seekers!

Vault Reports will e-mail job postings to you which match your interests and qualifications. This is a free service from Vault Reports. Here's how it works:

1. You visit www.VaultReports.com and fill out an online questionnaire, indicating your qualifications and the types of positions you want.

2. Companies contact Vault Reports with job openings.

3. Vault Reports sends you an e-mail about each position which matches your qualifications and interests.

4. For each position that interests you, simply reply to the e-mail and attach your resume.

5. Vault Reports laser prints your resume on top-quality resume paper and sends it to the company's hiring manager within 5 days.

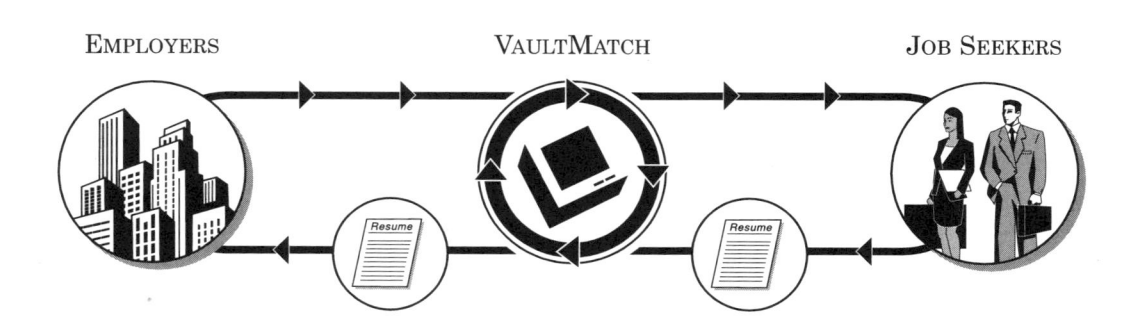

EMPLOYERS → VAULTMATCH → JOB SEEKERS

EMPLOYERS: PUT VAULTMATCH TO WORK FOR YOU. CONTACT VAULT REPORTS AT 888-562-8285.

www.VaultReports.com

JOB INTERVIEWS ARE COMING!

Your competition is prepared...are you?

VAULT REPORTS™

Vault Reports Employer Profiles are 50- to 70-page reports on leading employers designed to help you ace your job interviews. **Vault Reports Industry Guides** are 100- to 400-page guides providing in-depth information on leading industries, including industry trends, sample interview questions, and snapshots of the top firms. Filled with "insider" details, the Profiles and Industry Guides provide the hard-to-get company info that no recruiting brochure would dare reveal. Profiles are available on hundreds of leading companies.

Price: $25 per Employer Profile*
$35 per Industry Guide*

As Featured in
Newsweek
& The Wall Street Journal

Employer Profiles

American Express
American Management Systems
Andersen Consulting
Arthur Andersen
Arthur D. Little
AT Kearney
Bain & Co.
Bankers Trust
Bear Stearns
Booz Allen & Hamilton
Boston Consulting Group
Cargill
Chase
Citicorp/Citibank
Coca-Cola
Credit Suisse First Boston
Deloitte & Touche
Deutsche Bank
Donaldson Lufkin & Jenrette
Enron
Ernst & Young
Fidelity Investments
Ford Motor
Gemini
General Mills
Goldman Sachs
Hewlett Packard
Intel
JP Morgan

KPMG
Lehman Brothers
McKinsey & Co.
Mercer
Merrill Lynch
Microsoft
Mitchell Madison
Monitor
Morgan Stanley Dean Witter
Oracle
PricewaterhouseCoopers
Procter & Gamble
Salomon Smith Barney
Sprint
Walt Disney

.......100s more!

Industry Guides

Advertising
Brand Management
Fashion
Healthcare
High Tech
Internet and New Media
Investment Banking
Management Consulting
MBA Employers
Media and Entertainment

To order call 1-888-JOB-VAULT or order online at www.VaultReports.com

Founded by Wharton, Harvard, Yale and Stanford alums, Vault Reports is dedicated to helping job seekers ace their interviews.
Copyright © 1998 Vault Reports, Inc., 80 Fifth Avenue, 11th Floor, New York NY 10011.

VAULT REPORTS INDUSTRY GUIDES

The first career guides of their kind, Vault Reports' Industry Guides offer detailed evaluations of America's leading employers. Enriched with responses from thousands of insider surveys and interviews, these guides tell it like it is – the good and the bad – about the companies everyone is talking about. Each guide includes a complete industry overview as well as information on the industry's job opportunities, career paths, hiring procedures, culture, pay, and commonly asked interview questions..

Each employer entry includes:

- **The Scoop**: the juicy details on each company's past, present, and future.
- **Getting Hired**: insider advice on what it takes to get that job offer.
- **Our Survey Says**: thousands of employees speak their mind on company culture, satisfaction, pay, prestige, and more.

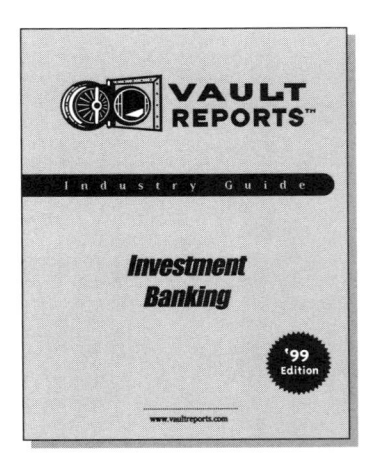

PRICE: $35 PER GUIDE

GUIDE TO ADVERTISING™
Reviews America's top employers in the advertising industry, including Bozell Worldwide, Grey Advertising, Leo Burnett, Ogilvy & Mather, TBWAChiat/Day, and many more!
100pp.

GUIDE TO FASHION™
Reviews America's top employers in the fashion industry, including Calvin Klein, Donna Karan, Estee Lauder, The Gap, J. Crew, IMG Models, and many more!
100pp.

GUIDE TO HEALTHCARE™
Reviews America's top employers in the healthcare industry, including Amgen, Eli Lilly, Johnson & Johnson, Oxford, Pfizer, Schering-Plough, and many more!
120pp.

GUIDE TO HIGH TECH™
Reviews America's top employers in the high tech industry, including Broderbund, Cisco Systems, Hewlett-Packard, Intel, Microsoft, Sun Microsystems, and many more!
400pp.

GUIDE TO INTERNET AND NEW MEDIA™
Reviews America's top employers in the Internet and new media industry, including Amazon.com, CDNow, DoubleClick, Excite, Netscape, Yahoo!, and many more!
130pp.

GUIDE TO INVESTMENT BANKING™
Reviews America's top employers in the investment banking industry, including Bankers Trust, Goldman Sachs, JP Morgan, Morgan Stanley, and many more!
400pp.

GUIDE TO MANAGEMENT CONSULTING™
Reviews America's top employers in the management consulting industry, including Andersen Consulting, Boston Consulting Group, McKinsey, PricewaterhouseCoopers, and many more!
400pp.

GUIDE TO MARKETING AND BRAND MANAGEMENT™
Reviews America's top employers in the marketing and brand management industry, including General Mills, Procter & Gamble, Nike, Coca-Cola, and many more!
150pp.

GUIDE TO MBA EMPLOYERS™
Reviews America's top employers for MBAs, including Fortune 500 corporations, management consulting firms, investment banks, venture capital and LBO firms, commercial banks, and hedge funds.
500pp.

GUIDE TO MEDIA AND ENTERTAINMENT™
Reviews America's top employers in the media and entertainment industry, including AOL, Blockbuster, CNN, Dreamworks, Gannett, National Public Radio, Time Warner, and many more!
400pp.

Vault Reports Guide to Case Interviews

VAULT REPORTS™

The Vault Reports Guide to Case Interviews is a must for anyone preparing for the management consulting case interview! With this 150-page guide, you'll find:

THE KEY FRAMEWORKS, TOOLS AND MODELS YOU NEED TO SHAPE YOUR CASE INTERVIEW RESPONSE

- Cost-benefit analysis
- Value chain analysis
- Porter's Five Forces
- Benchmarking
- Opportunity cost
- The "Five Cs"
- 2 x 2 and BCG matrices
- Basic accounting concepts

Price: $30 per Case Interviews Guide

A STEP BY STEP BREAKDOWN OF CASE INTERVIEW QUESTIONS

- Types of case questions
- Key questions you should ask
- How to structure your response
- What qualities interviewers look for
- Over 30 actual case interview questions
- "Guesstimating" and market sizing
- Brainteasers and curveball questions
- Much more!

Consulting interviewers expect candidates to be prepared. Make sure you're ready to crack your consulting interviews with the Vault Reports Guide to Case Interviews.

To order call 1-888-562-8285 or order online at www.VaultReports.com